Culinary Adventures

Techniques and Recipes

Cooking Club
of
America®

Minnetonka, Minnesota

Culinary Adventures

Techniques and Recipes

Printed in 2010

Janice Cole
Recipe Development

Tom Carpenter
Creative Director

Jen Weaverling
Managing Editor

Wendy Holdman
Cover Design and Production

Gina K. Germ
Book Design and Production

Stafford Photography
Commissioned Photography

Special thanks to: Kathy Bauwens, Mike Billstein, Terry Casey, Lori Grosklags, Ruth Taswell and Betsy Wray.

On the cover: Chocolate Angel
Food Cake with Triple-Chocolate
Glaze, p. 119
On the back:
Traditional Guacamole, p. 74
Tomato-Olive Pizza with Fresh
Mushrooms, p. 24
Pasta with Roasted Tomatoes
and Mussels, p. 50

Cooking Club of America
12301 Whitewater Drive
Minnetonka, MN 55343
www.cookingclub.com

Table of Contents

Introduction

Every cook has their established favorites, sure success specialties and guaranteed masterpieces. These are the old stand-by main dishes, sides, baked goods, sweets and desserts that we really know how to make, and how to make well. Sometimes, among friends and family, we're even famous for them!

But cooking is also about expanding your horizons. Why else would you belong to a leading organization like the Cooking Club of America? That's where *Culinary Adventures* comes in. Compiled from the award-winning pages of *Cooking Club* magazine, these cooking *Techniques and Recipes* assure you a bountiful resource of new skills and ideas to really grow your culinary pleasure and enjoyment.

More than just a cookbook, each section of *Culinary Adventures* brings you essential techniques you need to know to become an even better cook. Of course, we include plenty of recipes as well, to help you put your new-found skills to work.

Great cooking combines proper technique with wonderful recipes. That's exactly what we've brought together in these pages, to help you continue your quest for *Culinary Adventures*.

Main Dishes

Oven-Dried Tomatoes

Feta Chicken Salad with Oven-Dried Tomatoes

Oven-drying is a simple, reliable way to preserve the taste of juicy, ripe summer tomatoes for use throughout the year. While sun-drying may sound romantic, it takes days, and the weather does not cooperate with any regularity in most parts of the country. You need a constant source of heat—like an oven—to dry tomatoes.

If you regularly use commercial sun-dried tomatoes, you'll find that oven-dried tomatoes are more versatile: They're more pliable, so they can be used without being reconstituted, and they're often less salty.

Once you've dried a batch, you can use the tomatoes to add a hint of tomato flavor to all kinds of dishes: Sprinkle them over a sandwich filling, toss them into a green salad, add them to spaghetti sauce, or mix them into dips or spreads.

Feta Chicken Salad with Oven-Dried Tomatoes

GARLIC DRESSING

- 1 tablespoon red wine vinegar
- 1 garlic clove, minced
- ½ teaspoon Dijon mustard
- ¼ teaspoon salt
- ¼ teaspoon freshly ground pepper
- 3 tablespoons extra-virgin olive oil
- 1 tablespoon purchased garlic oil

SALAD

- 1 lb. boneless skinless chicken breast halves
- 4 cups mixed salad greens
- ¾ cup coarsely chopped fresh mint
- ½ large cucumber, unpeeled, halved lengthwise, sliced
- 4 radishes, halved, sliced
- ¾ cup halved oven-dried tomatoes
- ½ cup (2 oz.) crumbled feta cheese

1 In small bowl, combine all dressing ingredients except oils. Slowly whisk in oils.
2 Brush chicken breasts with 1 tablespoon of the dressing. Place on gas grill over medium heat or charcoal grill 4 to 6 inches from medium coals. Cook 8 to 10 minutes or until juices run clear, turning once.
3 Meanwhile, in large bowl, combine salad greens, mint, cucumber and radishes. Toss with half of dressing. Place on serving platter.
4 Slice chicken diagonally; arrange over greens. Top with tomatoes. Drizzle remaining half of dressing over chicken and tomatoes. Top with cheese.

4 servings

PER SERVING: 330 calories, 20 g total fat (5 g saturated fat), 29 g protein, 9 g carbohydrate, 75 mg cholesterol, 585 mg sodium, 2.5 g fiber

Pan-Broiled Steak with Tomato-Balsamic Sauce

- 1½ lb. boneless beef sirloin steak (about 1 inch thick), cut into 4 pieces
- ½ teaspoon salt
- ¼ teaspoon freshly ground pepper
- 2 large shallots, minced
- ¼ cup balsamic vinegar
- 1 cup beef broth
- ¼ cup packed thinly sliced oven-dried tomatoes

1 Heat large skillet over medium-high heat until hot. Add oil. Season steaks with salt and pepper; add to skillet. Cook 5 to 8 minutes for medium rare or until of desired doneness, turning once.
2 Remove steaks from skillet; loosely cover to keep warm. Return skillet to heat. Add shallots; cook briefly. Add vinegar; bring to a boil, scraping any browned bits from bottom of skillet. Add broth and tomatoes. Increase heat to high; boil 3 to 5 minutes or until sauce is slightly thickened. Pour sauce over steaks.

4 servings

PER SERVING: 375 calories, 23 g total fat (8 g saturated fat), 37 g protein, 4 g carbohydrate, 105 mg cholesterol, 705 mg sodium, 1 g fiber

Using Oven-Dried Tomatoes

When you want chewy texture, use oven-dried tomatoes "as is" with no further preparation. For a softer texture, reconstitute them. Oven-dried tomatoes also can be marinated to infuse them with other flavors.

- Add whole, sliced or chopped oven-dried tomatoes directly to tossed salads or hearty sandwiches for chewy tomato flavor. Stir sliced oven-dried tomatoes into salsa for a double tomato hit.

- They can also be added directly to dishes where there will be enough cooking liquid to soften them during the cooking process. Try them in beef stews, vegetable soups and chunky pasta sauces.

- To reconstitute oven-dried tomatoes, place them in a small bowl and cover with hot water. (For additional flavor, use chicken, vegetable or beef broth.) Let stand 5 to 10 minutes or until the tomatoes are soft and tender; drain.

- Use reconstituted tomatoes in corn muffins, smooth tomato sauces, meat loaf and hamburgers. Sprinkle them on top of pizza or focaccia. Finely chop them and add them to mashed potatoes, along with parsley and chives. Or slice them and toss with fresh green beans and melted butter flavored with garlic.

- To infuse oven-dried tomatoes with other flavors, marinate them in olive oil and assertive herbs such as rosemary or thyme, along with pepper and chiles. Keep them in the refrigerator for up to one week. Add them to pastas and salads, serve them chopped over slices of fresh mozzarella cheese, or use them as a condiment for roast beef sandwiches. The flavored oil can be used as well.

Red Pesto Linguine

8 oz. linguine
3 large garlic cloves
1½ cups oven-dried tomatoes
1½ cups reduced-sodium
   chicken broth
1 tablespoon extra-virgin olive oil
¼ cup chopped fresh Italian
   parsley
¼ teaspoon salt
¼ teaspoon freshly ground pepper
½ cup (2 oz.) freshly shredded
   Asiago or Parmesan cheese

1 Cook linguine according to package directions.

2 Meanwhile, chop garlic in food processor until finely minced. Add tomatoes; process until finely chopped. While processor is running, slowly add broth; blend until mixture is pureed.

3 Heat oil in medium saucepan over medium heat until hot. Add tomato mixture; cook 3 to 4 minutes or until hot, stirring frequently. Stir in parsley, salt and pepper.

4 Drain linguine, reserving ½ cup linguine cooking water. Add reserved water to tomato mixture. In large bowl, toss linguine with tomato mixture. Place on serving platter; sprinkle with cheese. If desired, serve with additional cheese.

4 servings

PER SERVING: 380 calories, 9 g total fat (3 g saturated fat), 17 g protein, 59 g carbohydrate, 10 mg cholesterol, 1055 mg sodium, 5 g fiber

Drying Tomatoes

The drying process requires just a few basic pieces of equipment: baking sheet, wire rack, aluminum foil, sharp knife, spoon and tongs.

1. Heat the oven to 250°F. Line a 15x10x1-inch baking sheet with aluminum foil. Place a wire cooling rack in the foil-lined pan.

2. Wash 3 pounds of Italian plum tomatoes (about 26 medium), and cut out the stem core.

3. Slice the tomatoes in half lengthwise. Scoop out and discard the seeds, leaving just the shell. A grapefruit spoon works well.

4. Blot excess moisture from the tomatoes with paper towels.

5. Arrange the tomatoes on the rack cut side up. They can be placed closely together since they shrink considerably during baking.

6. Bake tomatoes 3 to 4 hours, checking them occasionally. If liquid collects in the tomatoes, turn them with tongs to remove water. (If you double the recipe, switch the oven rack position of the two pans halfway through baking.)

7. The tomatoes are done when they are dry but still pliable, not brittle. (Remove each tomato as it is done. The time the tomatoes take to cook will vary because their size and moisture content vary.) Store them in resealable plastic bags 3 to 4 days in the refrigerator or up to 8 months in the freezer.

Peppers On Fire

Roasted Red Pepper Crostini

Try roasting peppers before summer. Farmers' markets and gardens are rich with firm, bright green peppers ripening to vibrant red, orange, yellow, purple or even dusky brown. Many professional and home cooks agree that the rich, smoky aroma of roasting peppers makes this task a pleasant one.

Peppers are roasted to remove the tight, waxy skin that can shrivel unattractively during cooking and to add a complex, smoky flavor to the pepper. Roasted peppers give depth and richness to dishes that you can't achieve any other way.

Perfectly roasted peppers have skins that slip off easily and flesh that still has a bit of crunch. For easier roasting, choose peppers with thick skins and few crevices. Red bell peppers are the most popular, but yellow, orange and even green peppers can be roasted. (Because purple peppers turn green when heated, they must be used raw if you want to preserve the purple color.) Roasted peppers also freeze very well, so roast up a large batch while peppers are plentiful and less expensive. Then you'll have them on hand to use throughout the year.

Roasted Red Pepper Crostini

24 thin slices baguette
4 teaspoons extra-virgin olive oil
6 oz. goat cheese
1 roasted red bell pepper,
   cut into 24 pieces
24 small basil leaves
   Freshly ground pepper

1 Heat oven to 375°F. Place bread slices on baking sheet. Brush both sides lightly with oil. Bake 5 to 8 minutes, turning once. Set aside.
2 Spread toasted bread slices with cheese. Top each with piece of roasted pepper. Garnish with basil; sprinkle with pepper.

24 appetizers

PER APPETIZER: 95 calories, 3 g total fat (1.5 g saturated fat), 5 mg cholesterol, 170 mg sodium, 1 g fiber

Fettuccine with Roasted Red Pepper Sauce

3 roasted red bell peppers
¾ cup reduced-sodium
   chicken broth
1 tablespoon extra-virgin olive oil
2 large garlic cloves, minced
1 tablespoon chopped fresh
   thyme
¼ teaspoon salt
¼ teaspoon freshly ground pepper
1 (9-oz.) package fettuccine

1 Place bell peppers and broth in blender or food processor; blend until peppers are pureed.
2 Heat oil in medium saucepan. Add garlic; cook briefly. Add red pepper puree, thyme, salt and pepper; mix well. Bring to a boil. Reduce heat to medium; cook 15 to 20 minutes. (This sauce can be made up to 2 days ahead; cover and refrigerate.)
3 Meanwhile, cook fettuccine according to package directions. Drain; toss with red pepper sauce.

4 servings

PER SERVING: 275 calories, 6 g total fat (1 g saturated fat), 55 mg cholesterol, 615 mg sodium, 2.5 g fiber

Roasting Methods

You can roast peppers over a gas range, electric range or outdoor grill, or under the broiler.

Direct heat: Works with gas and electric ranges and outdoor grills.

1. Place whole peppers on grate over gas flame or hot coals, or directly on burner of electric stove.

2. Cook over high heat, turning the pepper with tongs every one to two minutes, until the skin is completely blackened.

3. Place the pepper in a heavy plastic bag, close the bag and let it stand 15 minutes or until it's cool enough to handle.

4. Peel the pepper under running water, removing the charred skin.

5. .Slit the pepper open and remove the seeds and veins.

Broiling: This method is well suited for large batches.

1. Cut the peppers into wedges. Remove the seeds and veins.

2. Flatten the wedges with the palm of your hand. Place them skin side up on a foil-lined 15x10x1-inch pan.

3. Place the pan under a preheated broiler, as close as possible to the heat source.

4. Broil until the skin is blackened.

5. Place the peppers in a heavy plastic bag, close the bag and let it stand 15 minutes or until the peppers are cool enough to handle. Peel peppers under running water, removing charred skin.

Peeling under water: The easiest way to peel roasted peppers is under running water. Some cooks believe the water washes away some of the essential oils of the pepper and, thus, the flavor. We've peeled peppers both with and without water and didn't notice a flavor difference. Many chefs tell us they also use the water method.

Roasted Red Pepper Mayonnaise

1 roasted red bell pepper
½ cup mayonnaise
1 small garlic clove, minced
¼ teaspoon lemon juice
⅛ teaspoon salt
⅛ teaspoon pepper
   Dash ground red pepper
   (cayenne)

Dry bell pepper between paper towels to remove any excess moisture. Chop and place in small bowl. (There should be about ⅓ cup.) Add remaining ingredients; blend to combine. Cover and refrigerate until ready to serve.

⅔ cup

PER 2 TABLESPOONS: 165 calories, 17.5 g total fat (2.5 g saturated fat), 15 mg cholesterol, 180 mg sodium, 0 g fiber

Mastering Omelets

Spring Herb Omelet

The French truly have a way with omelets. They've taken this simple little egg dish and elevated it to exquisite perfection.

Here is the simple secret to this typical French omelet: Keep the eggs moving. The French, or stirred, method of omelet-making requires both hands going in different directions at the same time. It's a little like rubbing your tummy while patting the top of your head. One hand continually stirs the eggs to create layers of soft eggs within the omelet, while the other hand keeps the pan moving to avoid overheating the bottom of the omelet. The constant stirring and shaking keep the eggs from becoming overcooked and tough.

This method requires just a few skills and a little practice. Read through the directions in the recipes and the tips, then take a dozen eggs and begin making one omelet after the other. (Don't worry about adding a filling; that can be done once you've mastered the technique.) After a few tries, you'll soon develop the abilities of an expert and be dazzling your guests with omelets worthy of a French café.

Caramelized Onion and Bacon Omelet

FILLING
- 1 strip bacon, coarsely chopped
- ½ cup sliced onion
- Dash sugar

OMELET
- 3 eggs
- ⅛ teaspoon salt
- Dash freshly ground pepper
- 1 tablespoon unsalted butter

1 Heat medium nonstick skillet over medium heat until hot. Add bacon; cook and stir 4 minutes or until brown and crisp. Place on paper towel-lined plate. Leave 1 tablespoon bacon drippings in skillet. Add onion; cook and stir over medium heat 1 minute. Cover and cook an additional 3 minutes or until wilted and soft. Remove cover; sprinkle with sugar. Cook 2 to 3 minutes or until golden brown. Place on plate; cover to keep warm.

2 In medium bowl, whisk eggs, salt and pepper until eggs are light and foamy (about 30 seconds).

3 Heat medium nonstick skillet over high heat 30 seconds or until hot. Add butter, swirling over bottom and sides of pan as it melts. Heat until foam subsides and butter just begins to turn light brown and smell nutty (watch carefully so butter does not turn deep brown and burn). Pour egg mixture into pan; immediately begin stirring eggs with flat side of fork while shaking pan back and forth over burner. When eggs begin to form curds and no longer flow over bottom of pan (about 30 seconds; top of eggs will still be very moist), spread eggs in single layer. Add onion; top with bacon.

4 Lift pan to 45-degree angle; fold top edge of omelet over filling to middle. Run rubber spatula over bottom edge to release omelet; place bottom edge of omelet on plate. Tip pan over plate to form omelet.

1 serving

PER SERVING: 510 calories, 43.5 g total fat (18 g saturated fat), 21.5 g protein, 7.5 g carbohydrate, 685 mg cholesterol, 575 mg sodium, 1 g fiber

Smoky Cheddar and Ham Omelet

FILLING
- ½ tablespoon unsalted butter
- 2 tablespoons finely diced unpeeled apple (Gala, Rome, Fuji)
- 2 tablespoons finely diced ham
- 2 tablespoons shredded smoked cheddar cheese

OMELET
- 3 eggs
- ⅛ teaspoon salt
- Dash freshly ground pepper
- 1 tablespoon unsalted butter

1 Melt ½ tablespoon butter in medium nonstick skillet over medium heat. Add apple; cook 2 to 3 minutes or until tender. Add ham; cook 2 to 3 minutes or until ham is hot. Place in small bowl; cover to keep warm.

2 In medium bowl, whisk together eggs, salt and pepper 30 seconds or until eggs are light and foamy.

3 Heat medium nonstick skillet over high heat 30 seconds or until hot. Add 3 tablespoon butter, swirling over bottom and sides of pan as it melts. Heat until foam subsides and butter just begins to turn light brown and smell nutty (watch carefully so butter does not turn deep brown and burn). Pour egg mixture into pan; immediately begin stirring eggs with flat side of fork while shaking pan back and forth over burner. When eggs begin to form curds and no longer flow over bottom of pan (about 30 seconds; top of eggs will still be very moist), spread eggs in single layer. Add ham mixture; top with cheese.

4 Lift pan to 45-degree angle; fold top edge of omelet over filling to middle. Run rubber spatula over bottom edge to release omelet; place bottom edge of omelet on plate. Tip pan over plate to form omelet.

1 serving

PER SERVING: 480 calories, 39.5 g total fat (19 g saturated fat), 26.5 g protein, 4.5 g carbohydrate, 705 mg cholesterol, 810 mg sodium, .5 g fiber

Spring Herb Omelet

- 3 eggs
- 1 tablespoon minced fresh herbs (tarragon, dill, chervil, parsley, chives and/or lemon balm)
- ¼ teaspoon salt
- ¼ teaspoon freshly ground pepper
- 1½ tablespoons unsalted butter

1 In medium bowl, whisk together eggs, herbs, salt and pepper until eggs are light and foamy (about 30 seconds).

2 Heat medium nonstick skillet over high heat 30 seconds or until hot. Add butter, swirling over bottom and sides of pan as it melts. Heat until foam subsides and butter just begins to turn light brown and smell nutty (watch carefully so butter does not turn deep brown and burn). Pour egg mixture into pan; immediately begin stirring eggs with flat side of fork while shaking pan back and forth over burner. When eggs begin to form curds and no longer flow over bottom of pan (about 30 seconds; top of eggs will still be very moist), spread eggs in single layer. Add filling, if desired.

3 Lift pan to 45-degree angle; fold top edge of omelet over filling to middle. Run rubber spatula over bottom edge to release omelet; place bottom edge of omelet on plate.

4 Tip pan over plate to form omelet.

1 serving

PER SERVING: 390 calories, 33 g total fat (15.5 g saturated fat), 19 g protein, 2.5 g carbohydrate, 685 mg cholesterol, 780 mg sodium, .5 g fiber

Tips For Perfect Omelets

For tender, fluffy omelets, follow these guidelines for ingredients, equipment and preparation.

BEFORE YOU BEGIN

Pan It's not necessary to have a specially designed omelet pan, but you do need a nonstick one. The best pan is a 10-inch nonstick skillet (the sides slope and the bottom measures 71/2 to 8 inches). This size is perfect for making one three-egg omelet.

Eggs Use the freshest eggs available. They give an omelet more body. If possible, use organic free-range eggs for better color and flavor. Beat the eggs thoroughly. They should be smooth, light in color and foamy. Don't rush the process—it will take about 30 seconds, or longer if you're mixing more than three eggs. The air beaten into the eggs creates a lighter omelet.

Butter Melting the butter until it turns light brown adds a rich, nutty taste to the eggs. And when the butter reaches this stage, the pan is at a perfect temperature for the eggs to coagulate. (Watch the butter carefully because it can quickly go from light brown to burnt.)

Multiple Omelets To make more than one omelet at a time, have all the ingredients ready in an assembly line fashion before you start to cook. It's best to make omelets individually in rapid order rather than trying to make one omelet to serve several people. You can easily make four to six omelets in a row, but more than that becomes difficult. To save time, beat all the eggs together in one bowl, then use approximately ⅔ cup per omelet.

READY, SET, GO!

Read the recipe thoroughly ahead of time. Omelets cook so quickly there's no time to stop in the middle.

Stirring and Shaking The key to a good omelet is to keep it moving. Eggs that are allowed to sit on the heat overcook and toughen. Once the butter is light brown, immediately pour the eggs into the pan and begin stirring them using the back of a fork **(photo 1)**. Keep the tines of the fork parallel to the bottom of the pan. Do not point the sharp tips of the fork into the pan or they may scratch the nonstick surface. Stir the eggs evenly around the pan. As the eggs are being stirred, shake the pan back and forth, but keep the pan on the burner.

Timing The difference between a perfect omelet and one that's overcooked can be as little as 30 seconds. As soon as the eggs begin to form curds and are no longer liquid (this will take 30 seconds or less), spread them in a single layer **(photo 2)**. Add the filling and lift the pan off the heat. The top of the eggs will be very moist, but the omelet will continue cooking once folded on a plate. For a firmer omelet, let the eggs sit on the burner with the heat turned off for 10 to 30 seconds or until of desired consistency; then add the filling and fold.

Folding To fold an omelet, hold the pan off the heat at a 45-degree angle. Using a fork or rubber spatula, fold the top edge of the omelet over the filling to the middle of the omelet **(photo 3)**. Release the bottom of the omelet by running a fork or rubber spatula under the edge; place the edge of the pan on a serving plate, and let the omelet begin to slide onto the plate **(photo 4)**. Tip the pan over the plate to make the final fold in the omelet and situate it on the plate. The top of the omelet should be a pale golden color. It should never be brown, an indication that the eggs are overcooked.

Eyes On the Rise

Gingered-Apple Omelet Soufflé

When you are searching for a breakfast entree that will rise to the occasion, look to souffléed omelets. A cross between an omelet and a soufflé, these light, airy creations are easy to make and spectacular to serve.

The secret behind souffléed omelets is simple—the eggs are separated and the whites are beaten until stiff. The beaten egg whites are gently folded into the egg yolk mixture, and the heat of the oven causes them to rise during baking. The result is a puffy omelet with a delicate airy center. And there's an added bonus: Because the eggs expand, you need fewer eggs per serving than in a typical omelet.

The risen omelet can be served like a traditional omelet—folded over a filling, as in the Gingered-Apple Omelet Soufflé—or it can be served open-faced, as in the Smoked Bacon, Mushroom and Potato Omelet. For a really spectacular treat, try your hand at individual souffléed omelets, such as the Orange-Glazed Asparagus Souffléed Omelets. Whatever your choice, you'll find souffléed omelets expanding your breakfast (or supper) horizons.

Gingered-Apple Omelet Soufflé

FILLING

- 2 tablespoons unsalted butter
- 4 large apples (Rome, Braeburn or Fuji), peeled, thinly sliced
- 1 tablespoon grated fresh ginger
- ¼ cup sugar
- ½ teaspoon cinnamon

OMELET

- 6 eggs, separated
- 1 teaspoon grated fresh ginger
- ½ teaspoon salt
- ⅛ teaspoon freshly ground pepper
- 2 tablespoons unsalted butter
  Powdered sugar

1 Heat oven to 400°F. Melt 2 tablespoons butter in large skillet over medium heat. Add apples; sauté 4 to 6 minutes or until soft. Add 1 tablespoon ginger; cook 30 seconds. Stir in sugar and cinnamon. Cook 30 to 60 seconds or until sugar is melted. Set aside.

2 In large bowl, combine egg yolks, 1 teaspoon ginger, salt and pepper; beat at medium speed 2 to 3 minutes or until thick and light colored. In another large bowl, beat egg whites at high speed until stiff peaks form. Add ⅓ of egg whites to egg yolk mixture; stir gently to combine. Gently fold in remaining egg whites.

3 Melt 2 tablespoons butter in large (12-inch) nonstick ovenproof skillet over medium heat. Add egg mixture; cook 1 minute. (Do not stir.) Immediately place skillet in oven; bake 4 to 6 minutes or until top is lightly browned and set.

4 While omelet is baking, reheat apple filling. Remove omelet from oven; slide onto serving platter. Spread warm apple filling over half of omelet; fold omelet over filling. Sprinkle with powdered sugar; serve immediately.

4 servings

PER SERVING: 380 calories, 19.5 g total fat (9.5 g saturated fat), 10 g protein, 44.5 g carbohydrate, 350 mg cholesterol, 390 mg sodium, 4 g fiber

Orange-Glazed Asparagus Souffléed Omelets

FILLING

- 2 tablespoons unsalted butter
- 1 lb. asparagus, peeled, cut into 2-inch pieces
- ⅛ teaspoon salt
- ⅛ teaspoon freshly ground pepper
- 2 teaspoons grated orange peel
- ¼ cup fresh orange juice
- 1 tablespoon chopped fresh tarragon
- 1 tablespoon chopped fresh chives

OMELET

- 6 eggs, separated
- 1 tablespoon chopped fresh tarragon
- 1 tablespoon chopped fresh chives
- 2 teaspoons grated orange peel
- 2 tablespoons fresh orange juice
- ¼ teaspoon salt
- ⅛ teaspoon freshly ground pepper

1 Place 2 oven racks in center area of oven, one above the other. Heat oven to 400°F. Spray 2 nonstick baking sheets with nonstick cooking spray. Melt 2 tablespoons butter in large skillet over medium heat. Add asparagus; sprinkle with ⅛ teaspoon each of the salt and pepper. Sauté 2 minutes. Add 2 teaspoons orange peel and ¼ cup orange juice; cook asparagus 2 to 3 minutes or until tender and orange juice has reduced to a glaze. Sprinkle with 1 tablespoon each of the tarragon and chives. Set aside.

2 In large bowl, combine egg yolks and all remaining omelet ingredients; beat at medium speed 2 to 3 minutes or until thick and light colored.

3 In another large bowl, beat egg whites at high speed until stiff peaks form. Add ⅓ of egg whites to egg yolk mixture; stir gently to combine. Gently fold in remaining egg whites.

4 Spoon ¼ of egg mixture onto each half of the 2 baking sheets; spread to 6-inch rounds.

5 Place baking sheets on oven racks, one above the other. Bake 3 minutes or until set. Reverse baking sheet positions in oven. Bake an additional 2 to 3 minutes or until lightly browned and puffed. While omelet is baking, reheat filling.

6 Remove omelets from oven; place each omelet on individual serving plate. Top each with ¼ of the filling; fold omelets over filling. Serve immediately.

4 servings

PER SERVING: 245 calories, 19.5 g total fat (9.5 g saturated fat), 11.5 g protein, 7 g carbohydrate, 350 mg cholesterol, 315 mg sodium, 1.5 g fiber

Smoked Bacon, Mushroom and Potato Omelet

FILLING

- 4 new potatoes, thinly sliced
- 6 slices thick-sliced bacon, chopped
- 6 oz. assorted mushrooms (shiitake, crimini or portobello), sliced
- ½ medium onion, sliced
- ¼ teaspoon salt
- ⅛ teaspoon freshly ground pepper

OMELET

- 6 eggs, separated
- ½ cup sliced green onions
- ¼ teaspoon salt
- ⅛ teaspoon freshly ground pepper
- 2 tablespoons butter
- ½ cup shredded Gruyère cheese

1 Heat oven to 400°F. Cook potatoes in boiling, salted water 6 to 10 minutes or until tender. Drain.

2 Meanwhile, cook bacon in large skillet over medium-high heat until browned. Remove bacon from skillet; drain on paper towels. Remove bacon drippings from skillet; return skillet to heat. Add mushrooms and onion; cook over medium heat 5 to 8 minutes or until tender.

3 Add potatoes to skillet; sprinkle with ¼ teaspoon salt and ⅛ teaspoon pepper. Cook and stir 1 to 2 minutes to heat. Stir in half of bacon; set aside.

4 In large bowl, combine egg yolks, green onions, ¼ teaspoon salt and ⅛ teaspoon pepper; beat at medium speed 2 to 3 minutes or until thick and light colored. Stir in remaining half of bacon.

5 In another large bowl, beat egg whites at high speed until stiff peaks form. Add ⅓ of egg whites to egg yolk mixture; stir gently to combine. Gently fold in remaining egg whites.

6 Melt butter in large (12-inch) nonstick ovenproof skillet over medium heat. Add egg mixture; sprinkle with cheese. Cook 1 minute. Immediately place skillet in oven; bake 4 to 6 minutes or until top is lightly browned and set.

7 While omelet is baking, reheat filling. Remove omelet from oven; slide onto serving platter. Spoon filling over omelet; serve immediately.

6 servings

PER SERVING: 280 calories, 18 g total fat (8 g saturated fat), 14.5 g protein, 16 g carbohydrate, 240 mg cholesterol, 515 mg sodium, 2 g fiber

Getting a Rise Out of Omelets

Egg whites are the reason souffléed omelets puff up. Understanding egg whites and giving them proper treatment guarantees spectacular results.

Separating eggs

Always crack eggs on a flat surface; there is less chance of an eggshell piercing the yolk.

- Use the two halves of the eggshell to separate the yolk from the white. Pass the yolk from one half to the other, letting the white run into a bowl. Or, when separating several eggs at a time, use impeccably clean hands. Let the egg white run between your fingers into a bowl while the yolk rests in your hand.

- Always place egg whites in a bowl that is free from any trace of oil, grease or yolk. The slightest bit of fat or yolk prevents the egg whites from expanding during beating.

- To retrieve bits of egg yolk or particles from the egg white, use the eggshell to scoop them out.

Beating egg whites

Room temperature egg whites beat up higher than cold egg whites.

- Beat egg whites in a metal bowl; never use a plastic one. The egg whites cling to the metal surface during beating, but they slip on plastic, causing them to become overbeaten around the edges.

- Begin beating egg whites at low speed, and beat just until frothy. This allows the egg whites to loosen and mix together.

- Once the egg whites are frothy, increase the speed to medium-high. Beat only until stiff peaks just begin to form.

- To test for stiff peaks, lift the beater horizontally. The egg whites at the end of the beater should hold a horizontal peak. The egg whites also should be shiny and have small air bubbles.

- Do not overbeat egg whites. Overbeaten whites form little cloud-like clumps in the mixture. When egg whites are too stiffly beaten, they do not mix well and, as a result, lose air and do not rise as high.

Folding mixtures

The objective when folding is to combine two mixtures together quickly and gently while keeping as much air in each mixture as possible.

- When folding egg whites into another mixture, first stir in about one-third of the egg whites to lighten the mixture. This step helps the mixture more easily accept the remaining egg whites and retain as much air as possible.

- Always add the egg whites to the egg yolks, never the other way around. Gently fold them together using a rubber spatula. Place the spatula in the center of the mixture and bring it down and up the side nearest you, bringing the yolk mixture over the whites. Turn the bowl one-quarter of the way and repeat until the two mixtures are combined.

- Do not overmix—a few remaining streaks of egg white in the mixture are just fine.

Invest in Stock

Homemade Chicken Stock

The secret of good cooking resides in the basics: Use quality ingredients and proper technique. One of the first basics every cook should learn is how to make stock. While stock begins simply enough—water simmers with meat, bones, vegetables and seasonings—the result is liquid gold, a rich and complex-flavored broth.

There are several types of stock—brown, white, fish and vegetable—but chicken is the easiest and most versatile to make. It's considered a white stock because the bones are not browned before cooking. With chicken stock on hand, you can make sauces that rival your favorite restaurant's version, as well as simple soups and savory sides, all on a moment's notice.

Technique for Making Stock

Chicken stock requires a few minutes to prepare, then a couple of hours to simmer. A long cooking time extracts the flavor, protein and gelatin from chicken bones—the foundation of rich stock. Use these tips to obtain rich, clear stocks.

Proper pot Stocks can be made in any large pot; however, the best ones are tall with narrow openings. This limits the amount of evaporation that occurs and forces the liquid to simmer through several layers of meat and bones for richer flavor. The recipe for stock can be increased to accommodate larger stockpots. A six-quart stockpot holds a single recipe with room to spare. If you have an 8- or 10-quart pot, you can easily double the recipe.

Saving bones You can collect uncooked chicken bones over time. Keep a resealable plastic bag in the freezer; whenever you work with chicken, save breast bones, rib bones, necks, gizzards, back bones, wings and wing tips until there is enough for a pot of stock. Or buy chicken bones and parts from butchers who trim their own chickens. In a pinch, you can also use a whole chicken.

Making stock Start with bones Rinse excess blood from the bones, but save the skin—it adds flavor, and the fat it contains is removed before the stock is used. Place the bones in the stockpot and cover them with cold water—never use hot water. Slowly bring the mixture to a boil. As the water begins to simmer, impurities coagulate and form a scum on the surface. Skim off the scum as it appears.

Vegetables and seasoning Once the liquid is gently boiling and the scum is no longer rapidly forming, add the vegetables and seasonings but no salt. Salt is never used when making stock because the stock reduces as it cooks; any added salt would intensify in flavor. Simmer the stock gently; never let it come to a full boil or it will become cloudy. The bubbles should be constant but gentle, not vigorous.

Strain and skim When the stock has simmered long enough for the flavor to be extracted (3 to 4 hours), strain it twice to remove all particles. Put the stock in several smaller containers to chill it in the refrigerator. Chilling stock causes the fat to congeal on the surface. Once the stock is chilled, remove the fat and taste the stock. A well-made stock should be strong-tasting, clear and slightly gelatinous. When it's chilled, it should wiggle like weak gelatin. If the stock tastes weak or is watery, bring it to a full boil and boil vigorously to reduce it and concentrate the flavor.

Storing stock Store stock in the refrigerator for up to 2 days. For longer storage, freeze stock in 1- or 2-cup portions. Try freezing stock in resealable plastic bags—they lay flat in the freezer and take up very little space.

Skim off the scum.

Strain the stock.

Remove the fat.

Slightly gelatinous chilled stock.

Homemade Chicken Stock

- 3 lb. chicken wings, backs, necks and/or bones
- 12 cups water
- 2 medium onions, coarsely chopped
- 1 carrot, coarsely chopped
- 1 rib celery, coarsely chopped
- 2 large garlic cloves, coarsely chopped
- 2 sprigs fresh parsley
- ¼ teaspoon peppercorns
- 1 small sprig fresh thyme or ¼ teaspoon dried
- 1 bay leaf

1 Place chicken parts in large stock pot or Dutch oven. Add water. Bring to a boil over medium-high heat, skimming off foam as it rises to surface.

2 Reduce heat to low; skim surface. Add all remaining ingredients; simmer, uncovered, 3 to 3½ hours, skimming surface occasionally. Strain stock through colander into large pot or bowl. Strain stock again through fine strainer or cheesecloth to remove all particles from stock. Refrigerate, uncovered, until thoroughly chilled, 6 to 8 hours or overnight.

4 Remove and discard any fat that has solidified on top of stock. Taste stock; if it tastes watery and lacks flavor, place over high heat and boil until stock has concentrated and has strong flavor. Stock is now ready to use. To store, place 1- to 2-cup amounts in resealable plastic freezer bags. Store flat in freezer up to 4 months.

About 7 cups

PER CUP: 25 calories, 1 g total fat (.5 g saturated fat), 2.5 g protein, 1.5 g carbohydrate, 0 mg cholesterol, 55 mg sodium, 0 g fiber

Roast Chicken Breasts with Caramelized Onion Sauce

SAUCE
- 3 tablespoons butter
- 1½ cups thinly sliced onions
- ⅛ teaspoon sugar
- 2 tablespoons all-purpose flour
- 1½ cups Homemade Chicken Stock (pg. 20)
- ¼ cup dry white wine
- 1 teaspoon tomato paste
- ¼ teaspoon salt
- ⅛ teaspoon freshly ground pepper

CHICKEN
- 6 boneless skinless chicken breast halves
- ¼ teaspoon salt
- ¼ teaspoon freshly ground pepper
- 1 tablespoon olive oil

1 Heat oven to 425°F. Melt butter in medium skillet over medium heat. Add onions; stir until onions are coated with butter. Cover; cook 5 minutes or until onions are wilted and have begun to soften.

2 Uncover skillet; sprinkle onions with sugar. Cook 7 to 10 minutes or until onions are golden brown, stirring occasionally, increasing heat to medium high if necessary.

3 Stir in flour; cook 1 minute, stirring constantly. Add stock, wine and tomato paste; mix well. Bring to a

boil. Stir in ¼ teaspoon salt and ⅛ teaspoon pepper. Reduce heat to low; simmer 10 to 15 minutes or until sauce is slightly thickened.

4 Meanwhile, sprinkle chicken with ¼ teaspoon salt and ¼ teaspoon pepper. Heat large ovenproof skillet over medium-high heat until hot. Add oil; heat until hot. Add chicken; cook 3 to 5 minutes or until golden brown, turning once.

5 Bake 7 to 10 minutes or until chicken juices run clear. Serve chicken with sauce.

6 servings

PER SERVING: 240 calories, 11.5 g total fat (5 g saturated fat), 27.5 g protein, 5.5 g carbohydrate, 80 mg cholesterol, 315 mg sodium, .5 g fiber

Basmati-Sun-Dried Tomato Rice Pilaf

- 1 tablespoon olive oil
- 3 tablespoons finely chopped shallots
- 1 cup basmati rice
- ⅓ cup coarsely chopped dried sun-dried tomatoes
- ½ teaspoon salt
- ¼ teaspoon freshly ground pepper
- 2 cups Homemade Chicken Stock (pg. 20)
- ½ cup (2 oz.) shaved Parmesan cheese

1 Heat oil in medium saucepan over medium heat until hot. Add shallots; sauté 1 to 2 minutes or until soft. Add rice; cook 1 minute, stirring constantly.

2 Add tomatoes, salt, pepper and stock; mix well. Cover; bring to a boil. Reduce heat to low; simmer 15 minutes or until liquid is absorbed and rice is tender. Place in serving bowl; top with cheese.

6 (⅔-cup) servings

PER SERVING: 195 calories, 5.5 g total fat (2.5 g saturated fat), 7.5 g protein, 27.5 g carbohydrate, 5 mg cholesterol, 450 mg sodium, 1 g fiber

Shiitake Mushroom-Corn Chowder

- ¼ lb. bacon, chopped
- 1 large onion, chopped
- 1 rib celery, sliced
- 2 cups (4 oz.) shiitake mushrooms, sliced
- 2 large garlic cloves, minced
- 2 tablespoons all-purpose flour
- 2 medium russet potatoes, peeled, chopped
- 1½ teaspoons salt
- ½ teaspoon freshly ground pepper
- 3 cups Homemade Chicken Stock (pg. 20)
- 2 cups frozen corn
- 1½ cups whipping cream or milk
- 1 teaspoon lemon juice
- ½ cup chopped green onions

1 Sauté bacon in large saucepan over medium heat 4 to 5 minutes or until brown. Remove bacon from saucepan; set aside.

2 Remove all but 2 tablespoons bacon drippings from saucepan. Add onion, celery and mushrooms; sauté 3 minutes or until onion begins to soften. Add garlic; sauté 30 seconds. Stir in flour; cook 2 minutes, stirring constantly.

3 Add bacon, potatoes, salt, pepper and stock; mix well. Bring to a boil, scraping brown bits from bottom of saucepan. Reduce heat to low; simmer 20 to 25 minutes or until potatoes are tender, stirring occasionally.

4 Add corn, cream and lemon juice; mix well. Cook 5 to 8 minutes or until corn is tender. Garnish with green onions.

6 (1⅓-cup) servings

PER SERVING: 360 calories, 26.5 g total fat (14.5 g saturated fat), 7.5 g protein, 27 g carbohydrate, 75 mg cholesterol, 730 mg sodium, 3 g fiber

Making Pizza at Home

Tomato-Olive Pizza with Fresh Mushrooms

Making good pizza is not difficult. The dough takes very little hands-on time, and it can be prepared ahead. The real key is in the baking. The best pizzerias have a brick oven; you can imitate the effect by using a baking stone. The stone sits on the oven rack and absorbs moisture, resulting in an authentic crust that's crisp and crunchy on the outside, soft and chewy in the center. Be sure to heat the stone completely (about 45 minutes) before sliding the pizza onto it. Then get ready to enjoy hot-from-the-oven pizza that rivals the best in town.

Pizza Baking Essentials

Cornmeal helps prevent the dough from sticking to the pizza peel.

A pizza peel is handy for transferring the pizza to the oven, but a baking sheet also works. Shake the pizza often to make sure it's not sticking to the peel.

Move the peel towards the back of the stone and gently shake the pizza onto the baking stone.

- A large baking stone is essential for making pizza. The hot stone cooks the pizza quickly and absorbs moisture from the dough, creating a crisp, crackling crust. Choose the largest, thickest stone that will fit in your oven. With use, the stone darkens; this is normal and doesn't adversely affect baking. Baking stones can be purchased at many kitchen, retail and discount stores. (Visit www.cookingclub.com and click on Featured Links for online resources.)

- Place the oven rack in the bottom position to gain the most heat from the oven. Pizzas need to cook quickly at very hot temperatures.

- Heat the baking stone at least 45 minutes before baking. The stone needs to be very hot to produce a crisp crust.

- Restaurants use a pizza peel to transfer pizzas to the oven. Its long handle keeps the baker's hands from getting too close to the intense heat of the brick oven. Although a pizza peel is not essential—a cookie sheet with no sides can accomplish the same task—it's nice to have if you make pizza often.

- Sliding the pizza onto the baking stone can be daunting at first. It's a task that needs to be completed quickly so you don't lose too much of the oven's heat. Make sure the pizza doesn't stick to the peel (or baking sheet) by shaking it on the peel before opening the oven door. Then open the door, position the peel towards the back of the baking stone and gently shake the pizza off in one motion. Don't worry if the pizza becomes misshapen or hangs off the edge of the stone slightly—it will still bake up beautifully.

Rustic Pizza Crust

DOUGH
¾ cup warm water (110° F. to 115° F.)
½ teaspoon sugar
1 teaspoon active dry yeast
1 tablespoon extra-virgin olive oil
2 to 2¼ cups bread flour
1 teaspoon salt
1 to 2 tablespoons cornmeal

GARLIC OIL
1 large garlic clove
Dash salt
1½ tablespoons extra-virgin olive oil

1 Place water, sugar and yeast in large bowl; let stand 5 to 10 minutes or until foamy. Add 1 tablespoon olive oil and 1 cup of the flour; stir to combine. Add 1 teaspoon salt; stir to combine. Slowly stir in enough of the remaining flour to form a soft dough.
2 On lightly floured surface, knead dough 6 to 8 minutes or until smooth and elastic. Place in greased medium bowl; cover with plastic wrap and clean towel. Let rise in warm place 1 hour or until doubled in size.
3 Meanwhile, place baking stone on bottom oven rack; heat oven to 475°F. for at least 45 minutes. To make garlic oil, smash garlic clove on cutting board with side of knife; sprinkle with dash salt. With knife, mash garlic and salt together to form paste; place in small cup. Stir in 1½ tablespoons oil.
4 Gently punch down dough to deflate; place on lightly floured surface. Roll into 14- to 16-inch round, making sure dough doesn't stick to surface during rolling. (Or divide dough in half; roll into 2 (10-inch) rounds.) Sprinkle cornmeal on pizza peel or rimless baking sheet. Place dough on peel; brush with garlic oil.
5 Top with desired sauce, toppings and cheese, shaking pizza occasionally to make sure it isn't sticking to peel. (If sticking occurs, sprinkle with additional cornmeal.) Slide pizza directly onto baking stone.

Bake 9 to 12 minutes or until bottom of crust is brown and cheese is melted and bubbly.

1 (14- to 16-inch) pizza

PER ⅙ OF CRUST: 115 calories, 3 g total fat (.5 g saturated fat), 2.5 g protein, 18.5 g carbohydrate, 0 mg cholesterol, 220 mg sodium, .5 g fiber

Parmesan-Herb Pizza Sauce

- 1½ teaspoons olive oil
- 1 small garlic clove, minced
- 1½ teaspoons all-purpose flour
- ⅓ cup milk
- ¼ cup whipping cream
- 3 tablespoons freshly grated Parmigiano-Reggiano cheese
- 1 to 2 tablespoons chopped fresh herbs (chives, tarragon, oregano and/or basil)
- ⅛ teaspoon salt
- ⅛ teaspoon freshly ground pepper

Heat oil in medium saucepan over medium heat until hot. Add garlic; cook 30 seconds or until fragrant. Whisk in flour; cook 1 minute. Whisk in milk and cream until smooth. Bring to a boil; boil 1 to 2 minutes or until slightly thickened, stirring constantly. Stir in cheese, herbs, salt and pepper. Place in small bowl; cool to room temperature. (Sauce can be made up to 1 day ahead. Cover and refrigerate.)

½ cup

PER 2 TABLESPOONS: 95 calories, 8 g total fat (4 g saturated fat), 3 g protein, 2.5 g carbohydrate, 20 mg cholesterol, 170 mg sodium, 0 g fiber

Tomato-Basil Pizza Sauce

- 1 tablespoon olive oil
- 2 medium garlic cloves, minced
- 1 (14½-oz.) can diced tomatoes, undrained
- ¼ teaspoon salt
- ⅛ teaspoon freshly ground pepper
- 2 tablespoons coarsely chopped fresh basil or 2 teaspoons dried

Heat oil in medium saucepan over medium heat until hot. Add garlic; cook 30 seconds or until fragrant. Stir in tomatoes, salt and pepper; cook 8 to 10 minutes or until slightly thickened, stirring and mashing tomatoes with potato masher until crushed. Stir in basil. Place in small bowl; cool to room temperature. (Sauce can be made up to 3 days ahead and refrigerated or up to 2 months ahead and frozen.)

1 cup

PER 2 TABLESPOONS: 25 calories, 2 g total fat (0 g saturated fat), .5 g protein, 2.5 g carbohydrate, 0 mg cholesterol, 150 mg sodium, .5 g fiber

Topping your Pizza

Pizza toppings are limited only by your imagination. Use restraint, however, with the amount you pile on. A pizza heavy with sauce and a mountain of toppings will never develop the crisp and light crust that characterizes the best pizzas. Here are two topping suggestions to get you started.

Tomato-Olive Pizza with Fresh Mushrooms

- 1 recipe Rustic Pizza Crust (pg. 23)
- ½ cup Tomato-Basil Pizza Sauce
- ½ cup diced seeded fresh tomatoes
- ½ cup sliced mushrooms
- ⅓ cup sliced pitted Kalamata olives
- 3 tablespoons coarsely torn fresh basil, divided
- 2 tablespoons freshly grated Parmigiano-Reggiano cheese
- 1 cup (4 oz.) shredded mozzarella cheese

Prepare pizza dough through Step 4. Spoon and spread Tomato-Basil Sauce over dough to within ½ inch of edge. Arrange tomatoes, mushrooms, olives and 2 tablespoons of the basil over sauce; sprinkle with Parmesan cheese and mozzarella. (Don't sprinkle cheese over ½-inch border.) Bake pizza according to directions in recipe. Sprinkle with remaining 1 tablespoon basil.

1 (12-slice) pizza

PER SLICE: 150 calories, 5 g total fat (1.5 g saturated fat), 6 g protein, 21 g carbohydrate, 5 mg cholesterol, 400 mg sodium, 1.5 g fiber

Artichoke-Onion Pizza with Fresh Herbs

- 1 recipe Rustic Pizza Crust (pg. 23)
- 1 recipe Parmesan-Herb Pizza Sauce
- 1 cup chopped canned artichoke hearts
- ½ cup diced seeded fresh tomatoes
- ½ cup coarsely chopped red onions
- 1 tablespoon chopped fresh herbs (basil, oregano, tarragon, chervil and/or thyme)
- 1 cup (4 oz.) shredded mozzarella cheese

Prepare pizza dough through Step 4. Spoon and spread Parmesan-Herb Pizza Sauce over dough to within ½ inch of edge. Arrange artichoke hearts, tomatoes, onions and herbs over sauce; sprinkle with cheese. (Don't sprinkle cheese over ½-inch border.) Bake pizza according to directions in recipe.

1 (12-slice) pizza

PER SLICE: 165 calories, 6 g total fat (2.5 g saturated fat), 7 g protein, 22 g carbohydrate, 10 mg cholesterol, 345 mg sodium, 1.5 g fiber

Stand-Up Ribs

Easy Baby-Back Barbecued Ribs

Ribs are at once easy and challenging. The ease comes in the simplicity of it all — heat up the grill, start with a rub, create a great barbeque sauce, and you're set. Well, almost. As with most culinary creations, the devil is in the details, and here are some pointers to keep in mind when pursuing rib masterpieces of your own.

Get rid of any large portions of fat from the ribs. While you're at it, trim away any membrane so that the smoke from your grill can permeate the meat. Season liberally with your rub, which is really the heart and soul of good ribs. Don't cook ribs too fast — you want to let that smoke do its thing, and you don't want a crusty outside surrounding a raw instead. Slow and steady heat is your best bet. Finally, don't overdo the sauce … a little bit goes a long way. Let the rub and the smoke work their subtle magic.

3 Easy Steps to Grilled Ribs

1. Spread a seasoning rub all over the ribs, and arrange them standing upright in a circle. Join the circle of ribs using 1 or 2 metal turkey lacing pins.

2. Place the circle of ribs upright over low heat and grill, covered, 60 minutes or until they're fork-tender, turning them halfway through grilling.

3. Remove the lacing pins; lay the ribs flat on the grill. Brush them with barbecue sauce and grill an additional 15 minutes, turning once and brushing with sauce halfway through.

Easy Baby-Back Barbecued Ribs

2   full racks baby-back pork ribs
¼   cup purchased or homemade
     seasoning rub
2⅔ cups purchased or homemade
     barbecue sauce divided

1 Heat grill. Rub both sides of ribs with seasoning rub. Arrange each rack in a circle (like a crown roast); secure with turkey lacing pins.
2 Grill ribs, covered, standing upright on tips of bones over low heat or coals 30 minutes. Turn; grill an additional 20 to 30 minutes or until meat between rib bones is fork-tender. Meanwhile, place 1 cup of the barbecue sauce in small bowl; reserve remaining sauce.

3 Remove lacing pins; lay ribs flat. Brush with ½ cup of the barbecue sauce. Grill 15 minutes, turning once and brushing with remaining ½ cup barbecue sauce. Serve ribs with reserved sauce.

4 servings

PER SERVING: 940 calories, 50.5 g total fat (18.5 g saturated fat), 49.5 g protein, 73 g carbohydrate, 200 mg cholesterol, 2320 mg sodium, 3 g fiber

Kickback BBQ Sauce

½   cup finely chopped onion
1½ tablespoons olive oil
3   garlic cloves, minced
2¼ cups tomato sauce
¼   cup cider vinegar
¼   cup molasses
¼   cup water
3   tablespoons tomato paste
3   tablespoons Worcestershire
     sauce
½   teaspoon chipotle chile powder

Cook onion in oil in medium saucepan over medium to medium-low heat 5 to 8 minutes or until soft, stirring occasionally. Add garlic; cook 30 seconds or until fragrant. Stir in all remaining ingredients; bring to a boil. Reduce heat to medium-low to low; simmer 15 minutes to blend flavors.

2⅔ cups

PER 1/3 CUP: 90 calories, 3 g total fat (.5 g saturated fat), 1.5 g protein, 17 g carbohydrate, 0 mg cholesterol, 480 mg sodium, 1.5 g fiber

Smoky Seasoning Rub

2   tablespoons smoked paprika
2   teaspoons paprika
1   teaspoon chili powder
1   teaspoon coarse salt
½   teaspoon dried thyme
½   teaspoon garlic powder
½   teaspoon onion powder
½   teaspoon pepper

Combine all ingredients in small bowl.

¼ cup

PER TABLESPOON: 20 calories, .5 g total fat (0 g saturated fat), 1 g protein, 3.5 g carbohydrate, 0 mg cholesterol, 405 mg sodium, 2 g fiber

Rubs and Sauces

If you don't want to make your own seasoning rub and sauce, purchase ready-made versions. But be wary of sauces and rubs with too much salt and artificial smoke flavor. And don't choose a rub with sugar in it. Because this recipe cooks for more than an hour over direct heat, the sugar will caramelize and begin to burn, imparting a burnt taste to the ribs. However, it's fine if the barbecue sauce contains sugar because it's applied only during the last 15 minutes of cooking.

Perfectly Seasoned

Citrus-Glazed Turkey

As the crown jewel of a Thanksgiving meal, a perfectly roasted turkey should be more than good—it should be memorable. Starting with a bird that is naturally moist and flavorful is the first step. But to liven up your Thanksgiving memories, try adding a glistening glaze, a rich spice blend or fragrant fresh herbs. These additions not only enhance the turkey, they also provide an important function. Current roasting wisdom calls for baking stuffing separately. By doing so, you don't risk overcooking the turkey to properly cook the stuffing. Seasoning a turkey with glazes, rubs or herbs replaces the richness, moisture and flavor the stuffing used to provide. Turkey's mild taste is the perfect backdrop for a variety of seasonings, so why not take this succulent centerpiece to new heights?

Use one of three simple techniques. The first is a glaze that creates a crisp, golden skin and adds a slight sweetness to the meat. The second borrows a technique from grilling, using a combination of spices in a dry rub seasoning to spice up the bird. The third uses fresh ingredients, such as herbs and garlic, to enhance the flavor of the meat by getting under the turkey's skin and basting the meat as it bakes.

Three Ways to Season

Each of these techniques adds flavor in a different way. They are all easy and adapt well to a variety of flavors. Get started with the recipes here, then try your hand at creating your own variations.

Method 1: Glazing

Glazes contain sugar (often from fruit juices) and fat, such as butter, to add moisture and richness and to help the turkey brown to a deep golden finish. Baste the bird throughout cooking so it retains moisture and absorbs more of the flavor. You can experiment with ingredients, but if you use a sugar, such as brown sugar or jam, make sure the sugar content doesn't get too high. Too much sugar will cause the skin to burn before the meat is cooked through.

Method 2: Dry Rub

A dry rub seasoning is easy to use with a large turkey. Apply the rub the evening before roasting; then refrigerate the turkey until you're ready to roast it the next day. This gives the seasonings time to flavor the bird. You can also apply a dry rub under the skin to get the seasoning directly onto the meat. A dry rub mixture contains many spices, and the heat level of the spices can be adjusted to suit your style.

Method 3: Under the Skin

To get the seasonings closer to the meat, loosen the skin from the breast meat to form a pocket; then slip the seasonings into it. I like to use olive oil, fresh rosemary and garlic. The garlic cooks slowly to a soft, mellow flavor and the oil bastes the meat as it roasts. The skin protects the fresh rosemary and prevents it from burning. If you have time, use this method for seasoning the entire turkey by loosening the skin around the legs, thighs and wings. Vary the seasonings by using lemon slices, minced shallots or herb butters.

GLAZE
- ¼ cup butter, melted
- 2 teaspoons grated orange peel
- 2 teaspoons grated lemon peel
- 2 teaspoons grated lime peel
- ¼ cup fresh orange juice
- 1 tablespoon fresh lemon juice
- 1 tablespoon fresh lime juice

TURKEY
- ½ orange, cut into wedges
- 1 (12-lb.) turkey
- 1 teaspoon salt
- ½ teaspoon freshly ground pepper

1 Heat oven to 400°F. In small bowl, combine all glaze ingredients; mix well. Set aside.

2 Place orange wedges in body cavity of turkey. Place turkey on rack in large roasting pan. Brush turkey with glaze; sprinkle with salt and pepper.

3 Bake at 400°F. for 30 minutes. Brush turkey with glaze. Cover loosely with foil. Reduce oven temperature to 325°F.; bake an additional 2½ to 3 hours or until internal temperature reaches 180°F. to 185°F., brushing with remaining glaze and basting with any accumulated juices every 30 minutes. Remove foil during last half hour of baking for additional browning, if necessary.

8 servings

PER SERVING: 225 calories, 8 g total fat (3 g saturated fat), 33 g protein, 1.5 g carbohydrate, 100 mg cholesterol, 170 mg sodium, 0 g fiber

Barbecue-Seasoned Roast Turkey

SEASONING
 2 tablespoons ground cumin
 2 tablespoons paprika
 2 tablespoons chili powder
 2 teaspoons salt
1½ teaspoons garlic powder
 1 teaspoon brown sugar
 ½ teaspoon ground allspice
 ¼ teaspoon ground red
     pepper (cayenne)
 ¼ teaspoon freshly ground
     black pepper

TURKEY
 1 (12-lb.) turkey
 2 small onions, coarsely chopped
 2 cups chicken broth
 ¼ cup vegetable oil

1 In small bowl, combine all seasoning ingredients; mix well. Reserve half of seasoning mixture; set aside. Sprinkle remaining seasoning mixture over turkey and into body cavity of turkey. Cover and refrigerate 12 hours to marinate.
2 Heat oven to 400°F. Place turkey on rack in large roasting pan. Place onions in cavity of turkey. Pour broth into pan around turkey.
3 Bake uncovered at 400°F. for 30 minutes. Meanwhile, combine oil with reserved seasoning mix. Brush turkey with seasoning mixture. Cover loosely with foil. Reduce oven temperature to 325°F.; bake an additional 2½ to 3 hours or until internal temperature reaches 180°F. to 185°F., brushing with remaining seasoning mixture and basting with accumulated juices every 30 minutes. Remove foil during last half hour of baking for additional browning, if necessary.

8 servings

PER SERVING: 240 calories, 9 g total fat (2.5 g saturated fat), 34 g protein, 3.5 g carbohydrate, 95 mg cholesterol, 305 mg sodium, 1 g fiber

Rosemary-Garlic-Basted Turkey

 1 (12-lb.) turkey
 4 large garlic cloves, thinly
     sliced
 ¼ cup coarsely chopped fresh
     rosemary or 1½ teaspoons
     dried
 3 tablespoons olive oil
 1 medium onion, coarsely
     chopped
 1 teaspoon salt
 ½ teaspoon freshly ground
     pepper
 2 cups chicken broth

1 Heat oven to 400°F. Loosen turkey skin from breast meat by hand or with rubber scraper, creating a pocket between skin and meat.
2 In small bowl, combine half each of the garlic and rosemary with 1 tablespoon of the oil; mix well. Place mixture between skin and breast meat, distributing evenly. Place onion and remaining garlic and rosemary in body cavity of turkey.
3 Place turkey on rack in large, shallow roasting pan. Brush with remaining 2 tablespoons oil; sprinkle with salt and pepper. Pour broth into pan around turkey.
4 Bake at 400°F. for 30 minutes. Baste with accumulated juices; cover loosely with foil. Reduce oven temperature to 325°F.; bake an additional 2½ to 3 hours or until internal temperature reaches 180°F. to 185°F., basting with accumulated juices every 30 minutes. Remove foil during last half hour of baking for additional browning, if necessary.

8 servings

PER SERVING: 240 calories, 10 g total fat (2.5 g saturated fat), 34 g protein, 2 g carbohydrate, 95 mg cholesterol, 225 mg sodium, 0 g fiber

Roasting Tips

Start with a flavorful, moist bird. I like the quality of local free-range organic turkeys. If they are not available, look for fresh, unfrozen birds. If you use a frozen turkey, thaw it carefully in the refrigerator, allowing several days thawing time for large birds. Here are some additional tips:

- Leave the legs untied so the heat can reach the thigh meat quickly.

- Pour stock, water or wine on the bottom of the roasting pan; replenish it as needed while cooking. The moisture rises during roasting, keeping the meat and skin moist.

- Start with a high oven temperature (400°F.) and roast the turkey for 30 minutes to begin browning the skin; then reduce the heat to 325°F. for slower cooking. Loosely cover the bird with foil during roasting to avoid excessive browning. Remove it for final browning near the end of the cooking time.

- Turkey should be cooked to an internal temperature of 180°F. to 185°F. Use a meat thermometer inserted into the center of the thigh near the body to check for doneness.

- Let the turkey sit loosely covered for 20 to 30 minutes before carving so the juices can resettle in the bird.

Taming Tough Cuts

Country Pork Ribs with Hoisin Sauce and Shiitake Mushrooms

In today's world of fast food, quick-to-fix dinners and three-ingredient recipes, we sometimes forget the joys of simple slow-cooked food, the kind that brings back memories of favorite childhood meals. For me, dishes such as pot roast and country ribs, with their hearty richness, come to mind. While these meals may seem like distant memories, they're easy to re-create using the simple technique of braising.

Braising involves slowly cooking browned meat or vegetables with a small amount of liquid in a tightly covered pot. The beauty of braising is the transformation that takes place: Tough cuts of meat are turned into fork-tender, succulent dishes with rich, glossy sauces. The results are home cooking at its best, with flavors that run the gamut from an updated pot roast with olives to Asian-inspired country pork ribs.

While many of us rely on fast-cooking techniques to keep on schedule during the week, braises are perfect for the weekend. They require several hours of cooking but need little attention, leaving you free to do other things.

How to Braise

Braising and stewing are often erroneously assumed to be the same technique. Braises use whole roasts or larger cuts of meat, whereas stews require small pieces. And with braises, the meat is cooked in a small amount of liquid instead of being covered with liquid, as is done for stews.

Selecting meat When buying meat to braise, look for cuts that contain the most heavily used muscles of the animal. These parts are generously marbled with intramuscular fat, which provides a lot of flavor. They also have a lot of connective tissue, which makes them tough. Long, slow cooking breaks down the muscle fiber and connective tissue, however, making these muscular cuts tasty and tender.

Don't buy lean, tender cuts of meat, such as tenderloin or steak, for braising. Long, moist cooking makes them dry and tough.

Equipment Use a heavy Dutch oven or large pot. Enameled cast iron works very well because the weight of the pan promotes even heating without scorching the meat, and the enameled inside won't react with ingredients. Don't use uncoated cast iron or aluminum if you're cooking with acidic ingredients, such as wine or tomatoes.

Browning Part of the rich flavor in a good braise comes from the browning process, when the meat juices caramelize. It's necessary to brown the meat first because once liquid is added, no additional browning takes place. To brown, make sure the meat is dry, patting it with paper towels, if necessary. Heat the empty Dutch oven until hot (this helps keep the meat from sticking). To tell if the Dutch oven is hot enough, place your hand several inches above its bottom; you should feel heat emanating from the center. Add the oil and heat it until it's hot. (The oil should sizzle when the meat is added.) Brown all sides of the meat. If the meat sticks when you try to turn it, let it cook longer and try again. After the meat is browned, cook the vegetables either until they begin to soften or, for extra flavor, until they're browned.

Liquid The sauce that forms during cooking is an integral part of the braising process. Start with a liquid that adds flavor, such as wine, beef broth or chicken broth. It should only come partway up the side of the meat, not fully cover it.

Temperature and time The slower the cooking, the more tender the meat. The liquid should bubble lazily and gently throughout the process, never boil fast. Meats braised at a high temperature become tough, not tender. Although braised dishes can be made either on top of the stove or in the oven, most are done in the oven because it's easier to maintain an even temperature.

During cooking, collagen, a tough, stringy substance present in the connective tissues, converts to gelatin. The connective tissue becomes soft and dissolves into the sauce, creating tender meat with a shiny, shimmering sauce.

Doneness Braised meats need to be cooked until very tender. A fork should be able to pierce the meat with no resistance, and the meat should begin pulling away from the bone. The meat, if cooked properly, should be well-done. Be careful, however, not to overcook it because it will become dry and stringy.

Braising works best with well-marbled cuts of meat, such as this beef rump roast.

Browning, an important step in braising, creates rich flavor.

The braising liquid should come partway up the side of the meat but not fully cover it.

When the meat is done, it should be fork-tender and begin to pull away from the bone.

Country Pork Ribs with Hoisin Sauce and Shiitake Mushrooms

1 oz. dried shiitake
    mushrooms (about 1⅓ cups)
1 cup boiling water
2 tablespoons vegetable oil
3 lb. bone-in country-style pork ribs
1½ cups chopped onion
4 large garlic cloves, minced
1 tablespoon minced fresh ginger
½ cup apple cider
⅓ cup hoisin sauce
2 tablespoons soy sauce
2 teaspoons dark sesame oil
4 tablespoons sliced green
    onions, divided

1 Heat oven to 325°F. Place mushrooms in small bowl; add boiling water to cover. Let stand 10 to 20 minutes or until soft. Drain, reserving liquid (there should be about ½ cup). Remove and discard stems; slice mushrooms.

2 In large ovenproof skillet, heat oil over medium-high heat until hot. Add ribs in batches; cook 8 to 10 minutes or until browned on all sides. Place on plate.

3 Reduce heat to medium. Add onion to same skillet; cook 2 to 3 minutes or until onion begins to soften. Add garlic and ginger; cook 1 minute or until fragrant. Stir in apple cider, hoisin sauce, soy sauce and reserved mushroom liquid. Return ribs, any accumulated juices and mushrooms to skillet. Cover; place in oven. Bake 1 hour 15 minutes to 1 hour 30 minutes or until tender, turning ribs every 30 minutes.

4 Place ribs on platter; if necessary, skim off any accumulated fat from pan juices. Place skillet with pan juices over high heat; boil 4 to 5 minutes or until slightly thickened. Stir in sesame oil and 2 tablespoons of the green onions; pour over ribs. Sprinkle with remaining 2 tablespoons green onions.

4 servings

PER SERVING: 565 calories, 32.5 g total fat (9.5 g saturated fat), 45 g protein, 23.5 g carbohydrate, 115 mg cholesterol, 595 mg sodium, 3.5 g fiber

Braised Beef Roast with Country Olives

2 tablespoons olive oil
1 (2½-lb.) beef rump roast
½ teaspoon salt
½ teaspoon freshly ground pepper
1 sprig fresh thyme or
    1 teaspoon dried
1 sprig fresh Italian parsley
    or 1 teaspoon dried
1 large fresh or dried bay leaf
3 medium onions, cut into
    1-inch wedges (about 2 cups)
4 large garlic cloves, minced
1 (28-oz.) can crushed
    tomatoes (not in puree)
    or diced tomatoes
1 (14-oz.) can reduced-
    sodium beef broth
2 cups pitted mixed country
    olives

1 Heat oven to 325°F. Heat large nonreactive Dutch oven over medium-high heat until hot. Add oil; heat until hot. Add beef; cook 8 to 10 minutes or until well browned on all sides. Place on plate; sprinkle with salt and pepper.

2 Meanwhile, make bouquet garni by tying fresh thyme, parsley and bay leaf together with string. (If using dried herbs, place in cheesecloth; tie cheesecloth with string.)

3 Add onions to same Dutch oven; cook over medium heat 5 to 7 minutes or until browned, stirring occasionally. Add garlic; cook 30 seconds or until fragrant, stirring constantly. Stir in tomatoes and beef broth; add beef, any accumulated juices and bouquet garni. Bring to a gentle boil over medium heat.

4 Cover and bake 2 hours, turning beef every 30 minutes. Add olives; bake an additional 30 to 40 minutes or until beef is tender.

5 Place beef on platter; cover loosely with foil. Let stand 10 minutes. Skim off any accumulated fat from sauce, if desired. Bring to a boil over high heat; boil 3 to 5 minutes or until slightly thickened. Thinly slice beef; serve with sauce. (Roast may be made up to 2 days ahead. Slice and place in sauce. Cover and refrigerate. Reheat over medium heat until hot.)

6 servings

PER SERVING: 350 calories, 15.5 g total fat (3.5 g saturated fat), 38 g protein, 14.5 g carbohydrate, 90 mg cholesterol, 950 mg sodium, 4 g fiber

The Golden Goose

Roast Goose with Cranberry Fruit Stuffing

If you want to serve a truly festive meat this holiday season, consider a roast goose. Not only does it evoke scenes of Victorian Christmas extravaganzas from Charles Dickens' novels, it's a sumptuous choice for today's celebrations. And the dark, rich meat of goose goes well with stuffing, squash, potatoes and cranberries, so your favorite side dish traditions are the perfect accompaniments.

Roasting a goose is no more difficult than roasting a turkey. Contrary to popular belief, its meat is moist, not greasy. Like ducks, geese have a thick layer of protective fat under their skin. However, that fat drains away if a goose is properly cooked, resulting in a glistening, golden-brown bird that's teeming with class and flavor.

Goose Know-How

Geese are available frozen year-round and often fresh during the holidays. The quality of frozen goose is excellent, but be sure to allow at least 3 days for thawing.

Prepare the goose as directed. Start roasting it at 400°F. to render the fat quickly and start browning the skin. Reduce the temperature to 350°F. to allow the meat time to cook thoroughly. Cover the bird with foil partway through roasting to keep the skin from getting too brown while the legs and thighs continue to cook. If necessary, remove the foil during the last 15 minutes to allow for additional browning.

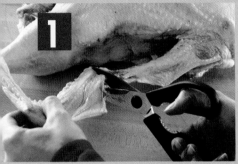

1. There's no meat on the lower parts of the wings, so remove and discard them.

2. Cut away the long neck skin. It's not necessary and contributes excess fat.

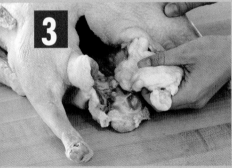

3. Remove excess fat and skin from around and inside the cavity to reduce grease that gathers in the pan.

4. Pierce the skin with a small knife so fat drains during cooking. Don't pierce the meat or juices will be lost during roasting.

5. To eliminate splattering during roasting, barely cover the bottom of the pan with water.

6. Use a baster to remove the fat at least every 30 minutes during roasting.

Roast Goose with Cranberry-Fruit Stuffing

STUFFING
- 6 cups cubed hearty white bread (¾ inch)
- 2 cups cubed hearty cinnamon bread (¾ inch)
- 1 tablespoon butter
- 1 medium onion, chopped
- 1½ cups orange-flavored or regular dried cranberries
- 1 cup coarsely chopped dried apricots
- ¾ cup coarsely chopped dates
- 1 cup lower-sodium chicken broth
- 1 egg, beaten
- 1 tablespoon chopped fresh rosemary
- ¼ teaspoon ground allspice
- ¼ teaspoon salt
- ¼ teaspoon pepper

GOOSE
- 1 (10- to 12-lb.) goose
- ½ teaspoon salt
- ½ teaspoon pepper

1 Heat oven to 350°F. Bake white and cinnamon bread cubes on large rimmed baking sheet 15 minutes or until lightly toasted; place in large bowl. Increase oven temperature to 400°F.

2 Meanwhile, melt butter in small skillet over medium heat. Add onion; cook and stir 3 minutes or until just softened. Add to bread. Stir in cranberries, apricots and dates. Add broth and egg; stir until bread is moistened. Add all remaining stuffing ingredients; stir gently but thoroughly.

3 Cut away and discard excess neck skin and excess fat and skin from cavity of goose. Remove and discard lower 2 portions of wing at joint with knife or kitchen shears.

4 Spoon about 4 cups of the stuffing into cavity of goose (cavity will be about three-fourths full). Loosely tie legs together. Spoon remaining stuffing into greased 11x7-inch glass baking dish; cover with foil. Refrigerate until ready to bake.

5 With small knife, pierce skin all over to allow fat to drain during roasting, being careful not to pierce meat. Rub outside of goose with ½ teaspoon salt and ½ teaspoon pepper; place on rack in roasting pan. Add enough water to just cover bottom of roasting pan to keep juices from splattering.

6 Bake, uncovered, 30 minutes; remove fat that accumulates in pan. Bake an additional 15 minutes; remove fat. Cover goose with foil. Reduce oven temperature to 350°F.; bake an additional 1 hour 15 minutes to 1 hour 30 minutes or until internal temperature of inner thigh reaches 175°F. to 180°F. and stuffing reaches 165°F., basting goose and removing excess fat every 30 minutes. Remove foil during last 15 minutes of cooking to brown skin, if necessary. Cover loosely with foil; let stand 20 minutes before carving.

7 Meanwhile, bake remaining stuffing at 350°F. for 30 minutes or until hot.

8 servings

PER SERVING: 670 calories, 32 g total fat (10 g saturated fat), 37.5 g protein, 60.5 g carbohydrate, 145 mg cholesterol, 890 mg sodium, 5 g fiber

Golden Goose with Caramelized Yukon Gold Potatoes and Olives

GOOSE
1 (10- to 12-lb.) goose
1 medium onion, coarsely chopped
2 teaspoons coarse salt, divided
1½ teaspoons pepper, divided
2 teaspoons dried sage, divided
2 teaspoons dried thyme, divided
1½ lb. Yukon gold potatoes, unpeeled, cubed (1¼ inches)
2 large onions, cut into 1-inch wedges
2 tablespoons grated lemon peel
2 cups pitted mixed olives

GLAZE
3 tablespoons honey
1½ tablespoons orange juice

1 Heat oven to 400°F. Cut away and discard excess neck skin and excess fat and skin from cavity of goose. Remove and discard lower 2 portions of wing at joint with knife or kitchen shears.

2 Place onion in cavity of goose; sprinkle cavity with ½ teaspoon each of the salt and pepper. Loosely tie legs together. With small knife, pierce skin all over to allow fat to drain during roasting, being careful not to pierce meat. Rub outside of goose with ½ teaspoon of the salt, ½ teaspoon of the pepper, 1 teaspoon of the sage and 1 teaspoon of the thyme; place on rack in roasting pan. Add enough water to just cover bottom of roasting pan to keep juices from splattering.

3 Bake, uncovered, 30 minutes; remove fat that accumulates in pan. Bake an additional 15 minutes; remove fat. Cover goose with foil.

4 Meanwhile, combine honey and orange juice. Toss potatoes, onions, lemon peel, and remaining 1 teaspoon salt, ½ teaspoon pepper, 1 teaspoon sage and 1 teaspoon thyme in large bowl. Add to roasting pan; scatter olives over potatoes. Shake pan to evenly distribute potatoes.

5 Reduce oven temperature to 350°F. Bake 1 hour, basting goose and removing excess fat after 30 minutes. Remove foil; brush goose and potatoes with glaze. Bake an additional 15 to 30 minutes or until internal temperature of inner thigh reaches 175°F. to 180°F. Cover loosely with foil; let stand 20 minutes before carving.

8 servings

PER SERVING: 540 calories, 33 g total fat (9.5 g saturated fat), 34 g protein, 27 g carbohydrate, 115 mg cholesterol, 1165 mg sodium, 4 g fiber

Carving 1, 2, 3

Carving a goose is similar to carving a turkey, but keep in mind that a goose has more bone in relation to meat than turkey.

1. Start by thinly slicing the breast meat, carefully following the contour of the breastbone.

2. Pull the leg and thigh away from the body to find the joint that joins the thigh to the cavity; then cut between the joint and the cavity.

3. Separate the thigh and leg at the joint, and cut the meat off the bones. You may need to wiggle the bones (more than you would in carving a turkey) to find the joint areas.

Discovering the Versatile Brisket

Meltingly Tender Pot Roast

What do pot roast, corned beef and Texas BBQ have in common? They're all made from brisket, one of the most versatile cuts of meat available. From a Rosh Hashanah dinner to a Sunday night boiled supper, brisket is the foundation for celebration and casual meals alike. Its versatility is reflected in the many ways it can be prepared — simmered, brined, boiled or barbecued.

Brisket is inexpensive, and it has great flavor. The cut comes from a hardworking muscle in the front of the cow. The more a muscle is used, the more flavor it develops. But hardworking muscles also are tough. To make this cut edible, it requires long, slow cooking. Barbecue masters in Texas get up early in the morning to put their briskets on low, slow fires that are tended all day, giving the meat its unique tenderness and smoky taste. Luckily, you don't have to spend the day at a grill to enjoy brisket. Slow, moist cooking in the oven requires little hands-on tending. The heat and moisture gradually melt the connecting tissues in the brisket, creating a tender piece of meat. Once you master this easy technique, you can take full advantage of this popular cut.

A Slow, Moist Method for Brisket

A whole beef brisket is very large, weighing from 12 to 15 pounds. It's sold in sections called the flat-cut (also called first-cut) and the point-cut. The flat-cut is flatter and leaner, and it's the most commonly available. Here's how to cook it.

Brown for flavor An initial browning develops flavor in the meat and the pan juices that form. For best results, heat a large, heavy and dry ovenproof pot over medium-high heat until hot. Once the pot is hot, add the oil. Cook the beef until all sides are nicely browned. The process doesn't seal in flavor as is commonly thought; instead, it caramelizes the proteins and sugars on the outside of the meat, creating a tasty crust.

Keep it moist Brisket needs to be cooked in a moist environment, but it doesn't need to be totally covered by liquid. Use a heavy cover to trap the moisture inside the pan, creating steam. Turn the brisket halfway through cooking so that all sides of the meat receive equal amounts of moisture.

Check for doneness A 2 - to 3-pound flat-cut brisket takes about 2 hours to cook, but it's important to do a doneness test. The meat should be cooked until a small knife can be easily inserted into the meat. If it's difficult to insert the knife, increase the baking time. Don't use a fork; it can be misleading and can result in an overcooked and dry brisket.

Cut against the grain Always slice brisket across the grain. Slicing it with the grain results in tougher meat.

Cook today, eat tomorrow A brisket often is better the day after it's been cooked because flavors mellow and develop as it sits. After cooking, cool the brisket, refrigerate it overnight, and then slice and reheat the meat in the pan juices until it's hot.

Flat-cut is the most common type of brisket.

Browning develops flavor in the meat and juices.

Turn the meat to cook all sides evenly.

When a knife can be easily inserted, the brisket is done.

Cut the brisket across the grain for the most tender meat.

Meltingly Tender Pot Roast

- 1 tablespoon olive oil
- 1 (2½- to 2¾-lb.) beef brisket (flat-cut or first-cut)
- 2 teaspoons dried thyme
- ½ teaspoon salt
- ½ teaspoon freshly ground pepper
- 1 tablespoon butter
- 4 large onions, halved, sliced (½ inch)
- 4 large garlic cloves, minced
- ¾ cup reduced-sodium beef broth
- ¾ cup red wine or additional beef broth
- 1 tablespoon Worcestershire sauce
- 4 medium carrots, cut into 2-inch pieces
- 4 medium Yukon Gold potatoes (1¾ lb.), unpeeled, quartered, or halved if small

1 Heat oven to 350°F. Heat heavy large pot over medium-high heat until hot. Add oil; heat until hot. Add brisket; cook 5 to 7 minutes or until browned, turning once. Place on plate; sprinkle both sides with thyme, salt and pepper.

2 Melt butter in pot over medium heat. Add onions; stir to coat with butter. Cover and cook 5 minutes or until wilted. Uncover; increase heat to medium high. Cook 5 minutes or until onions start to brown, stirring occasionally. Add garlic; cook 30 seconds or until fragrant, stirring constantly. Stir in broth, wine and Worcestershire sauce.

3 Return brisket to pot; spoon onions over brisket. Cover; bake 1 hour. Turn brisket; spoon onions over brisket. Arrange carrots and potatoes around brisket. Cover; bake an additional 1 hour or until brisket and vegetables are tender when pierced with knife.

4 Place brisket on cutting board; cover loosely with foil. Let stand 10 to 15 minutes. Thinly slice brisket; serve with onions, potatoes and carrots. Spoon any accumulated pan juices over brisket.

6 servings

PER SERVING: 440 calories, 14.5 g total fat (5.5 g saturated fat), 37.5 g protein, 40.5 g carbohydrate, 70 mg cholesterol, 345 mg sodium, 6.5 g fiber

Chipotle-Smoked Chile Brisket

    2 tablespoons packed brown
        sugar
 1½ tablespoons ground cumin
    2 to 3 teaspoons ground chipotle
        chile powder
    1 tablespoon paprika
   ½ teaspoon salt
   ½ teaspoon freshly ground pepper
    1 (2½- to 2¾-lb.) beef brisket
        (flat-cut or first-cut)
    2 tablespoons olive oil, divided
    1 large onion, halved, sliced
    4 large garlic cloves, minced
    1 (15-oz.) can tomato puree
 1¼ cups reduced-sodium beef broth
    2 tablespoons molasses
 1½ tablespoons red wine vinegar

1 Heat oven to 350°F. In small bowl, stir together brown sugar, cumin, chipotle chile powder, paprika, salt and pepper. Sprinkle over both sides of brisket.

2 Heat heavy large pot over medium-high heat until hot. Add 1 tablespoon of the oil; heat until hot. Add brisket; cook 5 to 7 minutes or until browned, turning once. Place on plate.

3 Add remaining 1 tablespoon oil and onion to pot; cook over medium heat

3 to 4 minutes or until slightly wilted. Add garlic; cook 30 seconds or until fragrant, stirring constantly. Stir in all remaining ingredients. Return brisket to pot; spoon sauce over brisket.

4 Cover; bake 2 hours or until tender when pierced with knife, turning halfway through baking.

5 Place brisket on cutting board; cover loosely with foil. Let stand 10 to 15 minutes. Thinly slice brisket; serve with sauce.

6 servings

PER SERVING: 365 calories, 15.5 g total fat (4.5 g saturated fat), 36 g protein, 22 g carbohydrate, 60 mg cholesterol, 575 mg sodium, 3 g fiber

Italian Beef Brisket

    1 tablespoon olive oil
    1 (2½- to 2¾-lb.) beef brisket
        (flat-cut or first-cut)
    1 teaspoon dried sage
    1 teaspoon dried basil
   ½ teaspoon salt
   ½ teaspoon freshly ground pepper
    2 large onions, chopped
    6 large garlic cloves, minced
 1½ cups red wine or reduced-
        sodium beef broth
    1 (28-oz.) can diced tomatoes
   ¾ cup reduced-sodium beef broth
        Pinch saffron threads, crushed
   ½ cup mixed pitted olives

1 Heat oven to 350°F. Heat heavy large pot over medium-high heat until hot. Add oil; heat until hot. Add brisket; cook 5 to 7 minutes or until browned, turning once. Place on plate; sprinkle both sides with sage, basil, salt and pepper.

2 Add onions to pot; cook over medium heat 2 minutes or until beginning to soften, stirring occasionally. Add garlic; cook 30 seconds or until fragrant, stirring constantly. Increase heat to high. Add wine; bring to a boil, scraping up any browned bits from bottom of pot. Boil 4 to 5 minutes or until reduced by half. Stir in tomatoes, broth and saffron. Return brisket to pot; spoon some of the tomatoes over brisket.

3 Cover; bake 1 hour. Turn brisket; spoon some of the tomatoes over brisket. Bake, covered, an additional 45 minutes. Stir in olives; bake, covered, 15 minutes or until brisket is tender when pierced with knife.

4 Place brisket on cutting board; cover loosely with foil. Let stand 10 to 15 minutes. Meanwhile, with potato masher, crush tomatoes in pot. Thinly slice brisket; serve with tomato sauce.

6 servings

PER SERVING: 330 calories, 13.5 g total fat (4.5 g saturated fat), 35.5 g protein, 14.5 g carbohydrate, 60 mg cholesterol, 545 mg sodium, 2.5 g fiber

Duck Demystified

Roast Duck with Sherry Vinegar Sauce

A flawless roast duck is considered a major accomplishment by most cooks' standards. Indeed, producing a bird with golden, crisp skin and rich, tender meat can be challenging. That's because duck's flavorful dark meat is protected by a layer of fat just under the skin. While that fat makes the duck meat rich and tasty, it can also make it greasy. For a crackling skin and meat without greasiness, the fat must be removed during cooking.

This method produces a fine roast duck, but after experimenting with other techniques, you'll want to add a step that improves the process: an Asian technique for air-drying the duck in the refrigerator before roasting. This tightens the skin and helps eliminate excess fat. You'll love the results of this method—crisp skin and moist, tender meat. It's easy, and each step can be done ahead, making roast duck an ideal entree for entertaining.

Three Steps to Roasting Duck

1. AIR-DRY

Drying the duck before roasting tightens its skin and helps release and eliminate excess fat. Begin by cutting away excess skin and visible fat from the neck and rear portion of the duck (1). Then prick the skin with the tip of a knife so that fat drains during roasting (2). Be careful not to pierce the meat. Season the duck and place it on a rack set over a baking sheet. Refrigerate it, uncovered, for 12 to 24 hours, making sure there is good air circulation around the duck. The skin of the duck may darken slightly (3).

2. PARTIALLY ROAST

During this step, which can be done up to 8 hours before serving, the duck cooks at a moderate temperature for 50 to 60 minutes. The fat drains away, the skin remains soft and moist, and the meat is still red near the bone. After the duck cools, carve it. Remove the leg and thigh portion from the bird, cutting between the joint (4). This joint is located farther back on the duck than it is on a chicken. Cut between the leg and thigh joint to separate them. Remove the breast from the rib cage. The wings have no meat on them so they are not used. You can save the carcass to make duck stock.

3. FINISH ROASTING

In a hot oven, roast the duck pieces until the skin is crispy and the internal temperature reaches 175°F. to 180°F. This renders the remaining fat and creates a crispy texture.

1. Trim away excess skin and visible fat.

2. Prick the skin with the tip of a knife.

3. The duck is seasoned and dried. The skin may darken during the process.

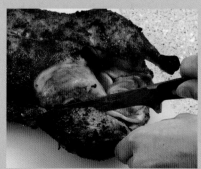

4. Carve the partially roasted and cooled duck.

oven; let stand 30 minutes or until cool enough to handle.

5 Line rimmed baking sheet with foil. With sharp knife, carve duck into 4 pieces: 2 legs and thighs, and 2 breasts. (If desired, cut between leg and thigh, and cut each breast in half.) Place pieces on baking sheet. (Duck may be made to this point up to 8 hours ahead. Cover and refrigerate. Baking time may need to be increased by 5 minutes.)

6 When ready to serve, heat oven to 425°F. Bake duck, uncovered, 20 to 25 minutes or until skin is crispy and internal temperature reaches 175°F. to 180°F. To serve, pass sauce separately. Or spoon sauce over individual serving plates; place duck on sauce.

4 servings

PER SERVING: 655 calories, 44.5 g total fat (18 g saturated fat), 57 g protein, 5 g carbohydrate, 235 mg cholesterol, 750 mg sodium, .5 g fiber

Lemon-Ginger Roast Duck

1 (4½- to 5-lb.) duck
8 slices fresh ginger (¼ inch)
4 lemon slices (¼ inch)
3 tablespoons soy sauce
1 tablespoon honey
2 teaspoons grated lemon peel
1 teaspoon grated fresh ginger
1 teaspoon ground anise or fennel seeds
½ teaspoon freshly ground pepper
1 teaspoon lemon juice

1 Remove and discard excess skin, fat and tail from duck. Rinse duck; pat dry with paper towels. Place ginger and lemon slices in duck cavity; tie legs together.

2 In small bowl, stir together all remaining ingredients. Prick skin of duck with knife; generously brush with soy mixture. Pour remaining soy mixture into duck cavity.

3 Place duck on roasting rack in shallow pan. Refrigerate, uncovered, at least 12 hours or up to 24 hours to allow skin to dry.

4 When ready to roast duck, heat oven to 350°F. Place duck with roasting rack in shallow roasting pan. Bake 50 to 60 minutes or until internal temperature reaches 155°F. (Juices will still run pink and meat will be red near the bone.) Remove from oven; let stand 30 minutes or until cool enough to handle.

5 Line rimmed baking sheet with foil. With sharp knife, carve duck into 4 pieces: 2 legs and thighs, and 2 breasts. (If desired, cut between leg and thigh, and cut each breast in half.) Place pieces on baking sheet. (Duck may be made to this point up to 8 hours ahead. Cover and refrigerate. Baking time may need to be increased by 5 minutes.)

6 When ready to serve, heat oven to 425°F. Bake duck, uncovered, 20 to 25 minutes or until skin is crispy and internal temperature reaches 175°F. to 180°F.

4 servings

PER SERVING: 490 calories, 27 g total fat (7.5 g saturated fat), 54.5 g protein, 3 g carbohydrate, 175 mg cholesterol, 365 mg sodium, 0 g fiber

Crispy Roast Duck with Glazed Kumquats

DUCK
1 (4½- to 5-lb.) duck
½ teaspoon kosher (coarse) salt
½ teaspoon freshly ground pepper
8 kumquats, quartered
2 shallots, quartered
1 cup reduced-sodium chicken broth

KUMQUATS
1 cup sliced kumquats, seeded
2 tablespoons sugar
1 teaspoon grated fresh ginger
¼ cup water
1 teaspoon balsamic vinegar

1 Remove and discard excess skin, fat and tail from duck. Rinse duck; pat dry with paper towels. Sprinkle inside of duck cavity with ¼ teaspoon of the salt and ¼ teaspoon of the pepper; sprinkle outside of duck with remaining ¼ teaspoon salt and ¼ teaspoon pepper.

2 Place 8 kumquats and shallots in duck cavity; tie legs together. Place duck on roasting rack in shallow roasting pan. Refrigerate, uncovered, at least 12 hours or up to 24 hours to allow skin to dry.

3 Meanwhile, place all kumquat ingredients in small saucepan. Bring to a boil over medium heat; boil 3 to 4 minutes or until liquid is reduced and kumquats are lightly glazed. Cool to room temperature. (Kumquats can be made up to 3 days ahead. Cover and refrigerate. Bring to room temperature before serving.)

4 When ready to roast duck, heat oven to 350°F. Prick skin of duck all over with small knife, being careful not to prick meat. Place duck with roasting rack in shallow roasting pan. Bake 50 to 60 minutes or until internal temperature reaches 155°F. (Juices will still run pink and meat will be red near the bone.) Remove from oven; let stand 30 minutes or until cool enough to handle.

5 Meanwhile, remove fat from roasting pan, leaving meat drippings. Set pan over medium-high heat. When pan is hot, add broth; bring to a boil. Boil until reduced by half. (If making ahead, cover and refrigerate. To serve, heat until hot.)

6 Line rimmed baking sheet with foil. With sharp knife, carve duck into 4 pieces: 2 legs and thighs, and 2 breasts. (If desired, cut between leg and thigh, and cut each breast in half.) Place pieces on baking sheet. (Duck may be made to this point up to 8 hours ahead. Cover and refrigerate. Baking time may need to be increased by 5 minutes.)

7 When ready to serve, heat oven to 425°F. Bake duck, uncovered, 20 to 25 minutes or until skin is crispy and internal temperature reaches 175°F. to 180°F. Serve duck with pan sauce and glazed kumquats.

4 servings

PER SERVING: 535 calories, 27.5 g total fat (7.5 g saturated fat), 56 g protein, 13 g carbohydrate, 175 mg cholesterol, 480 mg sodium, 2.5 g fiber

41

Mastering the Tenderloin

Marinated Beef Tenderloin with Roasted Shallots and Port Reduction

Beef tenderloin is one of the simplest and easiest cuts of meat to prepare, and it always makes a spectacular presentation. It's a versatile meat that can be served in an array of appetizers, as the main course at an open-house buffet or as the centerpiece of a sit-down dinner. The ease of preparation and do-ahead steps make it the perfect choice for busy times.

Tenderloin Tips

Beef tenderloin is the most tender cut of beef and, accordingly, the most expensive. Protect your investment by following these tips.

Buying Purchase beef tenderloin that has been trimmed by the butcher. Whole, untrimmed beef tenderloin is less expensive per pound but, because of the amount of fat surrounding the muscle, you actually pay more per pound of usable meat when trimming it yourself.

Browning Roast beef tenderloin cooks quickly in a hot oven, but because the cooking time is short, it doesn't have enough time to get evenly browned. Browning the tenderloin on the stovetop solves this problem by caramelizing the sugars and proteins before roasting for added color and flavor. Before browning, compare the size of the tenderloin to the pan. You may need to curl the tenderloin in the pan or cut the tenderloin into two pieces to fit.

To prevent the meat from sticking to the pan during browning, first place a dry heavy skillet over the heat until hot. Once the pan is hot, add the oil and swirl to coat. Heat the oil briefly, until it's hot but not smoking. Add the meat and cook it until brown, turning each side only when it becomes brown.

Roasting Roast the tenderloin in a shallow heavy pan. A rimmed baking sheet works well for whole tenderloins. Avoid deep roasters; the high sides keep the heat from penetrating the beef quickly and less browning occurs.

Tenderloins roast quickly at high temperatures, so timing is crucial. It's also important to have an instant-read thermometer for checking the internal temperature. Beef tenderloin is best served rare to medium rare (125°F. to 135°F.). Never cook beef tenderloin past medium; the meat begins to dry out and becomes tough the longer it cooks. If you prefer your meat medium-well to well done, it may be best to use another cut of meat because the flavor and tenderness of the tenderloin is lost at those temperatures.

After roasting, let the tenderloin stand, loosely covered with foil, at least 15 minutes to allow the juices to distribute evenly (the internal temperature continues to rise during this time). During roasting, the juices inside the meat flow towards the center; once cooking has stopped, the juices need time to redistribute evenly. If the resting time is too short, the juices run out during carving and the slices are pale brown around the outside edge and bright red in the center. Proper standing time yields uniformly pink slices.

Browning tenderloin.

Marinated Beef Tenderloin with Roasted Shallots and Port Reduction

MARINADE
- 3 cups port
- ½ medium orange, sliced
- ½ medium lemon, sliced
- 3 garlic cloves, minced
- 1 tablespoon chopped fresh sage
- 1 bay leaf
- Dash allspice

BEEF AND SAUCE
- 1 (2-lb.) center-cut beef tenderloin
- 12 large shallots, peeled, quartered
- 1 tablespoon plus 1 teaspoon olive oil
- 1 teaspoon kosher (coarse) salt
- ½ teaspoon freshly ground pepper
- 1½ cups beef broth
- 2 tablespoons unsalted butter, softened

1 In large, resealable plastic bag, combine all marinade ingredients. Place beef and shallots in bag; seal bag. Refrigerate 24 hours, turning bag occasionally.

2 Heat oven to 425°F. Spray shallow roasting pan with nonstick cooking spray. Remove beef from marinade; pat dry with paper towels. Strain marinade, reserving liquid. Remove shallots from marinade ingredients; set shallots aside. Discard remaining marinade ingredients. Pat shallots dry with paper towels; place in medium bowl. Add 1 teaspoon of the oil; toss to coat.

3 Heat large skillet over medium-high heat until hot. Add remaining 1 tablespoon oil; heat until hot. Add tenderloin; cook 4 to 6 minutes or until browned on all sides, turning occasionally. (Tenderloin can be browned up to 4 hours ahead. Cover and refrigerate until ready to bake. Immediately skip to step 6 and make sauce.)

4 Place tenderloin in roasting pan; set unwashed skillet aside. Sprinkle tenderloin with salt and pepper. Arrange shallots around beef.

5 Bake 20 to 25 minutes or until internal temperature reaches 130°F. for medium rare or until of desired doneness. Remove from oven. Cover loosely with foil; let stand 15 minutes before slicing.

6 Meanwhile, heat same skillet over high heat until hot. Add reserved marinade; bring to a boil, scraping browned bits from bottom of skillet. Add broth; return to a boil. Boil over high heat until slightly thickened and syrupy, stirring once or twice. (Liquid will be reduced to about ⅔ cup.) Reduce heat to medium; whisk in butter just until melted. Serve immediately. (Sauce can be made up to 4 hours ahead. If making ahead, reheat and whisk in butter immediately before serving.)

7 To serve, cut tenderloin in half lengthwise. Cut each half crosswise into ⅜-inch-thick slices. Mound shallots in center of each dinner plate. Arrange sliced beef over shallots. Drizzle sauce around shallots and beef.

6 servings

PER SERVING: 375 calories, 17.5 g total fat (7 g saturated fat), 35 g protein, 18.5 g carbohydrate, 95 mg cholesterol, 615 mg sodium, 1.5 g fiber

Herb-Crusted Beef Tenderloin with Balsamic Mustard

- 3 tablespoons olive oil
- 1 (4½-lb.) whole beef tenderloin, trimmed
- 1 teaspoon kosher (coarse) salt
- 1 teaspoon freshly ground pepper
- ¼ cup coarse-ground mustard
- 3 tablespoons balsamic vinegar
- 1 tablespoon fennel seeds, crushed

- 1 tablespoon grated lemon peel
- 2 garlic cloves, minced
- 2 tablespoons chopped fresh thyme
- 2 tablespoons chopped fresh rosemary
- 2 tablespoons chopped fresh sage

1 Heat oven to 425°F. Line 17x12x1-inch pan with foil. Heat large skillet over medium-high heat until hot. Add oil; heat until hot.

2 Add tenderloin. (It may be necessary to curve tenderloin to fit in skillet. If skillet is not large enough to hold tenderloin, cut in half crosswise.) Cook 8 to 10 minutes or until browned on all sides, turning occasionally. (Tenderloin can be browned up to 4 hours ahead. Cover and refrigerate until ready to bake.)

3 Place tenderloin in pan. Sprinkle with salt and pepper.

4 In small bowl, stir together mustard, vinegar, fennel, lemon peel and garlic. Spread over tenderloin. In another small bowl, combine thyme, rosemary and sage. Sprinkle herb mixture over mustard mixture.

5 Bake 25 to 30 minutes or until internal temperature reaches 130°F. for medium rare or until of desired doneness.

6 Remove tenderloin from oven. Cover loosely with foil; let stand 15 minutes before slicing.

14 servings

PER SERVING: 200 calories, 11 g total fat (3.5 g saturated fat), 23.5 g protein, 1 g carbohydrate, 60 mg cholesterol, 225 mg sodium, .5 g fiber

Molasses Roast Tenderloin with Wasabi Cream

CREAM
- 1 cup plain yogurt
- 3 tablespoons chopped fresh chives
- 1 teaspoon grated fresh ginger
- 1 to 2 teaspoons wasabi paste
- ¼ teaspoon kosher (coarse) salt
- ¼ teaspoon freshly ground pepper

BEEF
- 3 tablespoons olive oil
- 1 (4½-lb.) whole beef tenderloin, trimmed
- 1 teaspoon kosher (coarse) salt
- 1 teaspoon freshly ground pepper
- ½ cup molasses
- 1 tablespoon dark sesame oil
- 3 garlic cloves, minced

1 Place all cream ingredients in food processor; process until well blended and smooth. Cover; refrigerate until ready to serve. (Cream can be made up to 2 days ahead.)

2 Heat oven to 425°F. Line 17x12x1-inch pan with foil. Heat large skillet over medium-high heat until hot. Add 3 tablespoons oil; heat until hot. Add tenderloin. (It may be necessary to curve tenderloin to fit in skillet. If skillet is not large enough to hold tenderloin, cut in half crosswise.) Cook 8 to 10 minutes or until browned on all sides, turning occasionally. (Tenderloin can be browned up to 4 hours ahead. Cover and refrigerate until ready to bake.)

3 Place tenderloin in pan. Sprinkle all sides with 1 teaspoon salt and 1 teaspoon pepper. In small bowl, combine molasses, sesame oil and 3 garlic cloves; mix well. Spoon and spread over tenderloin.

4 Bake 25 to 30 minutes or until internal temperature reaches 130°F. for medium rare or until of desired doneness. Remove from oven. Cover loosely with foil; let stand 15 minutes before slicing. (Tenderloin can be roasted up to 6 hours ahead. Cover and refrigerate; bring to room temperature before serving.) Serve beef with cream.

14 servings

PER SERVING: 245 calories, 12 g total fat (3.5 g saturated fat), 24 g protein, 10 g carbohydrate, 65 mg cholesterol, 210 mg sodium, 0 g fiber

Cooking Lobster at Home

**Grilled Lobster with
Shallot Red Pepper Butter**

Whether you live near the ocean or are landlocked a thousand or two miles away, lobster is the king of seafood. And with modern shipping timing and techniques, ocean-fresh lobster is at practically everyone's disposal. There is something that happens when cracking the shells and prying out the meat that makes the lobster seem even sweeter. It brings dreams of the ocean and the adventure that awaits.

Lobster How-To

Before boiling.

BUYING, STORING LOBSTERS

Begin by selecting lobsters that are active. Look for tails that curl tightly and claws that hold firm, not limp. It's best to purchase and cook lobsters on the same day. However, they can be stored overnight in a cardboard box or paper bag with holes in the lowest section of the refrigerator. Never store lobsters on ice, and never hold them in fresh (tap) water.

COOKING LOBSTERS

Some people are squeamish about cooking a lobster while it's alive, but it really is necessary: Once a lobster dies, the meat begins to deteriorate quickly and can become toxic. If you don't like handling an active lobster, you can numb it by placing it in the freezer for 1 to 2 hours. It may then be cooked according to any of the methods below.

After boiling.

Equipment You'll need a very large pot to cook several lobsters at once—a large stock or canning pot will cook up to four lobsters comfortably. If you don't have a pot large enough to hold all the lobsters, cook the lobsters in batches. Lobster cooks quickly, so the wait isn't long.

Boiling Boiling is the easiest method for cooking lobsters. Make sure the lobsters are completely submerged; cover and begin timing once the water returns to a boil.

Steaming Some people prefer the steaming method because they believe the lobsters contain less liquid when steamed rather than boiled. Place lobsters on a steaming rack over the liquid, and begin timing when the liquid is at a full boil.

Parboiling Grilled or roasted lobster should be split before being cooked. The easiest and most humane way to prepare lobsters for these methods is to partially boil them for 3 to 4 minutes rather than splitting them while alive.

Cutting in half.

Doneness To check for doneness, turn the lobster upside down and look at the tail where it joins the body. The tail meat should be firm, white and creamy, not translucent.

CUTTING LOBSTERS IN HALF

Place the lobster on a cutting board shell side up. Place the tip of a large chef's knife behind the head of the lobster and press firmly down. Cut through the tail portion of the lobster. Then turn the lobster and cut through the head.

PARTS OF A LOBSTER

Sand sac This is located directly behind the eyes of the lobster and is actually the stomach of the lobster. Remove the sand sac with a spoon.

Halved lobster.

Intestine The intestine runs down the side of the tail and is often dark gray in color. It should be removed.

Tomalley The soft light green substance found in the body of the lobster is the tomalley. It is the liver and pancreas of the lobster and acts as a filter to keep the meat wholesome. Because the tomalley can accumulate contaminants from the environment, it is currently suggested that you remove and not consume the tomalley.

Roe Female lobsters will often contain eggs, or roe, which are located in the body cavity and are bright red in color. Many people find this a delicious prize when they split apart their lobster.

Grilled Lobster with Shallot-Red Pepper Butter

BUTTER
- 1 cup butter
- ½ cup finely chopped shallots
- ¼ cup fresh lemon juice
- 2 teaspoons crushed red pepper flakes

LOBSTER
- 4 quarts (16 cups) water
- ¼ cup sea salt
- 4 (1¼- to 1½-lb.) lobsters

1 Melt butter in small saucepan over medium heat. Add shallots; sauté 60 to 90 seconds or until shallots are fragrant and begin to soften. Stir in lemon juice and red pepper flakes; remove from heat. Divide butter mixture in half. Set aside half of mixture to brush on lobster during grilling; reserve remaining half to serve warm with lobster.

2 Place water and salt in large pot. Cover; bring to a boil over high heat. Add lobsters; cover and return to a boil. When water boils, cook lobsters 3 to 4 minutes or until lobster shells begin to turn a mottled red. Remove lobsters from pot; immediately plunge into large bowl of ice water to stop cooking.

3 Place lobsters on cutting board; cut in half lengthwise. Remove sand sac, intestinal track and liver (see p. 46). Crack claws to allow heat from grill to penetrate. (Lobster can be made up to 3 hours ahead. Cover and refrigerate.)

4 Heat grill. Brush lobster halves with half of butter mixture. Place on gas grill over medium heat or on charcoal grill 4 to 6 inches from medium coals. Cook 6 to 8 minutes or until lobster meat is opaque, turning once and brushing occasionally with butter mixture. Heat remaining butter mixture in small saucepan until warm. Serve lobsters with warm butter mixture.

4 servings

PER SERVING: 405 calories, 29.5 g total fat (18 g saturated fat), 31 g protein, 4 g carbohydrate, 185 mg cholesterol, 1240 mg

Ginger-Herb Roasted Lobster

sodium, .5 g fiber

SAUCE
- 1 cup chopped fresh Italian parsley
- ½ cup chopped fresh basil
- ½ cup chopped fresh dill
- ⅓ cup water
- 2 tablespoons chopped fresh ginger
- 2 large garlic cloves
- 2 tablespoons olive oil
- ¼ teaspoon salt
- ⅛ teaspoon freshly ground pepper

LOBSTER
- 4 quarts (16 cups) water
- ¼ cup sea salt
- 4 (1¼- to 1½-lb.) lobsters

1 In blender, combine all sauce ingredients; blend until smooth. Set aside.

2 Place water and salt in large pot. Cover; bring to a boil over high heat. Add lobsters; cover and return to a boil. When water boils, cook lobsters 3 to 4 minutes or until lobster shells begin to turn a mottled red. Remove lobsters from pot; immediately plunge into large bowl of ice water to stop cooking.

3 Place lobsters on cutting board; cut in half lengthwise. Remove sand sac, intestinal track and liver (see p. 46). Place lobsters cut side up in 2 (15x10x1-inch) pans. Spread herb sauce over lobster halves. (Lobster can be made up to 3 hours ahead. Cover and refrigerate.)

4 When ready to cook, arrange 2 oven racks, one above the other, in center third of oven. Heat oven to 425°F. Bake lobsters 8 to 12 minutes or until lobster meat turns opaque, switching positions of pans halfway through baking.

4 servings

PER SERVING: 215 calories, 8 g total fat (1 g saturated fat), 31 g protein, 4 g carbohydrate, 105 mg cholesterol, 1200 mg sodium, .5 g fiber

Boiled Lobster

- 4 quarts (16 cups) water
- ¼ cup sea salt
- 4 (1¼- to 1½-lb.) lobsters

1 Place water and salt in large pot. (There should be enough water in pot to cover lobsters, but not too much or water will boil over. Depending on size of pot, you may need more or less water.) Cover; bring to a boil over high heat.

2 Add lobsters, head first, to boiling water; cover and return to a boil.

3 Once water returns to a boil, cook 9 to 12 minutes or until lobster meat is opaque. Remove lobsters from water, allowing excess water to drain off. Serve with dipping sauces or melted butter and fresh lemon juice.

4 servings

PER SERVING: 145 calories, 1 g total fat (0 g saturated fat), 30 g protein, 2 g carbohydrate, 105 mg cholesterol, 1045 mg sodium, 0 g fiber

Steamed Lobster

- 6 cups water
- 1 tablespoon salt
- 4 (1¼- to 1½-lb.) lobsters

1 Place steaming rack in large pot. Add water and salt. Cover; bring to a boil over high heat.

2 Add lobsters; cover and return to a boil.

3 Once water is boiling, cook lobsters 10 to 14 minutes or until lobster meat is opaque. Serve with dipping sauces or melted butter and fresh lemon juice.

4 servings

PER SERVING: 145 calories, 1 g total fat (0 g saturated fat), 30 g protein, 2 g carbohydrate, 105 mg cholesterol, 560 mg sodium, 0 g fiber

Black Beauties

Pasta with Roasted Tomatoes and Mussels

Mussels have never gained the spotlight in this country like they have in Belgium, one of the world's top consumers of mussels. But their popularity is growing—U.S. production of mussels has doubled during the past eight years. Mussels are one of the best seafood bargains in the market today, both at restaurants and in grocery stores. For the home cook, they are easy to prepare and quick to cook. Simple one-dish recipes where the mussels are served in their shells are the best. Add a loaf of hearty bread and a bottle of wine, and you have a meal that will brighten even the dreariest winter day.

Buying and Cooking Mussels

Mussels are available year-round. The traditional peak season has been from fall to early spring, but Mediterranean mussels, which spawn during the opposite season, are now cultivated in the Northwest and are available throughout the summer.

BUYING MUSSELS

Types There are several types of mussels available. All are commercially cultivated and can be used interchangeably. The most common are blue mussels. Their shells range in color from blue to almost black. They're found along the Atlantic Coast, particularly in New England and near Prince Edward Island, as well as in Europe. Green-lipped mussels come from New Zealand and Southeast Asia and have beautiful dark shells with green highlights. They're larger than blue mussels and have a meatier, firmer texture. Penn Cove and Mediterranean mussels from the West Coast are smaller and are available when blue mussel season ends.

Choosing Look for mussels with tightly closed shells. As with many shellfish, mussels need to be alive when cooked because they begin to deteriorate very quickly. The shells may open slightly as the mussels react to temperature changes, but if tapped sharply, they should close. If a shell doesn't close, discard the mussel. Also discard any mussels with broken shells.

Storing Store mussels in the coldest part of the refrigerator in a plastic bag with the top left open or in a bowl covered with wet paper towels (make sure liquid does not accumulate in the bottom of the bowl). Never store mussels in an airtight container; they need to breathe and remain moist. Also, never submerge them in water. Mussels should be cooked within one to two days after they are purchased.

PREPARATION

Cleaning Most mussels are farm-raised and often are cleaned before coming to market; they require only slight rinsing before use. If they haven't been cleaned, use a brush to scrub the shells to get rid of any mud or grit. Clean the mussels just before cooking.

Removing the beard The little tuft of wiry thread on the lip of a mussel is referred to as the beard; the mussel uses the beard, or byssus thread, to attach itself to ropes, rocks and other surfaces. The amount and thickness of the beard can vary according to where the mussels were grown. Mussels found in sheltered water have thin beards; those in windy, stormy water have strong, thick beards. The beard should be removed before the mussels are cooked. Using a small, sharp knife, cut off the beard level with the lip of the shell. Many farm-raised mussels are debearded before coming to market, so this step may not be necessary.

COOKING

Mussels cook very quickly and toughen if overcooked, so watch them carefully. They usually cook in 2 to 5 minutes, depending on their size. When the shells open wide, they are done. Remove and discard any shells that do not open.

SERVING

Mussels exude a flavorful liquid as they cook, so they should be served with their cooking liquid. Serve them in wide shallow bowls, accompanied by a fork as well as a spoon. Use the fork to detach the mussel from the shell (it detaches very easily) and the spoon for the liquid. Provide extra bowls for the discarded shells.

Scrub the shells to remove any grit.

Trim the beard, a wiry thread on the lip of the mussel.

When the shells open wide, mussels are done cooking.

Types of mussels: (Clockwise, from top) green-lipped, Penn Cove, blue (also called common).

Pasta with Roasted Tomatoes and Mussels

12 medium plum tomatoes, halved lengthwise
2 tablespoons olive oil
1 medium onion, halved, sliced lengthwise into thin wedges
2 medium fennel bulbs, fronds removed, bulb chopped
1 (14.5-oz.) can reduced-sodium chicken broth
½ cup white wine
½ cup chopped fresh basil
¼ teaspoon salt
¼ teaspoon freshly ground pepper
3 dozen mussels
8 oz. trecce di Giulietta (twisted pasta)

1 Heat oven to 450°F. Place tomatoes on rimmed baking sheet; bake 20 minutes or until soft and tops are slightly charred.
2 In large pot or nonreactive Dutch oven, heat oil over medium heat until hot. Add onion; cook 3 minutes. Add fennel; cook 5 to 8 minutes or until onions and fennel are soft. Add roasted tomatoes and any accumulated juices, broth, wine, basil, salt and pepper. Stir, breaking up tomatoes into smaller pieces.
3 Bring to a boil over medium-high heat; boil 3 to 4 minutes or until slightly thickened. Add mussels; cover and cook 2 to 5 minutes or until mussels open. Discard any that have not opened.
4 Meanwhile, cook pasta according to package directions. Serve mussels and sauce over pasta.

4 servings

PER SERVING: 490 calories, 10.5 g total fat (1.5 g saturated fat), 31.5 g protein, 65.5 g carbohydrate, 50 mg cholesterol, 735 mg sodium, 7.5 g fiber

Fishermen's Mussel Chowder

2 tablespoons olive oil
1 large onion, finely chopped
2 medium leeks, white and light-green parts only, chopped
3 large garlic cloves, minced
¼ teaspoon crushed red pepper
1 (28-oz.) can diced tomatoes
2 (8-oz.) bottles clam juice
2 cups water
3 Yukon gold potatoes, peeled, coarsely chopped
1 carrot, coarsely chopped
1 teaspoon crushed fennel seeds
1 teaspoon turmeric
½ teaspoon saffron threads, crushed
¼ teaspoon salt
¼ teaspoon freshly ground black pepper
4 dozen small mussels

1 Heat oil in large pot or Dutch oven over medium-high heat until hot. Add onion; cook 2 minutes. Add leeks; cook 2 to 3 minutes or until onions and leeks begin to soften. Add garlic and red pepper; cook 30 seconds or until fragrant. Add tomatoes, clam juice, water, potatoes, carrot, fennel seeds, turmeric, saffron, salt and black pepper. Bring to a boil. Reduce heat to low; simmer 20 to 30 minutes or until vegetables are tender.
2 Increase heat to high. Add mussels; cover and cook 2 to 5 minutes or until mussels open. Discard any that have not opened.

6 (1½-cup) servings

PER SERVING: 210 calories, 6 g total fat (1 g saturated fat), 14 g protein, 26.5 g carbohydrate, 30 mg cholesterol, 545 mg sodium, 4 g fiber

Steamed Cape Cod Mussels in White Wine

1 tablespoon olive oil
4 large shallots, minced
3 large garlic cloves, minced
1 tablespoon chopped fresh thyme
1½ cups dry white wine
½ cup water
¼ teaspoon salt
¼ teaspoon freshly ground pepper
6 dozen small mussels
2 tablespoons butter, softened
3 tablespoons chopped fresh Italian parsley
1½ teaspoons finely grated lemon peel

1 In large pot or Dutch oven, heat oil over medium heat until hot. Add shallots; cook 2 to 3 minutes or until shallots begin to soften. Add garlic and thyme; cook an additional 30 seconds or until fragrant.
2 Add wine, water, salt and pepper; bring to a boil over high heat. Add mussels; cover and boil 2 to 5 minutes or until mussels open. Discard any that have not opened.
3 Divide mussels among 4 shallow bowls. Cook liquid over high heat 1 to 2 minutes or until slightly reduced. Whisk in butter. Immediately pour sauce over mussels; sprinkle with parsley and lemon peel.

4 servings

PER SERVING: 245 calories, 11 g total fat (4 g saturated fat), 24 g protein, 9 g carbohydrate, 75 mg cholesterol, 820 mg sodium, 1 g fiber

A Seafood Classic

Eastern Shore Crab Cakes

With a crisp outside and moist inside, a cake is the perfect way to savor the delicacy of crabmeat. And crab cakes are easy to make. You don't need to catch or buy whole crabs; very good picked crabmeat is widely available. Crab cakes also are versatile because they can take on various flavors. These recipes include one spiced with traditional Old Bay seasoning and another with Asian ingredients. They're simply cooked and remain on the lighter side because they're not deep-fried.

51

Making Crab Cakes

A gentle touch is required when making crab cakes, from mixing them to cooking them. Follow these tips to keep them moist and tender on the inside and crisp, golden brown on the outside.

- Mix all of the ingredients thoroughly before adding the crabmeat. Gently and carefully stir in the crabmeat. Don't overstir or you will break up the delicate meat.

- To form the mixture into patties, scoop it into measured portions and gently but firmly press the mixture together (a fork works well). The patties should not be compacted but firm enough to hold together.

- If the crab cakes are breaded (as are Spicy Crab Cakes with Asian Dipping Sauce, pg. 59), coat them gently.

- Once formed and breaded, it's important to refrigerate crab cakes for 1 hour or until firm before cooking. Do not skip this step! It helps to evenly distribute the moisture, which holds the ingredients together and makes it easier to turn the crab cakes during cooking.

- Gently cook the crab cakes in batches until they're lightly browned. Wait until the first side is golden brown before turning, and turn only once to avoid breaking them.

Carefully add the crabmeat to the other ingredients. To keep crab pieces intact, don't overstir.

To bread, place the patties in the crumbs; sprinkle crumbs on the patties and gently press in place.

With a fork, gently but firmly press the mixture together just until it forms a patty.

When cooking, turn crab cakes when the first side is golden brown and crisp. Turn just once.

Eastern Shore Crab Cakes

½ cup mayonnaise
1 egg
1 tablespoon lemon juice
1 teaspoon seafood seasoning, such as Old Bay
½ teaspoon coarse Dijon mustard
½ teaspoon hot pepper sauce
14 saltine crackers
1 lb. crabmeat, drained
2 tablespoons vegetable oil, divided
Lemon wedges

1 In large bowl, whisk together mayonnaise, egg, lemon juice, seafood seasoning, mustard and hot pepper sauce until smoothly blended. Coarsely crush crackers by hand into mayonnaise mixture; gently stir until blended. Gently stir in crabmeat.

2 Using loosely packed scant ½ cup per crab cake, gently form mixture into 12 (2½-inch) patties about ½ inch thick. Place on foil-lined baking sheet. Cover and refrigerate 1 hour or until firm.

3 Heat 1 tablespoon of the oil in large nonstick skillet over medium heat until hot. Cook crab cakes in batches 5 to 8 minutes or until lightly browned, turning once and adding additional oil as needed. Drain on paper towels. (Crab cakes can be made up to 4 hours ahead. Cover and refrigerate. To reheat, heat oven to 425°F. Place wire rack on rimmed baking sheet; place crab cakes on rack. Bake 8 to 10 minutes or until hot and crisp.) Serve with lemon wedges.

12 crab cakes

PER CRAB CAKE: 145 calories, 11 g total fat (2 g saturated fat), 8 g protein, 3.5 g carbohydrate, 60 mg cholesterol, 255 mg sodium, .5 g fiber

Spicy Crab Cakes with Asian Dipping Sauce

CRAB CAKES
¾ cup mayonnaise
1½ teaspoons fish sauce
1½ teaspoons Asian chile paste
2 teaspoons grated fresh ginger
1 teaspoon grated lime peel
1 small garlic clove, minced
½ cup finely diced red bell pepper
1½ cups panko, divided
1 lb. crabmeat, drained
2 tablespoons chopped cilantro
2 to 3 tablespoons vegetable oil, divided
4 cups spinach

SAUCE
6 tablespoons water
3 tablespoons fish sauce
4 teaspoons lime juice
1 tablespoon minced green onions
1½ teaspoons sugar
1 garlic clove, minced
1 teaspoon Asian chile paste
½ teaspoon grated fresh ginger

1 In large bowl, stir together mayonnaise, 1½ teaspoons fish sauce, 1½ teaspoons chile paste, 2 teaspoons ginger, lime peel and 1 small garlic clove. Stir in bell pepper and ½ cup of the panko. Gently stir in crabmeat and cilantro.

2 Using loosely packed ½ cup per crab cake, form mixture into 12 (2½-inch) patties about ½ inch thick. Place remaining 1 cup panko in shallow dish; dip crab cakes in panko. Place on foil-lined baking sheet. Cover and refrigerate 1 hour or until firm.

3 Meanwhile, stir together all dipping sauce ingredients until sugar is dissolved.

4 Heat 1 tablespoon of the oil in large nonstick skillet over medium heat until hot. Cook crab cakes in batches 6 to 8 minutes or until golden brown, turning once and adding additional oil as needed. Drain on paper towels. (Crab cakes can be made up to 4 hours ahead. Cover and refrigerate. To reheat, heat oven to 425°F. Place wire rack on rimmed baking sheet; place

crab cakes on rack. Bake 8 to 10 minutes or until hot and crisp.) Serve crab cakes on spinach with dipping sauce.

12 crab cakes

PER CRAB CAKE: 190 calories, 14 g total fat (2 g saturated fat), 8.5 g protein, 7 g carbohydrate, 43.5 mg cholesterol, 655 mg sodium, 1 g fiber

Miniature Lemon Crab Cakes with Watercress Sauce

CRAB CAKES
½ cup mayonnaise
2 tablespoons sliced green onions
2 teaspoons lemon juice
1 teaspoon grated lemon peel
½ teaspoon hot pepper sauce
1¼ cups panko, divided
1 lb. crabmeat, drained
2 to 3 tablespoons vegetable oil, divided
48 (¼-inch) slices seedless cucumber

SAUCE
⅔ cup mayonnaise
½ cup finely chopped fresh watercress
3 tablespoons thinly sliced green onions
1 teaspoon lemon juice
⅛ teaspoon salt

1 In large bowl, stir together ½ cup mayonnaise, 2 tablespoons green onions, 2 teaspoons lemon juice, lemon peel and hot pepper sauce. Stir in ¼ cup of the panko. Gently stir in crabmeat.

2 Using 1 tablespoon per crab cake, gently form mixture into 48 (1-inch) patties, about ½ inch thick. Place remaining 1 cup panko in shallow dish; dip crab cakes in panko. Place on foil-lined baking sheet. Cover and refrigerate 1 hour or until firm.

3 Meanwhile, place all sauce ingredients in food processor or blender; process until smooth.

4 Heat 1 tablespoon of the oil in large nonstick skillet over medium heat until hot. Cook crab cakes in batches

4 to 5 minutes or until lightly browned, turning once and adding additional oil as needed. Drain on paper towels. (Crab cakes can be made up to 4 hours ahead. Cover and refrigerate. To reheat, heat oven to 425°F. Place wire rack on rimmed baking sheet; place crab cakes on rack. Bake 6 to 8 minutes or until hot and crisp.) Serve on cucumber slices; top with watercress sauce.

48 crab cakes

PER CRAB CAKE: 60 calories, 5 g total fat (1 g saturated fat), 2 g protein, 1.5 g carbohydrate, 10 mg cholesterol, 75 mg sodium, 0 g fiber

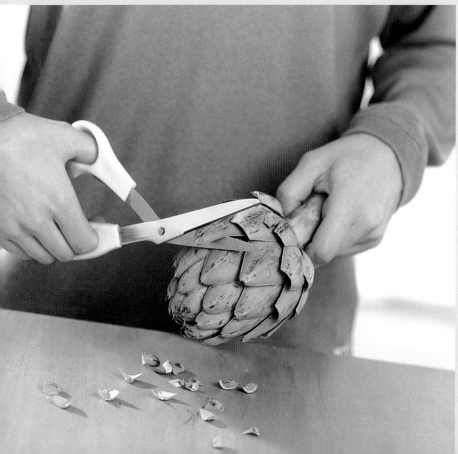

Vegetables

Garden Fresh Sauces

Linguine with Fresh Tomato Sauce and Melting Cheese

When tomato season is upon you, fresh tomatoes are a daily treat. At first, eating them plain, directly out of the garden, is perfectly satisfying. But as the weeks progress, we need to look for other ways to use the abundant supply that seems to appear daily.

There are several preparation methods, and each one produces different flavor nuances from the same tomatoes. Uncooked sauces give fleeting bursts of just-from-the-garden taste, while quickly cooked versions blend melting soft tomato notes with simple seasonings, such as garlic and olives. Slow-simmered sauces are a little heartier and have layers of flavor. All of these sauces can be varied easily, giving you endless ways to enjoy this hallmark of summer.

Using Fresh Tomatoes in Sauces

These fresh tomato sauces are meant for garden-ripe, in-season tomatoes. Don't use winter tomatoes; they may look nice, but they have very little flavor and won't provide the juiciness and taste necessary for these recipes. If you want to make the sauces out of season, canned tomatoes are a better choice.

All of these recipes use both the skin and the seeds of the tomato to capture its true flavor. If you prefer, the skin and seeds can be removed by passing the cooked sauces through a food mill.

UNCOOKED SAUCE

A fruity olive oil complements the sweetness of tomatoes in the uncooked sauce.

When tomatoes are in season and ripened naturally under the sun, the juiciness of the tomatoes is rich enough to make an uncooked sauce.

- Look for full-flavored, juicy tomatoes for this sauce; a variety of colors gives it visual interest. Use plum tomatoes or regular tomatoes.

- Use a fruity, full-flavored extra-virgin olive oil because the fruitiness of the oil complements both the acidity and sweetness of the tomatoes.

- Cook the sauce over medium-high heat, adjusting the heat if necessary, according to your stove. Cook the sauce no more than 6 to 8 minutes from start to finish.

- Use a potato masher to crush the tomatoes after cooking and to create a smoother sauce.

SLOW-SIMMERED SAUCE

The cooked tomatoes are passed through a food mill for a smoother slow-simmered sauce, but this step can be eliminated if you'd like.

This sauce cooks slowly over low heat, melding the flavors of the tomatoes, seasonings and aromatic vegetables. It's a light but full-flavored sauce that's perfect for freezing.

- Use plum tomatoes to create a full-bodied sauce.

- Cook the sauce about 30 minutes to help it gain complexity but still retain the fresh tomato taste.

- The amount of time it takes to simmer the sauce until slightly thickened varies, depending on the juiciness of the tomatoes. Adjust the heat and time accordingly.

QUICK-COOK SAUCE

Use a large, wide skillet for the quick-cook sauce.

This fast-cooking sauce preserves the tomatoes' freshness by using high heat. It's important to cook the sauce very rapidly and serve it immediately.

- Use plum tomatoes for best results. They have more pulp and less juice, which creates a thicker sauce.

- Use a large, wide skillet. It will cook the tomatoes and evaporate the tomato juices quickly, creating a slightly thickened sauce without overcooking.

Linguine with Fresh Tomato Sauce and Melting Cheese

4 cups finely chopped tomatoes (about 1¾ lb.)
¼ cup extra-virgin olive oil
2 garlic cloves, finely minced
2 tablespoons coarsely chopped fresh basil
2 tablespoons chopped mixed herbs, such as mint, tarragon, chives and/or additional fresh basil
¼ teaspoon kosher (coarse) salt
¼ teaspoon plus ⅛ teaspoon freshly ground pepper, divided
½ cup (2 oz.) crumbled soft goat cheese or feta cheese
12 oz. linguine

1 In large bowl, stir together tomatoes, oil, garlic, basil, mixed herbs, salt and ¼ teaspoon of the pepper. Gently stir in cheese. Let stand at room temperature 30 minutes or while preparing linguine.
2 Cook linguine in large pot of boiling salted water according to package directions; drain. Immediately add hot pasta to tomato mixture; stir to combine. Pour mixture into large pasta bowl or onto serving platter; sprinkle with remaining ⅛ teaspoon pepper.

4 servings

PER SERVING: 535 calories, 18.5 g total fat (4 g saturated fat), 16 g protein, 77 g carbohydrate, 5 mg cholesterol, 510 mg sodium, 5.5 g fiber

Pasta with Slow-Simmered Fresh Tomato Sauce

3 slices bacon, finely chopped
1 medium onion, chopped
4 garlic cloves, minced
¼ cup finely diced celery
1 bay leaf
5 cups chopped fresh plum tomatoes (about 2 lb.)
¼ cup chopped fresh basil
1 tablespoon chopped fresh thyme
¼ teaspoon kosher (coarse) salt
¼ teaspoon freshly ground pepper
12 oz. cavatappi, penne or other shaped pasta

1 Cook bacon in large skillet or pot over medium heat 5 to 7 minutes or until brown and crisp. With slotted spoon, place bacon on paper towel-lined plate.
2 Pour off all but 2 tablespoons of the bacon drippings. Add onion; cook over medium heat 5 to 8 minutes or until onion is golden brown, stirring occasionally. Add garlic, celery and bay leaf; cook 30 seconds or until garlic is fragrant. Add tomatoes, basil, thyme, salt and pepper; bring to a boil. Reduce heat to medium-low to low; simmer 30 minutes or until slightly thickened, stirring occasionally. Discard bay leaf.
3 For a smooth sauce, pass sauce through food mill or pulse in food processor or blender until of desired consistency. Return to skillet; stir in bacon. Heat over medium heat until hot. (Sauce can be made up to 3 days ahead and refrigerated or up to 4 months ahead and frozen.)
4 Cook cavatappi in large pot of boiling salted water according to package directions; drain. Top with sauce.

4 servings

PER SERVING: 480 calories, 11 g total fat (3.5 g saturated fat), 15 g protein, 80.5 g carbohydrate, 10 mg cholesterol, 535 mg sodium, 6.5 g fiber

Fettucine with Quick-Cook Fresh Tomato Sauce and Olives

12 oz. fettuccine
2 tablespoons extra-virgin olive oil
4 medium garlic cloves, minced
2 tablespoons finely chopped celery leaves
4 cups finely chopped fresh plum tomatoes (about 1¾ lb.)
½ teaspoon kosher (coarse) salt
½ teaspoon freshly ground pepper
½ cup quartered pitted Kalamata olives
½ cup lightly packed coarsely chopped fresh basil, plus additional for garnish
¼ cup (1 oz.) freshly grated Parmigiano-Reggiano cheese

1 Cook fettuccine in large pot of boiling salted water according to package directions; drain.
2 Meanwhile, heat oil in large skillet over medium heat until warm. Add garlic; cook 30 seconds or until fragrant. Add celery leaves; cook 15 seconds. Stir in tomatoes, salt and pepper. Increase heat to medium-high; cook 2 to 3 minutes or until tomatoes begin to soften. Crush tomatoes with potato masher until sauce is almost smooth with some pieces of tomato. Add olives and chopped basil; cook 2 to 3 minutes or until slightly thickened.
3 Toss fettucine with sauce. Place in large pasta bowl or on serving platter; sprinkle with cheese. Garnish with basil.

4 servings

PER SERVING: 450 calories, 14.5 g total fat (3 g saturated fat), 15 g protein, 66.5 g carbohydrate, 80 mg cholesterol, 840 mg sodium, 5.5 g fiber

Gnocchi Know-How

Watercress Gnocchi with Watercress Sauce

Dumplings epitomize comfort food, warming the body, satisfying the soul and kindling memories. Most cultures have their own version. Polish and Ukrainian folk make pierogi; Asians make pot stickers; and Italians make gnocchi.

Gnocchi (NYO-kee) are small pillows of light dumplings that are usually made with potatoes. They are served like pasta, with sauces, or simply tossed with seasoned butter or olive oil. Gnocchi have recently risen from their humble origins to star status in restaurants. However, while their delicacy and versatility have captured the attention of chefs, they remain essentially country food and are easy to make at home. Set aside an afternoon to stir up some dumpling memories of your own.

Making Gnocchi

Gnocchi can be made from potatoes, semolina flour, or even spinach and ricotta cheese. These recipes are potato-based.

Choosing potatoes Russet potatoes, also called baking potatoes, produce the best results. The dry, mealy texture combines with the egg to make the dumpling light. Yukon gold potatoes also work; they're slightly lower in starch but work well when combined with butternut squash in Golden Butternut Squash Gnocchi. Potatoes are baked rather than boiled to avoid adding excess moisture to the mixture.

To mash the potatoes, a potato ricer works best because it pushes the potatoes through tiny holes, mashing them evenly, with no lumps. You can also use a potato masher; just make sure there are no lumps in your mixture, and be careful not to overwork the potatoes.

Soft dough Gnocchi dough should be soft and slightly moist but not sticky. Add the flour slowly. If a soft dough forms without using all the flour called for, that's fine. If the mixture seems very sticky, you may need to add a little more flour, 1 teaspoon at a time. A word of

caution: Don't add too much flour; the gnocchi will become heavy. And avoid overworking the dough, which develops the gluten in the flour, resulting in tough rather than tender gnocchi.

Cutting and shaping Work with small pieces of dough. Each piece stretches into a long strand. To roll the dough into thin ropes, work on a very lightly floured surface. Too much flour causes the dough to slide around.

To form the characteristic ridges on gnocchi, use a dinner fork with rounded tines. Flour the fork and press the gnocchi into the tines with your thumb to create indentations. Gently roll the gnocchi off the fork, starting with the top edge and rolling downward. The gnocchi should have indentations from the fork on the outer edge and a little pocket formed on the inside edge. The indentations and pocket collect the sauce.

Cooking Cook the gnocchi in batches to avoid overcrowding the pot. Begin timing the gnocchi only after all of the gnocchi in the pot have risen to the surface of the water. At this point, cook them for 1 minute. Remove them using a strainer, and place them on a heated platter. The

gnocchi should be tender but firm. If they're overcooked, they begin to fall apart; if they're undercooked, they taste raw. Check the timing with the first batch.

Make ahead Gnocchi can be made up to one day ahead. Shape them and store them covered in the refrigerator until you're ready to cook them. They also can be frozen after shaping: Place them in a single layer on a baking sheet and freeze until firm. Store the frozen gnocchi in a resealable freezer bag for up to 1 month. Cook them frozen, adding 1 to 2 minutes to the cooking time.

Form ridges.

Gently roll off fork.

Watercress Gnocchi with Watercress Sauce

SAUCE
- 2 tablespoons unsalted butter
- ⅓ cup chopped green onions
- 1 teaspoon all-purpose flour
- 1 cup reduced-sodium chicken broth or vegetable broth
- ½ cup whipping cream
- 2 cups coarsely chopped watercress
- ¼ teaspoon salt
- ⅛ teaspoon freshly ground pepper

GNOCCHI
- 1 lb. russet potatoes
- 2 cups coarsely chopped watercress
- 2 cups whole-milk ricotta cheese
- 1 teaspoon salt
- ¼ teaspoon freshly ground pepper
- 1 egg, beaten
- 1 cup all-purpose flour

1 Melt butter in large skillet over medium heat. Add onions; cook 1 minute or until wilted. Add flour; stir until well blended. Whisk in broth and cream. Bring to a boil over medium heat. Cook 2 to 3 minutes or

until slightly thickened.

2 Stir in 2 cups watercress, ¼ teaspoon salt and ⅛ teaspoon pepper. Cook 1 minute or until watercress is just wilted. Remove from heat; cool slightly.

3 Place watercress mixture in blender; blend until very smooth.

4 Prick potatoes all over with fork to allow steam to escape. Microwave on high 7 to 10 minutes or until potatoes are tender. Let stand until cool enough to handle but still warm.

5 Meanwhile, blanch watercress by placing in small saucepan of boiling water 30 seconds or until watercress turns bright green and limp. Drain; rinse under cold running water to cool. Squeeze watercress to remove excess water. Place watercress, ricotta, 1 teaspoon salt and ¼ teaspoon pepper in food processor; process 1 to 2 minutes or until mixture is very smooth.

6 Peel potatoes; place in potato ricer. Rice potatoes into large bowl.

7 Add watercress mixture and egg to potatoes; stir gently to mix well. Slowly add flour, stirring until flour is incorporated and a soft dough forms.

8 Divide dough into 8 pieces. On very lightly floured surface, roll each piece of dough into long rope about ½ inch wide. Cut rope into 1-inch pieces. To shape gnocchi, press each piece onto floured fork to make indentation on one side; peel away from fork with thumb, curling gnocchi slightly. Place on lightly floured baking sheet.

9 Cook gnocchi in 4 batches in large pot of boiling salted water. Once gnocchi rise to surface, boil 1 minute or until firm and thoroughly cooked. Remove from water; place on large serving platter. Reheat sauce over medium heat 3 to 5 minutes or until hot. Spoon sauce over gnocchi.

6 servings

PER SERVING: 395 calories, 22 g total fat (13.5 g saturated fat), 15.5 g protein, 34 g carbohydrate, 110 mg cholesterol, 885 mg sodium, 2.5 g fiber

Golden Butternut Squash Gnocchi with Brown Butter–Hazelnut Sauce

1 lb. butternut squash
1 lb. Yukon gold potatoes (4 medium)
3 tablespoons freshly grated Parmigiano-Reggiano cheese
½ teaspoon salt
1 egg, beaten
1½ cups all-purpose flour
6 tablespoons unsalted butter
2 tablespoons finely chopped toasted hazelnuts

1 Heat oven to 375°F. Cut squash in half; remove seeds. Place squash, cut side up, in shallow baking pan. Prick potatoes all over with fork to allow steam to escape. Place potatoes on rack in oven.

2 Bake potatoes and squash 30 to 40 minutes or until tender. Let stand until cool enough to handle but still warm.

3 Peel potatoes; place in potato ricer. Rice potatoes into large bowl. Scoop squash out of shell; place in potato ricer. Rice squash into bowl. Sprinkle potatoes and squash with cheese and salt. Add egg; stir gently to mix well. Slowly add flour, stirring until flour is incorporated and a soft dough forms.

4 Divide dough into 8 pieces. On very lightly floured surface, roll each piece of dough into long rope about ½ inch wide. Cut rope into 1-inch pieces. To shape gnocchi, press each 1-inch piece onto floured fork to make indentation on one side; peel away from fork with thumb, curling gnocchi slightly. Place on lightly floured baking sheet.

5 Cook gnocchi in 4 batches in large pot of boiling salted water. Once gnocchi rise to surface, boil 1 minute or until firm and thoroughly cooked. Remove from water; place on large serving platter.

6 Melt butter in large skillet over medium heat. Continue cooking butter 1 to 3 minutes or until golden brown, stirring frequently. Add gnocchi to browned butter; cook over medium heat 2 to 3 minutes or until hot, stirring gently. Place on platter. Sprinkle with hazelnuts.

6 servings

PER SERVING: 350 calories, 15.5 g total fat (8 g saturated fat), 8 g protein, 47.5 g carbohydrate, 70 mg cholesterol, 490 mg sodium, 4.5 g fiber

Potato Gnocchi with Basil-Mint Tomato Sauce

SAUCE
2 large garlic cloves, minced
1 tablespoon olive oil
1 (28-oz.) can plum tomatoes, undrained
½ teaspoon salt
2 tablespoons chopped fresh basil
2 tablespoons chopped fresh mint

GNOCCHI
2 lb. russet potatoes (about 4 large)
6 tablespoons freshly grated Parmigiano-Reggiano cheese
1 teaspoon salt
1 egg, beaten
1½ cups all-purpose flour

1 In large saucepan, cook garlic in oil over medium heat 20 to 30 seconds or until fragrant. Reduce heat to medium-low to low. Add tomatoes and ½ teaspoon salt; cook 20 minutes or until slightly thickened. Cool slightly.

2 Place tomato mixture in food processor; pulse until sauce is almost smooth but some texture remains. Return sauce to saucepan. Stir in basil and mint. Cook over medium heat until hot.

3 Prick potatoes all over with fork to allow steam to escape. Microwave on high 7 to 10 minutes or until potatoes are tender. Let stand until cool enough to handle but still warm.

4 Peel potatoes; place in potato ricer. Rice potatoes into large bowl. Sprinkle potatoes with cheese and 1 teaspoon salt. Add egg; stir gently to mix well. Slowly add flour, stirring until flour is incorporated and a soft dough forms.

5 Divide dough into 8 pieces. On very lightly floured surface, roll each piece of dough into long rope about ½ inch wide. Cut rope into 1-inch pieces. To shape gnocchi, press each piece onto floured fork to make indentation on one side; peel away from fork with thumb, curling gnocchi slightly. Place on lightly floured baking sheet.

6 Cook gnocchi in 4 batches in large pot of boiling salted water. Once gnocchi rise to surface, boil 1 minute or until firm and thoroughly cooked. Remove from water; place on large serving platter. Meanwhile, reheat sauce over medium heat 3 to 5 minutes or until hot. Spoon sauce over gnocchi.

6 servings

PER SERVING: 290 calories, 5.5 g total fat (2 g saturated fat), 10 g protein, 50.5 g carbohydrate, 40 mg cholesterol, 1150 mg sodium, 3.5 g fiber

Art of the Artichoke

Grilled Artichokes with

Artichokes are certainly one of nature's more unusual vegetables. With their many layers and prickly leaves, they require the diner to use some ingenuity when eating them for the first time.

When I was growing up in the Midwest, artichokes were an exotic novelty. Today they're found in heaping piles in grocery stores, even in my hometown. And it's rare to find someone who hasn't tried a warm, gooey bowl of hot artichoke dip. One of the main reasons for artichokes' popularity is that eating them requires you to break some rules. When else is it proper to use your hands and scrape with your teeth? And what other food offers a treasure at the end, in the form of a heart?

Although artichokes take a little time to prepare, they're more than worth the effort. Try them simply steamed and served with melted butter or a dipping sauce. Stuff them with fresh tomatoes and herbs. Or grill them to add a smoky flavor. You'll love the different tastes, and everyone is guaranteed to have fun.

Working With Artichokes

TRIMMING

Artichokes need a little shaping before being cooked. To trim an artichoke, peel away the small outer leaves and any discolored leaves from the base of the artichoke. Then cut the stem even with the bottom of the artichoke, unless otherwise directed in the recipe. The stem is edible and can be peeled and cooked alongside the artichoke. Using a scissors, trim the tips from the artichoke leaves, if desired. (There are often thorns on the tips of the leaves that can be prickly when raw; however, the thorns soften during cooking, so this step is a matter of personal preference.)

Artichokes darken quickly when the cut surfaces are exposed to air. To counteract this, immediately rub the cut surfaces of the artichoke with a cut lemon.

REMOVING THE CHOKE

The heart of the artichoke, which is the sweetest part, is guarded by a dense layer of prickly purple-green leaves surrounding a hairy choke.

These leaves and the choke need to be removed and discarded before eating the heart. This can be done before cooking or after, depending on the recipe. If the artichoke is to be stuffed and baked, the choke must be removed before stuffing. If the recipe doesn't list a method, it is much easier to cook the artichoke, then remove the choke.

Spread apart the leaves in the center of the artichoke, exposing the undeveloped purple and pink-tinged leaves. Remove these leaves, exposing the hairy white choke beneath. Using a spoon (a grapefruit spoon with a serrated edge is perfect), scrape and remove the entire choke, exposing the artichoke heart.

COOKING

The most common ways to cook an artichoke are boiling and steaming. To test for doneness, insert a small knife into the bottom of the artichoke. The knife should glide in with little resistance.

Steaming This method retains more nutrients than boiling, and the artichokes are easier to work with because they drip less water. For

steaming directions, see steps 1 and 2 of Fresh Artichokes with Basil-Mint Dipping Sauce (pg. 64).

Boiling To boil artichokes, place them in a large pot and cover them with water. If necessary, place a small lid or heat-proof plate over the artichokes to keep them from rising above the water. Bring the water to a boil over medium-high heat; reduce the heat to low and simmer 20 to 30 minutes or until tender.

Microwaving Place up to four trimmed artichokes in a glass pie plate. Add enough water to come a scant ½ inch up the sides of the artichokes. Cover the pie plate with plastic wrap and microwave on high for 6 to 10 minutes or until tender.

EATING

Beginning with the outside leaves, use your fingers to gently pull away a leaf from the base. Place the base of the leaf into your mouth and scrape off the pulp with your teeth as you pull away the leaf. If the choke has not been removed, you eventually will get to the thin, undeveloped leaves; they should be removed and discarded. Using a spoon, scrape away the choke to reveal the heart.

Heart.
Choke.
Undeveloped leaves.

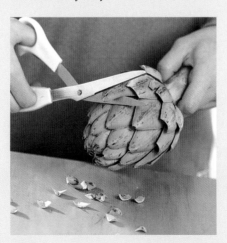

Before cooking, trim the tips of the artichoke leaves with scissors.

After cooking, spread the leaves to remove the choke.

4 medium artichokes
1 lemon, halved
¾ cup chopped fresh Italian parsley
½ cup extra-virgin olive oil
3 tablespoons fresh lime juice
2 small garlic cloves, minced
1 teaspoon grated fresh ginger
½ teaspoon salt, divided
½ teaspoon freshly ground
   pepper, divided

1 Leaving stem on, remove outer layer of leaves from artichokes to expose light-green, tender inside leaves. With small knife, trim outside edge of artichokes where leaves were removed; peel stem. Quarter artichokes lengthwise, cutting through head and stem. Remove fuzzy choke from inside. Rub cut edges with lemon halves.

2 Place parsley, olive oil, lime juice, garlic, ginger and ¼ teaspoon each of the salt and pepper in blender. Blend until smooth.

3 Heat grill. Brush artichokes with parsley mixture. Place on gas grill over medium heat or on charcoal grill 4 to 6 inches from medium coals. Grill 12 to 15 minutes or until tender, turning and basting with remaining parsley mixture about every 5 minutes. Sprinkle with remaining ¼ teaspoon each of the salt and pepper. Serve with remaining sauce.

4 servings

PER SERVING: 185 calories, 14 g total fat (2 g saturated fat), 4.5 g protein, 15 g carbohydrate, 0 mg cholesterol, 335 mg sodium, 7 g fiber

6.5 g fiber

ARTICHOKES
4 medium artichokes
1 lemon, halved

STUFFING
¼ cup unsalted butter, cut up

3 medium shallots, minced
1 garlic clove, minced
⅓ cup chopped prosciutto (1½ oz.)
2 medium plum tomatoes, chopped
2 cups coarse fresh bread crumbs
2 teaspoons chopped fresh thyme
½ cup white wine or orange juice

SAUCE
2 tablespoons olive oil
2 medium garlic cloves, minced
6 medium plum tomatoes,
   finely chopped (about 2 cups)
¼ teaspoon salt
⅛ teaspoon freshly ground pepper
½ cup orange juice

1 Heat oven to 375°F. Trim outside and remove inner chokes of artichokes. Rub cut surfaces with lemon halves.

2 Melt butter in large skillet over medium heat. Add shallots and 1 minced garlic clove; cook 1 minute, stirring constantly. Add prosciutto; cook 1 minute. Add 2 chopped tomatoes. Increase heat to medium-high; cook 2 to 3 minutes or until tomatoes begin to soften. Stir in bread crumbs and thyme; cook 2 to 4 minutes or until bread crumbs are lightly browned, stirring frequently.

3 Fill cavities and outside leaves of artichokes with stuffing. Place in 13x9-inch glass baking dish; pour wine around artichokes. Cover with buttered parchment or waxed paper, then aluminum foil. Bake 50 to 60 minutes or until tender.

4 Meanwhile, heat oil in another large skillet over medium-high heat until hot. Add 2 minced garlic cloves; cook 20 to 30 seconds or until fragrant. Add 6 chopped tomatoes, salt and pepper; cook 2 to 4 minutes or until tomatoes begin to soften. Add orange juice. Bring to a boil; cook 2 to 4 minutes or until slightly thickened. (For a smooth sauce, run sauce through food mill.) Place artichokes on individual plates; drizzle sauce around artichokes.

4 servings

PER SERVING: 345 calories, 21 g total fat (9 g saturated fat), 9.5 g protein, 34 g carbohydrate, 35 mg cholesterol, 465 mg sodium, 8.5 g fiber

ARTICHOKES
4 medium artichokes
1 lemon, sliced
1 cup loosely packed fresh
   mint sprigs

SAUCE
¼ cup coarsely chopped
   fresh basil
¼ cup coarsely chopped
   fresh mint
¼ teaspoon minced garlic
1½ teaspoons fresh lemon juice
¼ teaspoon salt
⅛ teaspoon freshly ground pepper
½ cup plain yogurt

1 Cut stem from base of artichokes; slice off top one-third of artichokes. Snip off tips of pointed leaves with scissors. Rub all cut edges with lemon slices. Place lemon slices and mint sprigs in large pot or nonreactive Dutch oven. Place steamer basket in pot; add enough water to reach just below basket. Bring to a boil over high heat.

2 Place artichokes right-side up on steamer rack. Cover; cook 30 to 40 minutes or until bottoms of artichokes are tender when pierced with knife or leaf comes out easily when pulled. Adjust heat as necessary to keep a rolling boil. Place artichokes in large bowl of ice water to cool quickly; drain well. With spoon, scrape out chokes from artichokes; discard chokes.

3 In food processor, combine basil, mint and garlic; process until finely chopped. Add lemon juice, salt, pepper and yogurt; process until smooth.

4 To serve, place artichokes on plates; serve dipping sauce alongside artichokes.

4 servings

PER SERVING: 80 calories, .5 g total fat (.5 g saturated fat), 6 g protein, 16 g carbohydrate, 0 mg cholesterol, 250 mg sodium,

Risotto Revealed

Lemon Asparagus Risotto with Chives

Risotto, the traditional Italian rice dish, may be haute cuisine on the restaurant scene but it is pure comfort food at heart. It's stirred constantly while it cooks, creating a creamy texture and the perfect backdrop for simple or exotic ingredients, which can be added during the process. The combined flavors make risotto satisfying and fulfilling.

The basic technique for making risotto is easy to master. You can start with this collection of recipes. Creamy Parmesan Risotto is a perfect choice if you have never made risotto. Lemon Asparagus Risotto with Chives is a delicate version in which the asparagus cooks with the rice to add a subtle flavor. Mushroom-Red Pepper Risotto with Pancetta has a hearty, bold flavor. Once you learn the technique, you can create endless variations of your own.

To make risotto, you must use plump, short-grain rice. It has a high starch content, which contributes to the creaminess of the dish. Arborio rice, a shorter and rounder form of short-grain rice, is the most common variety used. Other types such as carnoroli or maratelli can be used but may be difficult to find.

Meat, chicken, vegetable or seafood broth can all be used as the liquid in risotto, depending on the other ingredients. Wine is sometimes added for extra depth of flavor. The broth should be light in taste because the flavors concentrate as it evaporates and cooks with the rice. Homemade broth is always best, but canned, reduced-sodium broth can be used. If the reduced-sodium version is unavailable, use regular canned broth but dilute it by using half water.

The rice can be combined with a variety of ingredients including herbs, vegetables, seafood and meats. For risotto, it is important that flavors meld to produce a dish where no one ingredient stands out. The base for risotto usually contains sautéed onions, shallots or garlic. Ingredients needing longer cooking time, such as firm vegetables and uncooked meats, are added at the beginning. Other ingredients needing less time are added at the middle or the end of cooking.

Making Creamy Risotto

The technique for cooking risotto is different from the usual method for cooking rice. Follow these pointers for perfect risotto:

- Use a heavy, nonreactive saucepan such as enameled cast iron, stainless steel or lined aluminum. This type of pan allows for even cooking without scorching.

- Begin by sautéing the onion in butter or oil. Add the rice and sauté it as you would when making a rice pilaf.

- Then add the hot broth ½ cup at a time as you constantly stir the rice. Use a 4-ounce ladle—it's easier to handle than a measuring cup.

- Keep the rice moving. The starch from the grains dissolves in the liquid to create the creamy effect, while the stirring keeps the grains separated. Constant stirring is preferred, but risotto is fairly forgiving if you have to leave it alone for a short while during this process.

- Adjust your heat to keep the risotto simmering during cooking. If the heat is too high or too low, the broth will either evaporate or will not be absorbed by the rice. You may need to add a little more or a little less liquid, depending on the rice, pan and heat.

- When it's finished, the risotto should be creamy, not soupy. The grains should be separate and cooked al dente (there will be a slight resistance when you bite into them).

Arborio rice.　Long grain rice.

Sauté the rice with the onion and butter.

Add hot broth while constantly stirring the rice.

Lemon Asparagus Risotto with Chives

3 to 3½ cups reduced-sodium chicken broth
1 tablespoon butter
2 large shallots, minced
1 cup arborio rice
2 tablespoons julienned lemon peel
8 asparagus spears, peeled, cut into 1-inch pieces (about 1 cup)
6 tablespoons finely chopped fresh chives
⅛ teaspoon salt
⅛ teaspoon freshly ground pepper
2 tablespoons grated Asiago cheese

1 In medium saucepan, bring chicken broth to a boil. Reduce heat to low; cover and keep broth simmering while making risotto.
2 Melt butter in large saucepan over medium heat. Add shallots; cook 1 to 2 minutes. Add rice; stir to coat all grains with butter. Cook 1 minute, stirring constantly.
3 Add lemon peel and ½ cup of hot chicken broth to rice; cook until all liquid has been absorbed, stirring constantly. Adjust heat as necessary to keep rice mixture simmering. Continue to add chicken broth ½ cup at a time, cooking and stirring constantly.
4 After 2 to 2½ cups of chicken broth have been added, stir in asparagus and 4 tablespoons of the chives. (If asparagus spears are thin, add after 2½ cups broth have been added.) Continue adding chicken broth ½ cup at a time, cooking and stirring constantly until rice is tender with a slight firmness in the center.
5 Add salt, pepper, remaining 2 tablespoons chives and cheese; stir until cheese is melted. Serve immediately.

6 servings

PER SERVING: 160 calories, 3 g total fat (2 g saturated fat), 5 mg cholesterol, 130 mg sodium, 1 g fiber

Mushroom-Red Pepper Risotto with Pancetta

3 to 3½ cups reduced-sodium chicken broth
½ cup (2 oz.) diced pancetta
⅓ cup chopped onion
2 garlic cloves, minced
1 cup arborio rice
4 oz. crimini mushrooms, sliced (about 2 cups)
⅓ cup red wine
¼ cup diced roasted red bell peppers
¼ teaspoon salt
¼ teaspoon freshly ground pepper
½ cup freshly grated Parmigiano-Reggiano cheese

1 In medium saucepan, bring chicken broth to a boil. Reduce heat to low; cover and keep broth simmering while making risotto.
2 Heat large saucepan over medium heat until hot. Add pancetta; cook 3 to 4 minutes or until browned. Add onion; cook 3 to 4 minutes or until onion begins to soften. Add garlic; cook briefly. Add rice. Cook 1 minute, stirring constantly.
3 Add mushrooms; cook and stir 1 minute. Add wine; cook until wine is reduced by half. Add roasted peppers and ½ cup hot chicken broth to rice; cook until all liquid has been absorbed, stirring constantly. Adjust heat as necessary to keep rice mixture simmering. Continue to add chicken broth ½ cup at a time, cooking and stirring constantly until rice is tender with a slight firmness to the center.
4 Add salt, pepper and cheese; stir until cheese is melted. Serve immediately with additional grated cheese, if desired.

6 servings

PER SERVING: 195 calories, 5 g total fat (2.5 g saturated fat), 10 mg cholesterol, 325 mg sodium, 1 g fiber

Creamy Parmesan Risotto

3 to 3½ cups reduced-sodium chicken broth
3 tablespoons unsalted butter
½ cup finely chopped onion
1 garlic clove, minced
1 cup arborio rice
½ cup freshly grated Parmigiano-Reggiano cheese

1 In medium saucepan, bring chicken broth to a boil. Reduce heat to low; cover and keep broth simmering while making risotto.
2 Melt 2 tablespoons of the butter in large saucepan over medium heat. Add onion; cook 3 to 5 minutes or just until onion begins to brown. Add garlic; sauté briefly. Add rice; stir to coat all grains with butter. Cook 1 minute, stirring constantly.
3 Add ½ cup hot chicken broth to rice; cook until all liquid has been absorbed, stirring constantly. Adjust heat as necessary to keep rice mixture simmering. Continue to add chicken broth ½ cup at a time, cooking and stirring constantly until rice is tender with a slight firmness in the center.
4 Add cheese and remaining 1 tablespoon butter; stir until melted. Serve immediately with additional cheese, if desired.

6 servings

PER SERVING: 220 calories, 9 g total fat (5.5 g saturated fat), 20 mg cholesterol, 185 mg sodium, .5 g fiber

Sides & Condiments

The Magic of Caramelization

One of the greatest culinary magic tricks is the transformation of pungent raw onions into sweet, soft golden onions, called caramelized onions. The dramatic change is a prime example of how you can uncover layers of flavor in a food, depending on how it's cooked.

Caramelizing isn't a difficult technique; it's easy to do in the home kitchen. All you need are onions, butter, oil and patience. It's important to take the time required to adequately draw out the sugar in onions. Although there are quicker methods, too often they produce browned onions that don't have the sweetness of true caramelized onions. When you use the proper technique, the sulfur compounds (which are responsible for the strong taste and odor of the onion) dissolve and start to evaporate while the onions cook. At the same time, the sugars in the onions begin to melt and brown, and the starches begin to convert to sugar. When all of these processes work together correctly, the result is rich, subtly sweet, melt-in-your-mouth onions. The best way to appreciate the technique is to slice up a few onions and give it a try.

Caramelized Onions

Don't rush the cooking process for these onions. It takes about 30 minutes for heat to caramelize their sugars. For best flavor, cook the onions until they're soft, tender and a rich golden brown. While you start with a surprisingly large mound of onions, they wilt and reduce greatly in volume as they cook.

> 3 tablespoons unsalted butter
> 3 tablespoons olive oil
> 3 lb. onions (about 6 large),
>   thinly sliced (about 10 cups)
> ½ teaspoon sugar
> ½ teaspoon salt
> ¼ teaspoon freshly ground
>   pepper

Heat butter and oil in large skillet over medium heat until butter is melted. Add onions; stir to coat with butter mixture. Cover and cook 10 minutes or until onions have wilted, stirring occasionally. Remove cover; increase heat to medium high. Sprinkle with sugar; stir to combine. Cook 25 to 30 minutes or until onions are deep golden brown, stirring frequently. If necessary, reduce heat to medium to keep onions from sticking. Stir in salt and pepper. (Onions can be made up to 3 days ahead and refrigerated or up to 2 months ahead and frozen. To thaw onions, quickly microwave on defrost setting 4 to 5 minutes until thawed. Cook on high 30 seconds or until hot.)

1⅔ cups

PER 2 TABLESPOONS: 90 calories, 6 g total fat (2 g saturated fat), 1 g protein, 8.5 g carbohydrate, 5 mg cholesterol, 95 mg sodium, 2 g fiber

TIPS FOR SUCCESS

To best understand each step necessary for making outstanding caramelized onions, follow these guidelines:

Mound of onions Don't be alarmed by the amount; they cook down to less than 2 cups. Be sure to thinly slice the onions.

Butter and oil Use both for better taste and easier cooking. The butter adds flavor; the oil lets the onions cook at a higher heat without burning.

Cover and cook Cover the onions at the beginning so that they sweat or wilt and begin cooking before the browning process begins.

Add sugar A little sugar jump-starts the browning process while the onions cook.

Take your time Don't rush the process; it takes about 30 minutes. Stir frequently towards the end, and adjust the heat as necessary so the onions don't brown too fast before they are tender.

WAYS TO USE CARAMELIZED ONIONS

Make a batch of caramelized onions and store them in the refrigerator for 3 days or up to 2 months in the freezer. They add extraordinary taste to everyday food.

- Top sautéed or baked chicken breasts with warm caramelized onions.

- Stir caramelized onions into a quick stir-fry of beef and mushrooms; add sour cream for an upscale beef stroganoff.

- Top roast pork with caramelized onions during the last 15 minutes of baking.

- Toss steamed green beans with caramelized onions.

- Top tomato halves with caramelized onions and Parmesan cheese; broil until hot.

- Add caramelized onions to grilled ham and cheese sandwiches.

- Use caramelized onions as a pizza topping.

Balsamic-Glazed Steak with Caramelized Onions

ONIONS
  2 tablespoons unsalted butter
  1 tablespoon olive oil
  1½ lb. onions (about 3 large),
      thinly sliced (6 cups)
  ¼ teaspoon sugar
  ½ teaspoon salt
  ⅛ teaspoon freshly ground pepper

STEAK
  4 New York strip steaks
      (¾ inch thick)
  2 teaspoons chopped fresh thyme
  ¼ teaspoon salt
  ⅛ teaspoon freshly ground pepper
  1 tablespoon olive oil
  3 tablespoons balsamic vinegar

1 Heat butter and 1 tablespoon oil in large skillet over medium heat until butter is melted. Add onions; stir to coat with butter mixture. Cover and cook 5 minutes or until onions have wilted. Remove cover; increase heat to medium high. Sprinkle with sugar; stir to combine. Cook 25 to 30 minutes or until onions are deep golden brown, stirring frequently. If necessary, reduce heat to medium to keep onions from sticking. Stir in ½

teaspoon salt and ⅛ teaspoon pepper. (Onions can be made up to 3 days ahead and refrigerated or up to 2 months ahead and frozen.) Let stand while preparing steak.

2 Sprinkle steaks with thyme, ¼ teaspoon salt and ⅛ teaspoon pepper. Heat another large skillet over medium-high heat until hot. Add 1 tablespoon oil; heat until hot. Add steaks; cook 9 to 11 minutes for medium rare or until of desired doneness, turning once. Place steaks on plate. Drain drippings from skillet.

3 Return skillet to medium-high heat. Add vinegar; cook 1 to 2 minutes or until slightly thickened, scraping up any browned bits from bottom of skillet. Reheat caramelized onions over medium heat until hot; spoon onto individual plates. Top with steaks; pour balsamic glaze over steak and onions.

4 servings

PER SERVING: 625 calories, 33.5 g total fat (12.5 g saturated fat), 64.5 g protein, 14 g carbohydrate, 180 mg cholesterol, 595 mg sodium, 3 g fiber

Caramelized Onion Mashed Potatoes

Caramelized Onion Mashed Potatoes

ONIONS
- 3 tablespoons unsalted butter
- 3 tablespoons olive oil
- 2¼ lb. onions (about 4 large), chopped (about 7 cups)
- ½ teaspoon sugar
- ½ teaspoon salt
- ¼ teaspoon freshly ground pepper

POTATOES
- 4 lb. russet potatoes (3 to 4 large), peeled, cubed (1 inch)
- 3 teaspoons salt, divided
- ⅔ cup whole milk
- 2 tablespoons unsalted butter
- ¼ teaspoon freshly ground pepper

1 Heat 3 tablespoons butter and oil in large skillet over medium heat until butter is melted. Add onions; stir to coat with butter mixture. Cover and cook 10 minutes or until onions have wilted, stirring occasionally. Remove cover; increase heat to medium high. Sprinkle with sugar; stir to combine. Cook 25 to 30 minutes or until onions are deep golden brown, stirring frequently. If necessary, reduce heat to medium to keep onions from sticking. Stir in ½ teaspoon salt and ¼ teaspoon pepper. (Onions can be made up to 3 days ahead and refrigerated or up to 2 months ahead and frozen.)

2 Place potatoes in large saucepan; add enough water to cover potatoes by 1 inch. Add 2 teaspoons of the salt. Bring to a boil over medium-high heat. Reduce heat to medium-low to low; simmer 12 minutes or until potatoes are tender when pierced with fork. Drain. Return to saucepan; cover to keep warm.

3 Meanwhile, place milk and 2 tablespoons butter in small microwave-safe cup. Heat 30 to 60 seconds or until butter is melted and milk is hot. Reheat caramelized onions over medium heat until hot. Press potatoes through potato ricer into medium bowl or mash using potato masher. Stir in milk mixture until potatoes are creamy. Stir in caramelized onions, remaining 1 teaspoon salt and ¼ teaspoon pepper.

10 (¾-cup) servings

PER SERVING: 285 calories, 10.5 g total fat (4.5 g saturated fat), 4.5 g protein, 45 g carbohydrate, 20 mg cholesterol, 845 mg sodium, 5.5 g fiber

Guacamole Auténtico

Traditional Gua

Whether you use it for dipping chips or adding flair to other Mexican foods such a burritos, fajitas or tacos, there's nothing quite like fresh, homemade guacamole. Utilizing avocados from the Central American tropics and chiles from farther north in Mexico, nobody knows exactly where these two prime ingredients met to make the first bowl of guac, but thank goodness they did come together … likely among the Mayas or some other Mexican tribe.

For the best guacamole, always start with heavy, fully ripe avocados. As for chiles, that's a matter of taste: some like them hot, some not! Chiles are a good variable with which to experiment: Start with the basic recipes here and use them as starting points for your own personal brand of Guacamole Auténtico!

Molcajete

Guacamole is traditionally made with a molcajete *and tejolote, a Mexican mortar and pestle made of volcanic rock. Because it's so heavy, the* molcajete *is ideal for grinding spices as well as making sauces. The most versatile size is about 8 inches in diameter. You'll need to season the* molcajete *before the first use by scrubbing it with a brush and then grinding about ¼ cup of rice in the bowl to rid it of any loose rock and dust particles. Continue scrubbing and grinding the rice until it's clean.*

1. Crush the onion, cilantro, chile and salt until they form a smooth paste, which will blend well with the avocado. A large mortar and pestle is ideal, but a food processor or knife also works.

2. After you've pitted the avocados, scoop out the flesh with a large spoon and add to the paste. Coarsely crush the avocados, keeping the mixture chunky, not smooth.

3. Gently stir in the tomatoes and the remaining onion and cilantro. Plum tomatoes have fewer seeds and keep the guacamole from getting watery; chop them into bite-sized pieces.

Traditional Guacamole

- 5 tablespoons finely chopped white onion, divided
- 5 tablespoons chopped cilantro, divided
- 1 serrano chile, chopped
- ¼ teaspoon coarse salt
- 3 avocados
- 2 small plum tomatoes, chopped

1 Crush 3 tablespoons of the onion, 2 tablespoons of the cilantro, chile and salt in molcajete or pulse in food processor, until paste forms.
2 Cut avocados in half; remove pits. With large spoon, scoop out flesh; add to chile mixture. Coarsely crush avocados, keeping mixture chunky.
3 Gently stir in tomatoes, remaining 2 tablespoons onion and remaining 3 tablespoons cilantro.

2¼ cups

PER 2 TABLESPOONS: 50 calories, 4.5 g total fat (.5 g saturated fat), .5 g protein, 3 g carbohydrate, 0 mg cholesterol, 25 mg sodium, 2 g fiber

Roasted Guacamole

- 2 small plum tomatoes
- 1 small white onion, sliced (¼ inch)
- 1 serrano chile
- ¼ teaspoon coarse salt
- 5 tablespoons chopped cilantro, divided
- 3 avocados
- ⅓ cup crumbled cotija or feta cheese

1 Cook tomatoes, onion and chile in large cast-iron or nonstick dry skillet over medium-high to high heat 5 to 8 minutes or until blistered and charred on all sides. Cool completely.
2 Remove and discard tomato skins; coarsely chop roasted vegetables. Place in molcajete, large mortar or food processor; sprinkle with salt and 2 tablespoons of the cilantro. Crush or pulse ingredients until paste forms.
3 Cut avocados in half; remove pits. With large spoon, scoop out flesh; add to chile mixture. Coarsely crush avocados, keeping mixture chunky,

not smooth. Stir in remaining 3 tablespoons cilantro; sprinkle with cheese.

21/2 cups

PER 2 TABLESPOONS: 55 calories, 4.5 g total fat (1 g saturated fat), 1 g protein, 3 g carbohydrate, 0 mg cholesterol, 45 mg sodium, 2 g fiber •

Mastering the Cut

Chefs are on stage these days, whether it's in an open kitchen or on television, and everyone's watching. Many times, what turns heads and gains applause is knife skills. Chefs who easily chop piles of onions and vegetables in minutes, with a knife that never seems to stop, hold us in awe. Many people purchase the knives that chefs use in hopes that the key to efficiency lies in the equipment; they're often disappointed to find that knives alone are not enough. What's the secret, then?

After spending years in professional kitchens, I can tell you that there are no secrets. The keys to awe-inspiring knife skills are simply sharp knives and proper technique. If you spend a little time learning the proper methods for basic cutting and chopping and spend a lot of time practicing, you'll be surprised how quickly your speed and efficiency improve. You'll soon reduce the amount of time spent on mundane chopping tasks and may even impress guests with your chef-like skills.

Once you've learned the basic techniques, look for recipes to practice on. Gazpacho, an uncooked, highly seasoned, fresh vegetable soup, is a fun recipe to prepare and is the perfect test of your skills because it requires substantial chopping. When you're done, you'll have a meal that's a reward in itself.

Steps to Knife Proficiency

For most chopping jobs, use a chef's knife; its weight and structure are designed for efficient cutting and chopping. To practice, use soft vegetables, such as zucchini and cucumber. Practice until you are comfortable with the techniques and your speed increases.

CUTTING RULES There are a few things to keep in mind when cutting vegetables.

- With round food, slice off an edge to create a flat side. This makes the food more stable when it's being cut.

- Let the weight and structure of the knife help you move it. Use your full arm, not just your wrist.

- Always keep your fingers curved as you hold the food. They should be a guide, not part of the recipe!

- Keep your knives sharpened; dull blades are worthless.

GARLIC

Loosen the skin from garlic cloves by crushing the clove with the side of the knife; then slip off the skin. It's more efficient to chop several cloves of garlic at once instead of a single clove.

To mince garlic, first smash the clove with the side of the knife, using enough pressure to flatten the clove.

Keeping the tip of the knife on the cutting board, rock the knife up and down quickly until the garlic is finely chopped. This should take no more than 30 seconds (less time than it takes to clean a garlic press). If the garlic sticks to the knife, scrape the knife on the cutting board and continue chopping.

Crush clove.

Rock knife to chop.

Halve the onion.

Horizontal slices.

Vertical cuts.

Remove strip.

ONION

Peel and halve the onion, leaving some of the root end attached. Make horizontal slices through the onion (close together for a fine mince, further apart for a coarse chop). Instead of pushing the knife into the onion, slide it through, starting at the heel of the knife (above) and ending at the tip (below).

You'll find the knife slips through the onion much easier. (Do not cut all the way through the root end because it holds the onion together during chopping.)

Make vertical cuts through the onion, then slice it crosswise, rocking the tip of the knife on the cutting board. The onion should be either finely or coarsely chopped, depending on the recipe, and shouldn't need additional chopping.

CARROT

For safety, always cut with a flat surface of the carrot on the cutting board, even when you want the round shape. Slice a thin strip off the bottom of the carrot so it is stable during cutting.

Coursely Slice.

HERBS

Bunch fresh herbs together and coarsely slice them. With the knife tip on the cutting board, quickly rock the knife to coarsely chop the herbs.

Do not mince herbs too finely because they bruise easily and lose too much flavor.

Core.

Slice.

HERBS

To core a bell pepper easily, first slice off the top and bottom of the pepper; reserve the bottom, which can be chopped separately. Then cut a slit in the pepper and begin to run the knife around the inner edge, cutting off the veins and leaving the core and seeds in the center. For efficiency, stack sections of bell pepper and slice or chop them.

Summer Gazpacho with
Garlic-Cumin Sauce

Summer Gazpacho with Garlic-Cumin Sauce

GAZPACHO
4 cups chopped tomatoes (about 4 medium)
1 cup finely diced peeled cucumber
1 large green bell pepper, finely diced
½ cup chopped sweet onion
1 serrano chile, minced
¼ cup chopped mixed fresh herbs (basil, tarragon and/or chives)
1 large garlic clove, minced
1 teaspoon salt
¼ teaspoon freshly ground pepper
⅛ teaspoon crushed saffron threads
2 cups water
¾ cup tomato juice
1 tablespoon sherry vinegar or red wine vinegar
1 tablespoon extra-virgin olive oil

SAUCE
½ cup plain yogurt
1 medium garlic clove, finely minced
1 teaspoon fresh lime or lemon juice
¼ teaspoon ground cumin

1 In large bowl, stir together all gazpacho ingredients. Cover and refrigerate 30 to 60 minutes.
2 In small bowl, stir together all sauce ingredients; refrigerate until ready to serve. Drizzle soup with sauce; pass remaining sauce.

4 (about 1¾ cup) servings

PER SERVING: 125 calories, 4.5 g total fat (1 g saturated fat), 5 g protein, 19.5 g carbohydrate, 0 mg cholesterol, 790 mg sodium, 3.5 g fiber

Summer in a Jar

Blueberry-Raspberry Jam

Spiced Peach Jam

Gingered Plum Jam

Thoughts of a kitchen overflowing with fruit, jars and scalding kettles keeps many home cooks from making jam. But then it isn't necessary to make enough to supply everyone you know. The key to making jam is keeping the project small. In fact, it's better because making jam in small batches keeps the fruit tasting fresher and looking brighter.

The recipes here demonstrate the beauty of small. They make just four jars and use the natural pectin in the fruit for thickening, so they contain only fruit, sugar and flavorings. You can make the jam and store it in the refrigerator or, for longer storage on the shelf, you can process it in a water bath—it's your choice. Either way, it's easy, and it's gratifying knowing the taste of summer will return when you open the jars at a later date.

Jam-Making Tips

Follow these tips for brilliant jars of perfect jam.

- Use a wide, large, heavy pot. The mixture bubbles up high during boiling, so make sure there's plenty of room for it to rise.

- Bring the fruit mixture to a rolling boil. A rolling boil is a strong boil over the entire surface that can't be stirred down. Begin timing after the mixture reaches a rolling boil—not before.

- When the jam starts to thicken slightly, begin testing the set. It's slightly thickened when you start to see the bottom of the pot when stirring.

- To test the set, drop a spoonful of jam on an ice-cold plate and put the plate back in the freezer to cool for a minute or two. The jam is set when you can pull your finger through the cooled jam and the jam doesn't run together on the plate. Remember to remove the pot of jam from the heat when doing this test or it could overcook. If the test shows the jam is not ready, continue cooking the jam another 1 to 2 minutes and repeat the test until the jam sets.

- Jam also can be tested using a thermometer; the temperature should be about 221°F. The exact time it takes for each batch of jam to set will vary depending on the type and size of pan, the heat, and the amount of moisture in the fruit. The more jam you make, the more adept you'll get at recognizing the set point.

Use a wide, large, heavy pot to cook the fruit, which will bubble up as it starts to boil.

Bring the fruit to a full, rolling boil before you begin timing it.

The jam is starting to set when you can see the bottom of the pot when stirring.

The jam is set when you can pull your finger through it and it doesn't run back together.

Blueberry-Raspberry Jam

3 cups blueberries
3 cups raspberries, divided
3 cups sugar
3 tablespoons lemon juice

1 Place blueberries and 2 cups of the raspberries in heavy large pot. Add sugar and lemon juice; stir to combine. Cook over medium to medium-low heat until sugar has melted and juices begin to form, gently stirring occasionally. (Sugar and fruit will clump together before sugar begins to melt. Be patient and don't over-stir. Clumps will disappear when sugar melts.)
2 Increase heat to medium high; bring to a rolling boil. Boil, stirring occasionally, 15 minutes, adjusting heat as necessary to maintain an even boil. Add remaining 1 cup raspberries; boil 3 to 4 minutes, stirring frequently, or until slightly thickened (you'll begin to see bottom of pot when stirring) and set. (Temperature should be about 221°F.)
3 Pour hot jam into 4 sterilized 8-oz. jars. Carefully wipe jar rims; cover. (Jam can be made up to 1 month ahead and refrigerated or up to 6 months ahead and frozen.) To store at room temperature, immediately process in boiling water bath 5 minutes (see instructions on pg. 80).

4 (8-oz.) jars

PER TABLESPOON: 45 calories, 0 g total fat (0 g saturated fat), 0 g protein, 11.5 g carbohydrate, 0 mg cholesterol, 0 mg sodium, .5 g fiber

Processing Jam

STERILIZING JARS

All jars that are used for jam should be sterilized; use canning jars that are designed to withstand the heat of boiling water.

Place the jars on a rack in a large pot. (If you don't have a specially designed canning pot with jar holders, put a small, round cooling rack in the bottom of the pot to elevate the jars.) Fill the pot with enough hot water to completely cover the jars. Cover the pot, bring the water to a boil and boil the jars 10 minutes. To keep the jars warm until you're ready to fill them, keep them in hot water or on a small baking sheet in a 250°F. oven. (This prevents the jars from breaking when you add the hot jam.)

PROCESSING JAM FOR ROOM TEMPERATURE STORAGE

Sealing Use lids and screw bands that are designated for canning when storing jam at room temperature. These specially designed lids create an airtight seal. Paraffin is no longer recommended for sealing because an airtight seal may not form.

Warm the lids according to the manufacturer's directions. (Usually lids are kept in simmering, but not boiling, water for 5 minutes or until ready to use.) Lids can only be used once—do not reuse them. Screw bands should be washed but do not need to be sterilized or kept warm; they can be reused.

Boiling Fill warm, dry jars with hot jam, leaving at least ¼ inch at the top of the jar. Clean the rim of the jar with a damp cloth. Place a warm canning lid on the rim and tighten a screw band around the jar until it's finger tight; do not over-tighten.

Place the filled jars on a rack in a large pot of boiling water; the water should cover the jars by at least 1 inch. Cover the pot; bring the water to a boil and boil gently for 5 minutes. (Start timing only after the water has returned to a full boil.) Carefully remove the jars and place them on paper towel-lined baking tray.

Storing Let the jars stand 12 hours (moving them sooner could break the gel). As the jars cool, each lid should make a loud popping sound. To keep track, count each time you hear a lid pop. Make sure each jar has sealed and the lid is concave on top, not raised in the center. Screw bands can be removed at this point. Store in a dark, cool place for up to 1 year, keeping in mind that the shorter the storage time, the better the quality. When opening stored jam, make sure the lid is tight before opening. If the lid is loose or if there's leakage, mold or anything unusual, discard the jam.

stirring frequently, or until slightly thickened (you'll begin to see bottom of pot when stirring) and set. (Temperature should be about 221°F.)

2 Pour hot jam into 4 sterilized 8-oz. jars. Carefully wipe jar rims; cover. (Jam can be made up to 1 month ahead and refrigerated or up to 6 months ahead and frozen.) To store at room temperature, immediately process in boiling water bath 5 minutes (see instructions at left).

4 (8-oz.) jars

PER TABLESPOON: 45 calories, 0 g total fat (0 g saturated fat), 0 g protein, 12 g carbohydrate, 0 mg cholesterol, 0 mg sodium, .5 g fiber

Spiced Peach Jam

6 cups chopped peeled peaches (about 2½ lb.)
3 cups sugar
1 cinnamon stick
3 tablespoons lemon juice
½ teaspoon ground cardamom
½ teaspoon ground nutmeg

1 Place all ingredients in heavy large pot; stir to combine. Bring to a rolling boil over medium-high heat. Boil, stirring occasionally, 15 minutes, adjusting heat as necessary to maintain an even boil.

2 While mixture boils, mash fruit with potato masher to desired consistency. Boil an additional 5 to 10 minutes, stirring frequently, or until slightly thickened (you'll begin to see bottom of pot when stirring) and set. (Temperature should be about 221°F.) Remove from heat; remove cinnamon stick.

3 Pour hot jam into 4 sterilized 8-oz. jars. Carefully wipe jar rims; cover. (Jam can be made up to 1 month ahead and refrigerated or up to 6 months ahead and frozen.) To store at room temperature, immediately process in boiling water bath 5 minutes (see instructions at left).

4 (8-oz.) jars

PER TABLESPOON: 40 calories, 0 g total fat (0 g saturated fat), 0 g protein, 11 g carbohydrate, 0 mg cholesterol, 0 mg sodium, .5 g fiber

Gingered Plum Jam

6 cups finely chopped unpeeled plums (about 2 lb.)
3 cups sugar
3 tablespoons lemon juice
1½ teaspoons grated fresh ginger
Dash ground allspice

1 Place all ingredients in heavy large pot; stir to combine. Bring to a rolling boil over medium-high heat, adjusting heat as necessary to maintain an even boil. Boil 12 to 15 minutes,

Bottling Summer

Garlic-Ginger-Dill Vinegar

Roasted Red Pepper- Rosemary Vinegar

Citrus-Mint Vinegar

Making infused vinegar—vinegar flavored with fresh herbs and produce—is one way to preserve summer that doesn't take loads of time and effort. No special equipment or processing is needed. And the vinegar can be used throughout the coming months to add summertime flavors to cooking.

Experiment with various combinations of herbs, produce and seasonings, depending on what's available. Here are three new potential favorites: Citrus-Mint Vinegar, a light, almost sweet vinegar that pairs well with fruity salads; Garlic-Ginger-Dill Vinegar, which makes a perfect all-purpose vinegar; and Roasted Red Pepper-Rosemary Vinegar, a beautiful and seductive smoky-flavored vinegar. Get started today bottling the tastes of summer with these recipes, then go on to create your own.

How to Make Flavored Vinegar

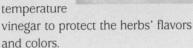

Making flavored vinegar is very simple. Be sure to wash herbs and produce well, and sterilize jars used to infuse and store the vinegar. These additional tips will ensure success:

Herbs and seasonings For optimum flavor, use herbs before they blossom. Choose seasonings that complement rather than dominate the flavors of the herbs and produce. Peppercorns, shallots, hot chiles, lemon peel, cinnamon sticks, edible flowers and fruit all add unique tastes to vinegar.

Vinegar Any type can be used, but keep in mind color and acidity.

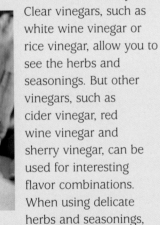

Clear vinegars, such as white wine vinegar or rice vinegar, allow you to see the herbs and seasonings. But other vinegars, such as cider vinegar, red wine vinegar and sherry vinegar, can be used for interesting flavor combinations. When using delicate herbs and seasonings, use a lighter vinegar, such as rice vinegar, which has a low acidity level of 4.2 percent. White wine vinegar is a good all-purpose choice at about 5 percent acid. Brands vary in acidity so check the label before purchasing. Distilled white vinegar tends to be a little harsh for infused vinegars.

Temperature Typically, the vinegar is heated until it's warm but not hot. The warmth begins to pull the essential oils and flavors from the herbs quicker than room temperature vinegar, so the flavor develops faster. When using delicate herbs, such as dill, or colorful herbs, such as opal basil or chive blossoms, it's better to use room temperature vinegar to protect the herbs' flavors and colors.

Containers Use glass containers, not metal or plastic, to infuse and store vinegar. Select a wide-mouth jar for infusing so that it's easy to add herbs and seasonings. For longer term storage, transfer the vinegar to decorative bottles, if desired, or recycle vinegar containers that have been cleaned and sterilized.

To sterilize jars and bottles, immerse them in a pan of boiling water for 15 minutes. Remove the pan from the heat, but let the jars stand in the hot water until ready to use.

Storage Store vinegar at room temperature unless otherwise indicated. Flavored vinegars keep for 6 months to 1 year. After 6 months, the flavor may begin to dissipate.

Creating your own recipes Use 1 to 2 cups lightly packed, coarsely chopped fresh herbs per 12-ounce bottle of vinegar. Use less of stronger herbs, such as thyme or rosemary, and more of delicate herbs, such as basil or tarragon. If you've never made flavored

vinegars, start with a single-herb vinegar; then experiment with your own special flavor combinations.

Roasted Red Pepper–Rosemary Vinegar

2 large red bell peppers
¾ cup white wine vinegar
3 sprigs fresh rosemary

1 Place bell peppers over high heat on gas or electric burner. Cook, turning with tongs every 1 to 2 minutes, until skins are completely blackened. Place peppers in heavy plastic bag; close bag and let stand 15 minutes or until cool enough to handle. Peel blackened skins under running water. Slit peppers and remove veins and seeds.
2 Place bell peppers in blender. Add vinegar; blend until almost smooth. Place in sterilized glass bottle; add rosemary. Cover; refrigerate (color stays nicer in refrigerator) 7 to 14 days or until vinegar is full-flavored.
3 Remove and discard rosemary. If desired, place fresh rosemary sprig in bottle for garnish. Store in refrigerator.

1½ cups

PER 2 TABLESPOONS: 5 calories, 0 g total fat (0 g saturated fat), 0 g protein, 2 g carbohydrate, 0 mg cholesterol, 0 mg sodium, 0 g fiber

---

Citrus-Mint Vinegar

2 large oranges
1 large lime
1 cup lightly packed fresh mint sprigs
1 (12-oz.) bottle rice vinegar

1 Sterilize 3-cup glass jar. With vegetable peeler, remove peel from oranges and lime, being careful not to include white pith below peel. (Reserve oranges and lime for another use.) Place orange and lime peels in jar. Add mint sprigs.
2 Heat vinegar in small saucepan over medium heat just until vinegar is warm but not hot. Pour vinegar over citrus peel and mint. Cover; let stand at room temperature 7 to 14 days or until vinegar is full-flavored.

3 Strain vinegar; place in sterilized 12-oz. bottle. Discard peels and mint. If desired, add fresh mint sprigs and large pieces of orange and lime peels to bottle for garnish. Store at room temperature.

1⅓ cups

PER 2 TABLESPOONS: 5 calories, 0 g total fat (0 g saturated fat), 0 g protein, 2 g carbohydrate, 0 mg cholesterol, 0 mg sodium, 0 g fiber

Garlic-Ginger-Dill Vinegar

1 cup packed coarsely chopped fresh dill
¼ cup coarsely chopped fresh ginger
3 large garlic cloves, minced
1 (12.7-oz.) bottle white wine vinegar

1 In large glass jar, combine all ingredients; stir to combine. Cover; let stand at room temperature 7 to 14 days or until vinegar is full-flavored.
2 Strain vinegar; place in sterilized glass bottle. Discard dill, ginger and garlic. If desired, add fresh dill sprigs to bottle for garnish. Store at room temperature.

1½ cups

PER 2 TABLESPOONS: 5 calories, 0 g total fat (0 g saturated fat), 0 g protein, 2 g carbohydrate, 0 mg cholesterol, 0 mg sodium, 0 g fiber

Using Infused Vinegar

Try these recipe suggestions with the flavored vinegars featured in this story.

CITRUS-MINT VINEGAR

Citrus-Mint Vinaigrette Combine 1 tablespoon Citrus-Mint Vinegar with ⅛ teaspoon Dijon mustard. Whisk in 3 tablespoons of mild olive oil or vegetable oil; season to taste with salt and pepper.

Grilled Summer Fruit Salad Combine apricot preserves with Citrus-Mint Vinegar to make a light glaze. Brush sliced peaches, pineapple, plums, pears and/or thinly sliced apples lightly with olive oil. Grill 5 to 8 minutes or until the fruit is tender, brushing with the glaze during the last 3 minutes of cooking. Serve on a bed of mixed salad greens and garnish with coarsely chopped fresh mint.

GARLIC-GINGER-DILL VINEGAR

Garlic-Ginger-Dill Vinaigrette Combine 1 tablespoon of Garlic-Ginger-Dill Vinegar with ½ small garlic clove, minced. Slowly whisk in 3 tablespoons of olive oil; season to taste with salt and pepper.

Garlic-Ginger Roasted Tomato Linguine Place sliced plum tomatoes in a large shallow pan. Drizzle with Garlic-Ginger-Dill Vinegar and olive oil. Bake at 425°F. for 15 minutes or until the tomatoes are tender. Toss with hot linguine, Parmesan cheese and freshly ground pepper.

ROASTED RED PEPPER-ROSEMARY VINEGAR

Roasted Red Pepper-Rosemary Vinaigrette Combine 1 tablespoon Roasted Red Pepper-Rosemary Vinegar with 1 small clove of garlic, minced. Slowly whisk in 3 tablespoons of olive oil; season to taste with salt and pepper.

Marinated Red Pepper Grilled Chicken Drizzle Roasted Red Pepper-Rosemary Vinegar over boneless skinless chicken breasts. Marinate in the refrigerator for 2 to 4 hours. Grill the chicken over medium heat. For added flavor, place rosemary stems that have been soaked in water at least 20 minutes directly on the coals while the chicken is grilling.

Homemade Fries

Sweet Potato Fries
All American Fries
Gold Yukon Fries

There's nothing more American than a heaping pile of golden fries. They're as much a part of our culinary heritage as Boston baked beans or homemade apple pie. When it comes to fries, however, most of us have left it up to the fast-food establishments to satisfy our tastes, and the results are often less than satisfying.

We knew we could do better. After numerous trials in which every variable was tested, from the type of oil and frying time to the variety of potato and the thickness of the cut, we came up with three versions that drew unanimous praise. Next time you get a french fry craving, head to the kitchen instead of the local burger joint. You'll create perfect fries, light golden brown on the outside, tender and melting on the inside—fries worthy of this American tradition.

Making Perfect Fries

Fries are simple to make; they only require potatoes, salt, pepper and oil for frying. In our quest for great french fries, we tested piles of potatoes using numerous methods. Here's what we found.

POTATOES

The type of potato you use has an impact on flavor, texture, cooking time and temperature.

Russet potatoes, also called baking potatoes, are great for french fries. Their low moisture and high starch content produce perfectly crisp fries with fluffy interiors.

Yukon gold potatoes, with their buttery color and delicate flavor, also make wonderful fries. Because they are moister than russets, Yukon golds are best when fried at a lower temperature; the excess moisture inside the potato is allowed to evaporate before the outside browns, resulting in crisp, golden fries. Yukon golds brown more quickly than russets.

Sweet potatoes make delicate, lightly crisp fries. They cook and brown very quickly, so the trick is not to overcook them. They are best when fried for a short time at lower temperatures.

A mandoline is handy for cutting perfectly even potato strips, which ensures even frying.

CUTTING

While hand-cut french fries always work well, use a mandoline, vegetable slicer or french fry cutter to create perfectly even potato strips and to save time. We found that ¼-inch strips give the optimum crisp-tender ratio. If your slices are bigger or smaller, you may need to adjust the cooking time. Whatever size you use, make sure all the slices are cut the same to ensure even frying.

OIL

Deep-fat frying involves high temperatures, so it's necessary to fry the potatoes in fat that holds up well to high heat. Vegetable oils are a good choice because they have a high smoke point, meaning they can be heated to a high temperature before they begin smoking. Peanut oil, corn oil, olive oil (not extra-virgin), safflower oil and soybean oil (oil labeled vegetable oil is usually pure soybean oil) also can be used. We prefer the slightly nutty taste of peanut oil for frying french fries. Olive oil also is excellent, but it costs more. Canola oil is not a good choice for deep-fat frying because it breaks down at higher temperatures and can leave a residue on the pan. Saturated fat, such as lard, produces fries with excellent crispness and taste, but most people prefer to avoid using saturated fat.

DOUBLE FRYING

This two-step process is crucial to obtain the perfect french fry. The first frying is done at a lower temperature and allows the inside of the potato to cook without browning the outside. The second frying, at a higher temperature, is done right before serving. It browns and crisps the outside of the potato while keeping the inside moist and tender. This process also allows you to get half of the frying out of the way early, requiring only a quick fry immediately before serving.

The first frying is done at a lower temperature, allowing the inside of the potato to cook.

COOKING TIME AND TEMPERATURE

To avoid problems, it's necessary to understand the frying process. When the potato hits the hot oil, the moisture on the outside of the potato evaporates and the exterior becomes brown and crisp. At the same time, the moisture inside the potato turns to steam, which cooks the potato, while pressure from the steam keeps oil out of the potato. Undercooking leaves moisture inside the potato and creates limp fries. Overcooking evaporates all of the moisture, causing oil to rush in and fill the void, creating soggy, greasy fries.

The outside of the potato browns and crisps during the second frying, done at a higher temperature.

If the oil temperature is too cool, the outside will not crisp and the inside moisture will not turn to steam, creating pale, damp fries. If the oil is too hot, the outside of the potato will crisp and brown before the inside is cooked, creating golden brown, limp fries. The goal is to find the delicate balance between the correct oil temperature and the right amount of cooking time.

All-American French Fries

2 lb. russet potatoes (about 3 medium), peeled
Oil for frying
¾ teaspoon kosher (coarse) salt
¼ teaspoon freshly ground pepper

1 Cut potatoes lengthwise into ¼-inch strips; pat dry with paper towels.
2 Heat 3 inches oil in heavy large saucepan over medium-high heat or in deep-fat fryer to 350°F., adjusting heat if necessary to maintain temperature. Line 2 baking sheets with several layers of paper towels. Fry in small batches 2½ minutes or until potatoes are pale white and just tender but not limp. (They will become limp as they cool.) Drain well; place on paper towels. Let stand, uncovered, at least 5 minutes or up to 3 hours.
3 When ready to serve, heat oil to 375°F. Fry potatoes in batches 2½ minutes or until golden brown. Drain well; place on paper towels. Sprinkle with salt and pepper.

6 servings

PER SERVING: 230 calories, 12.5 g total fat (2 g saturated fat), 2.5 g protein, 27.5 g carbohydrate, 0 mg cholesterol, 200 mg sodium, 2.5 g fiber

Golden Yukon Fries

2 lb. Yukon gold potatoes (about 5 medium), peeled
Oil for frying
¾ teaspoon kosher (coarse) salt
¼ teaspoon freshly ground pepper

1 Cut potatoes lengthwise into ¼-inch strips; pat dry with paper towels.
2 Heat 3 inches oil in heavy large saucepan over medium heat or in deep-fat fryer to 325°F., adjusting heat if necessary to maintain temperature. Line 2 baking sheets with several layers of paper towels. Fry in small batches 1½ minutes or until potatoes are pale yellow and just tender but not limp. (They will become limp as they cool.) Drain well; place on paper towels. Let stand, uncovered, at least 5 minutes or up to 3 hours.
3 When ready to serve, heat oil to 350°F. Fry potatoes in batches 2½ to 3 minutes or until golden brown. Drain well; place on paper towels. Sprinkle with salt and pepper.

6 servings

PER SERVING: 230 calories, 12.5 g total fat (2 g saturated fat), 2.5 g protein, 27.5 g carbohydrate, 0 mg cholesterol, 200 mg sodium, 2.5 g fiber

Sweet Potato Fries

2 lb. sweet potatoes (about 3 medium), peeled
Oil for frying
¾ teaspoon kosher (coarse) salt
¼ teaspoon freshly ground pepper

1 Cut potatoes lengthwise into ¼-inch strips; pat dry with paper towels.
2 Heat 3 inches oil in heavy large saucepan over medium heat or in deep-fat fryer to 325°F., adjusting heat if necessary to maintain temperature. Line 2 baking sheets with several layers of paper towels. Fry in small batches 1 minute or until potatoes are pale orange and almost tender with slight resistance but not limp. (They will become limp as they cool.) Drain well; place on paper towels. Let stand, uncovered, at least 5 minutes or up to 3 hours.
3 When ready to serve, heat oil to 350°F. Fry potatoes in batches 1 to 1½ minutes or until golden brown. Drain well; place on paper towels. Sprinkle with salt and pepper.

6 servings

PER SERVING: 230 calories, 12.5 g total fat (2 g saturated fat), 2 g protein, 28.5 g carbohydrate, 0 mg cholesterol, 205 mg sodium, 3.5 g fiber

The Art of Mashing

Crispy Onion-Topped Mashed Potatoes

Mashed potatoes are always a welcome side, whether they're served at a speedy weeknight supper or an all-out Thanksgiving dinner. When you mash in special seasonings or other extra ingredients, there are endless ways they can be made to match the occasion and accompanying foods. But even the most inspired efforts will disappoint if you don't first master the basics of making mashed potatoes.

Perfect mashed potatoes start with choosing the right potato. There are two general types: waxy and floury. Waxy potatoes hold their shape when cooked and work well for potato salad. Floury potatoes fall apart easily when cooked but are light and fluffy, making them perfect for mashed potatoes. Look for russet and Yukon gold, two varieties widely available.

Next, follow our tips for proper mashing. You can hone your skills with classic mashed potatoes. Then when you crave bolder spuds to accompany meats, poultry or fish, try one of the other tempting recipes. Mashed potatoes have never been better.

Three Steps to Fluffy Mashed Potatoes

Work quickly when making mashed potatoes so they stay hot throughout the process, which keeps them fluffy and light. If they cool down, they become heavy and compacted.

1. BOIL UNTIL TENDER

Put the cut potatoes in a large saucepan and cover them with 1 inch of water. Cover the saucepan and bring the water to a quick boil, watching carefully so it doesn't boil over. Uncover the saucepan and let the potatoes boil gently until they are tender when pierced with a fork (don't overcook). Drain immediately; potatoes become water-logged if left in water.

2. DRY QUICKLY

To remove excess water still clinging to the potatoes, return the well-drained potatoes to the same saucepan. Cook them over medium to medium-low heat for 1 to 2 minutes, shaking the pan constantly, until the potatoes look dull, not moist. The moisture evaporates, keeping the potatoes light and fluffy.

3. MASH WHILE HOT

For the smoothest texture, mash hot potatoes with a potato ricer or food mill. You also can use a potato masher. An electric mixer can be used for large batches as long as the potatoes are not whipped too fast or too long. Don't use a food processor; it turns mashed potatoes gluey. Stir warm cream or milk and butter into the potatoes until they reach the desired consistency. The amount of liquid needed depends on the starchiness of the potatoes. Stir quickly at the end to fluff the potatoes.

Rosemary-Olive Mashed Potatoes

¼ cup extra-virgin olive oil
1½ tablespoons chopped fresh rosemary
1 medium garlic clove, minced
2 lb. Yukon gold potatoes, peeled, cut into 2-inch pieces
3 sprigs fresh rosemary
1½ teaspoons salt, divided
⅓ to ½ cup heavy whipping cream
¼ teaspoon freshly ground pepper
½ cup pitted Kalamata olives, coarsely chopped

1 Heat oil, chopped rosemary and garlic in small skillet over medium-low heat until oil is hot (it will begin to sizzle). Reduce heat to low; cook 1 minute or until garlic is highly fragrant. Remove from heat.
2 Place potatoes in large saucepan; add enough water to cover by 1 inch. Add rosemary sprigs and 1 teaspoon of the salt; bring to a boil over medium heat. Boil gently 20 to 25 minutes or until tender when pierced with fork. Drain well; remove rosemary stems (leaves will fall off during cooking).
3 Meanwhile, bring ⅓ cup of the cream to a simmer in small saucepan over medium heat. Keep warm.
4 Return potatoes to large saucepan; cook over medium to medium-low heat 1 to 2 minutes or until excess moisture has evaporated, shaking pan (potatoes will look dull, not moist).
5 Press potatoes through potato ricer or food mill, or mash using potato masher until no lumps remain. Slowly stir in cream and garlic-rosemary mixture, adding additional warm cream for creamier texture if desired. Add remaining ½ teaspoon salt and pepper; stir vigorously to fluff. Fold in olives.

6 (¾-cup) servings

PER SERVING: 250 calories, 14.5 g total fat (4 g saturated fat), 3 g protein, 28.5 g carbohydrate, 15 mg cholesterol, 645 mg sodium, 3.5 g fiber

Crispy Onion-Topped Mashed Potatoes

ONIONS
⅓ cup butter
3 tablespoons olive oil
¾ cup chopped onions
¾ cup sliced shallots

POTATOES
1 lb. russet potatoes, peeled, cut into 2-inch pieces
1 lb. Yukon gold potatoes, peeled, cut into 2-inch pieces
1½ teaspoons salt, divided
⅓ to ½ cup whole milk
¼ teaspoon freshly ground pepper

1 Heat butter and oil in medium skillet over medium heat until butter is melted. Stir in onions and shallots; cover and cook 5 minutes or until softened. Remove cover; cook an additional 18 to 20 minutes or until onion mixture is golden brown, stirring occasionally.
2 Strain onion mixture through fine strainer, reserving butter mixture and pressing on onions to extract all liquid. Place on paper towels. Place 1 tablespoon of the onion mixture in small dry nonstick skillet; cook and stir over medium heat 1 to 2 minutes or until very crispy, taking care not to over-brown.
3 Meanwhile, place potatoes in large saucepan; add enough water to cover by 1 inch. Add 1 teaspoon of the salt; bring to a boil over medium heat. Boil gently 20 to 25 minutes or until tender when pierced with fork. Drain well.
4 Bring ⅓ cup of the milk and reserved butter mixture to a simmer in small saucepan over medium heat. Keep warm.
5 Return potatoes to large saucepan; cook over medium to medium-low heat 1 to 2 minutes or until excess moisture has evaporated, shaking pan (potatoes will look dull, not moist).
6 Press potatoes through potato ricer or food mill, or mash using potato masher until no lumps remain. Slowly stir in milk mixture, adding additional warm milk for creamier texture if desired. Add onion mixture and

remaining ½ teaspoon salt and pepper; stir vigorously to fluff. Top with crispy onions.

6 (¾-cup) servings

PER SERVING: 290 calories, 17.5 g total fat (7.5 g saturated fat), 3.5 g protein, 31.5 g carbohydrate, 30 mg cholesterol, 615 mg sodium, 3.5 g fiber

Spiced Smoky Mashed Potatoes

6 garlic cloves, divided
2 lb. russet potatoes, unpeeled, cut into 2-inch pieces
1½ teaspoons salt, divided
¼ cup butter, cut up
¼ to ½ teaspoon ground chipotle chile powder
⅓ cup whole milk
2 tablespoons sour cream
¼ teaspoon freshly ground pepper

1 Peel garlic. Smash 4 of the cloves; mince remaining 2 cloves. Place potatoes and smashed garlic in large saucepan; add enough water to cover by 1 inch. Add 1 teaspoon of the salt; bring to a boil. Boil gently over medium heat 20 to 25 minutes or until tender when pierced with fork; drain well.
2 Meanwhile, melt butter in small skillet over medium heat. Add minced garlic and chile powder; cook 30 to 60 seconds or until fragrant.
3 Bring milk to a simmer in small saucepan over medium heat. Keep warm.
4 Return potatoes to large saucepan; cook over medium to medium-low heat 1 to 2 minutes or until excess moisture has evaporated, shaking pan (potatoes will look dull, not moist).
5 Mash potatoes with potato masher until coarsely mashed. Add butter mixture; slowly stir in milk. Add sour cream, remaining ½ teaspoon salt and pepper; stir vigorously to fluff.

6 (¾-cup) servings

PER SERVING: 205 calories, 9 g total fat (5.5 g saturated fat), 3.5 g protein, 28.5 g carbohydrate, 25 mg cholesterol, 630 mg sodium, 3.5 g fiber

Baked
Goods

Puff Pastry from Scratch

Puff Pastry

While everyone acknowledges how wonderful it is, homemade puff pastry has the reputation of an aging diva: difficult to work with. Cooks instead often opt for frozen prepared puff pastry, which is convenient but in no way measures up to the grand dame herself. Real puff pastry, in fact, is not difficult to make, as our tester discovered; it only demands a little time.

Puff pastry made from scratch has incomparable taste and texture thanks to one ingredient: butter. (Frozen prepared puff pastry typically is made with shortening.) Butter is rolled between layers of dough. As the dough bakes, the butter melts and moisture evaporates, causing the layers to rise and air pockets to form. This is similar to what makes pie dough flaky, but on a grander scale. The process of layering the butter is simple. Butter is rolled into the dough, and then the dough is folded and turned. The process is repeated several times, with the dough resting between steps to stay cold to keep the layers separate.

Just as with many divas, puff pastry simply takes a little patience. Set aside an afternoon to discover this true culinary star.

Perfecting Puff Pastry

When making puff pastry, make sure you let the dough rest and always keep it cold.

1. Pound the butter with a rolling pin to soften it. Work quickly to keep it cold.

2. Fold the butter and pound it until it's 3/4-inch-thick and pliable but not sticky.

3. Roll the dough into a square. Place the butter on top and fold over the dough to meet in the center. Seal the seams.

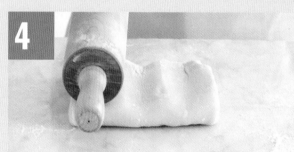

4. Pound the dough and butter with a rolling pin to soften slightly. Keep the surface well-floured for rolling.and rotate one-fourth turn. Repeat rolling and folding. If butter breaks through the surface, sprinkle it with flour and chill.

5. Roll the dough into a rectangle, shaping with your hands to keep it uniform.

6. Fold up the bottom third of the dough and brush off any excess flour.

7. Fold over the top third of the dough and rotate one-fourth turn. Repeat rolling and folding. If butter breaks through the surface, sprinkle it with flour and chill.

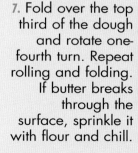

8. Make fingerprints in the dough to mark the number of times that it's been rolled, folded and turned. Chill. Repeat rolling, folding and turning as directed.

Puff Pastry

1½ cups (3 sticks) unsalted butter, chilled, divided
2 cups all-purpose flour
¼ teaspoon salt
½ to ¾ cup ice water

1 Reserve and refrigerate 3 tablespoons of the butter by cutting 1 tablespoon from each stick to keep the 3 sticks the same size.

2 Place 3 sticks of butter side by side on parchment paper, forming a block. Top with second piece of parchment. Pound butter with rolling pin until ¾ inch thick. Remove top piece of parchment; fold butter in half, using bottom piece of parchment to help guide. Cover with top piece of parchment. Continue pounding and folding butter 2 to 3 times or until butter is pliable but still cold and not sticky. Shape into 5-inch square; sprinkle both sides with flour. Cover and refrigerate 30 minutes or until chilled but not hard.

3 Meanwhile, in large bowl, stir together flour and salt. With pastry blender or 2 knives, cut in reserved 3 tablespoons butter until mixture resembles coarse crumbs with some pea-sized pieces. Add ½ cup of the ice water; mix with fork until soft dough forms, adding additional water 1 tablespoon at a time if necessary. On lightly floured surface, knead dough 30 seconds or until smooth and pliable. Cover and refrigerate 15 minutes.

4 On floured surface, roll dough into 12-inch square. Place butter in center of dough; fold ends over butter to meet in center. Fold sides of dough over butter; press dough with rolling pin to seal seams. Turn dough one-fourth turn.

5 Pound dough with rolling pin to soften slightly. Roll out dough to 18x6-inch rectangle. Fold dough like a letter, folding up bottom third and covering with top third. Press firmly with rolling pin 3 to 4 times to seal. Turn dough one-fourth turn so edges are facing you. Repeat rolling dough into 18x6-inch rectangle and folding like a letter; press with rolling pin to seal edges. Make two fingerprints in corner of dough to indicate it has been rolled and turned twice. Cover and refrigerate 15 minutes or until cold.

6 Repeat Step 5 two more times, for a total of 6 rolls. Indicate with fingerprints how many times the dough has been rolled and turned. If butter comes through dough or dough becomes sticky, stop immediately. Sprinkle flour on problem area and refrigerate until dough is well chilled before proceeding. (Dough can be refrigerated for 2 days or frozen for 1 month.)

About 2 lb. dough

PER ½ OF RECIPE: 280 calories, 23 g total fat (14.5 g saturated fat), 2.5 g protein, 16 g carbohydrate, 60 mg cholesterol, 55 mg sodium, .5 g fiber

Strawberry-Almond Puff Pastry Shortcakes

FILLING
1 cup sliced almonds
¼ cup sugar
2 tablespoons unsalted butter, softened
½ teaspoon almond extract

SHORTCAKES
½ recipe Puff Pastry (left)
1 egg white, lightly beaten
⅓ cup sliced almonds
⅓ cup plus 2 tablespoons sugar, divided
4 cups sliced strawberries
1 teaspoon vanilla extract, divided
1 cup whipping cream

1 Heat oven to 425°F. Line baking sheet with parchment paper. Place almonds and ¼ cup sugar in food processor; pulse until almonds are finely ground. Add butter and almond extract; pulse until butter is distributed and mixture is crumbly. Process 1 minute or until nuts just begin to form paste. Place in small bowl; cover and let stand at room temperature while baking pastry.

2 On lightly floured surface, roll pastry into 13x10-inch rectangle ⅛ inch thick. Trim edges even using a sharp knife, being careful to cut straight down. Cut pastry into 6 rectangles; place on baking sheet. Refrigerate 5 to 10 minutes or until pastry is chilled. (Rectangles can be made up to 1 day ahead. Cover and refrigerate.)

3 Bake 10 to 12 minutes or until pastry is puffed and light golden brown. Remove from oven. Brush with egg white; sprinkle each with almonds and scant 1 tablespoon of the sugar. Bake 3 to 5 minutes or until almonds are lightly toasted. Cool on wire rack.

4 Meanwhile, in large bowl, stir together strawberries, 1 tablespoon of the sugar and ½ teaspoon vanilla. In another large bowl, beat cream, remaining 1 tablespoon sugar and remaining ½ teaspoon vanilla at medium-high speed until soft peaks form. Cover and refrigerate.

5 To serve, carefully slice pastry rectangles in half horizontally. Place bottoms on individual plates. Place 2 tablespoons almond filling evenly over each pastry; top with half of the whipped cream and strawberries. Repeat with remaining whipped cream and strawberries. Cover with top half of pastry.

6 shortcakes

PER SHORTCAKE: 680 calories, 50 g total fat (25.5 g saturated fat), 9 g protein, 53.5 g carbohydrate, 115 mg cholesterol, 75 mg sodium, 5.5 g fiber

Tender-Hearted Rolls

Old-Fashioned Buttermilk Dinner Rolls

Artisan breads, with their dense textures and crispy crusts, have their place at the table, but there are times when only a soft, old-fashioned dinner roll will do. Large family get-togethers and holiday dinners beg for big, puffy rolls that soak up butter or the last drop of gravy.

Made from buttery white bread dough, these rolls are light and yeasty, chewy yet tender. While dinner rolls can be made from any bread recipe, buttermilk adds tenderness and a delicate tang to these. Try your hand at rolling the dough into a variety of shapes for a special presentation. It may take a little more effort, but at this time of the year, lovingly shaped rolls are a gift to your guests.

Shaping Technique

This dough is very versatile and can be formed into many different shapes. After dividing the dough into 16 pieces (Step 4 of opposite recipe), decide which shape you'd like to make.

For ease in shaping, the dough must rest after dividing to allow the gluten to relax. If the dough springs back during shaping and doesn't cooperate, stop and cover the dough. Let it sit 3 to 5 minutes or until it no longer springs back. Try not to work the dough too much, or the rolls may become tough. Always cover dough that is not being shaped to avoid forming a crust.

It's best to work on a very lightly floured surface. The surface should provide some resistance to the dough, so avoid using too much flour. In addition, extra flour can create dry, tough rolls. If the dough slides too much during shaping, you may be using too much flour. If the dough sticks, lightly flour your hands.

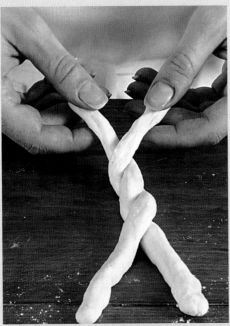

TWISTED ROLL

Divide each piece of dough into two pieces. Roll each piece into a thin rope 9 inches long. Twist the two strands, then gently press the strands together at each end.

BOW KNOT ROLL

Roll each piece of dough into a rope 12 inches long. Loosely tie a knot by making a circle and looping one end into the circle, pulling gently. Leave 1<None> inches at either end. Do not pull the dough tight; there should be room for the dough to expand during rising and baking.

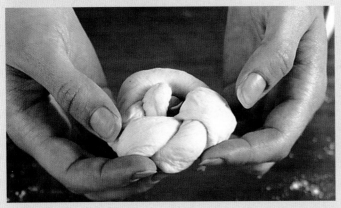

FLOWER ROLL

Follow the directions for the Bow Knot Roll, but start with a rope of dough 14 inches long. After tying the knot, tuck one end into the center from the bottom of the roll and the other end into the center from the top of the roll.

TWISTED CIRCLE

Follow the directions for the Twisted Roll, starting with 10-inch-long ropes. After twisting the strands, bring the ends together and press to form a circle.

RECTANGULAR ROLL

Form each piece of dough into a 4x2½-inch rectangle. After the final rise, use scissors to snip ½-inch-deep cuts across the top of the roll, forming a pattern if desired.

FOLDED ROLL

Press each piece of dough flat into a 4x3-inch rectangle. Fold one 4-inch side across to the other side. Press gently. After the final rise, use a knife to cut three ½-inch-deep slits across the top of the dough.

USING GLAZES

Glazes can be brushed onto the rolls for added shine, flavor and texture. They also help any seasonings, such as herbs or seeds, stick to the roll.

Butter Glaze A butter glaze turns a firm crust into a soft, buttery one. Brush 1 to 2 tablespoons melted butter over the rolls immediately after they come out of the oven. Let them stand 3 to 5 minutes before serving.

Egg Glaze An egg glaze adds a shine and is useful when sprinkling rolls with seasonings. Whisk 1 egg with 1 tablespoon of water in a small bowl. Strain the mixture to remove any small particles of egg white. Bake the rolls 15 minutes. Remove them from the oven and brush with the egg glaze. If desired, sprinkle with seasonings, such as poppy seeds, sesame seeds, caraway seeds or minced fresh herbs (basil, chives or rosemary). Continue baking 2 to 3 minutes or until brown.

Old-Fashioned Buttermilk Dinner Rolls

- ¾ cup warm water (110°F. to 115°F.), divided
- 1 (¼-oz.) pkg. active dry yeast (2¼ teaspoons)
- ½ cup warm buttermilk (110°F. to 115°F.)
- 1 egg, room temperature, beaten
- 2 tablespoons unsalted butter, melted
- 2 tablespoons sugar
- 1½ teaspoons salt
- 3½ to 3¾ cups bread flour

1 Place ¼ cup of the warm water in small bowl; stir in yeast. Let stand 10 minutes or until yeast is dissolved and foamy.
2 Meanwhile, in large bowl, whisk together remaining ½ cup water, buttermilk, egg, butter, sugar and salt. Whisk in yeast mixture to combine. Slowly stir in 3½ cups of the flour, using hands if necessary, until soft dough forms, slowly adding additional ¼ cup flour as necessary to form soft dough that pulls away from sides of bowl.
3 On lightly floured surface, knead dough 7 to 10 minutes or until smooth and elastic. Place dough in lightly buttered large bowl; turn to coat all sides with butter. Cover with plastic wrap and towel; let rise in warm place until doubled in size, about 1 hour.
4 Line baking sheet with parchment paper. Gently punch dough down; turn out onto lightly floured surface. Divide dough in half; cut each half into 8 pieces. Roll each piece into desired shape; place on baking sheet. Spray plastic wrap with nonstick cooking spray; cover rolls. Let rise in warm place 30 to 40 minutes or until doubled in size.
5 Meanwhile, heat oven to 375°F. Bake 17 to 20 minutes or until light golden brown.

16 rolls

PER ROLL: 135 calories, 2 g total fat (1 g saturated fat), 4 g protein, 25 g carbohydrate, 15 mg cholesterol, 235 mg sodium, 1 g fiber

Heavenly Challah

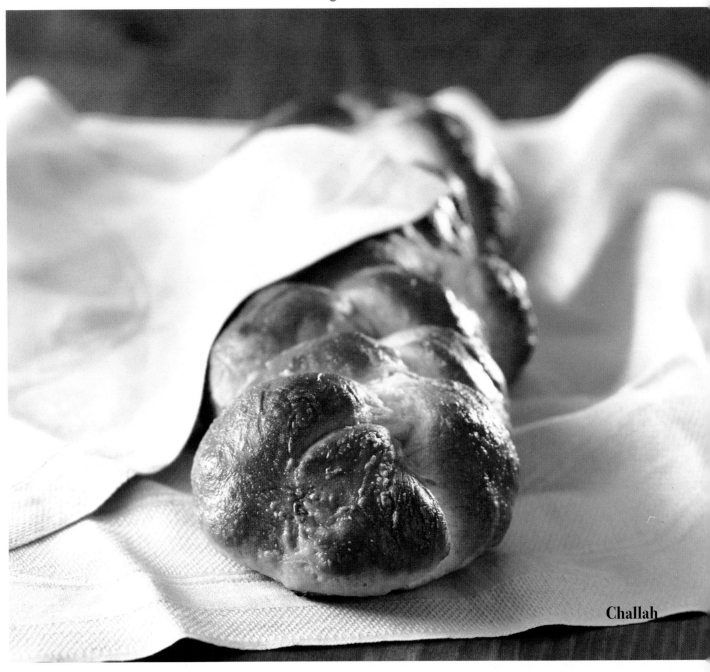

Challah

Challah is the light, almost cake-like egg bread traditionally baked for the Jewish Sabbath (or Shabbat) celebration held on Friday nights and Saturdays. But you don't have to be Jewish to enjoy challah. People from every background can agree on one thing: Challah made with love and care is truly is a heavenly creation!

A simple braiding process (outlined here) gives challah its unique look. Topped with an egg glaze and poppy seeds, sesame seeds or another accent seed of your choice, you can gently tweak your challah into exactly the creation you want it to be.

Serve challa with soft butter … it goes with any meal! And, truth be told, challah can even serve as dessert — just provide a selection of fruit jams or marmalades, and a little jar of honey too. Heavenly!

Challah

½ cup warm water (110°F. to
   115°F.)
1 (¼-oz.) pkg. active dry yeast
¼ teaspoon sugar

DOUGH
1 cup warm water (110°F. to
   115°F.)
⅓ cup canola oil
¼ cup sugar
3 eggs, room temperature*
1 egg yolk, room temperature
1 teaspoon salt
4½ to 5½ cups bread flour

GLAZE
1 egg
2 teaspoons poppy seeds or
   sesame seeds, if desired

1 Combine all yeast ingredients in
small bowl; let stand 10 minutes or
until foamy.
2 Meanwhile, combine 1 cup water,
oil and ¼ cup sugar in large bowl.
Add 3 eggs, egg yolk and salt; beat at
medium speed until combined.
3 Add yeast mixture and 1 cup of
the flour; beat at low speed until
smooth. Slowly beat in enough of the
remaining flour to make soft dough.
(Resist the urge to add too much
flour; dough should be sticky and
won't pull away from sides of bowl
cleanly.)
4 Knead dough 5 minutes with
mixer or gently by hand on lightly
floured surface 10 minutes or until
dough is soft and smooth. Gently
form into large ball; lightly dust
outside with flour. Spray large bowl
with cooking spray. Place dough in
bowl; cover with plastic wrap
sprayed with cooking spray. Cover
with towel; place in warm place. Let
rise until double, about 1 hour.
5 Heat oven to 350°F.; line large
baking sheet with parchment paper.
Gently punch down dough; turn out
onto lightly floured surface. Divide
dough in half; divide each half into 3
pieces. Roll each piece into rope 18
inches long and 1 inch wide.
6 Place 3 ropes next to each other.

Mixing and Braiding Challah

Sticky dough

Challah dough should be soft and
sticky. To keep the bread light, resist
the urge to add a lot of flour when
kneading, and use a light touch. If the
dough is difficult to work with, spray
your hands with cooking spray.

Making ropes

After the first rise, divide the dough in
half to form 2 loaves, and divide each
loaf into 3 pieces. On a lightly floured
surface, roll each piece into an 18-
inch rope. If the dough pulls back as
you roll, the gluten has begun to
form. Cover the dough and let it rest
for a minute or two; then try again.
Using too much flour on the surface
also can cause rolling problems.

Braiding

Arrange the 3 ropes on the surface
parallel and close to each other, but
not touching. Starting in the middle,
braid one half of the loaf. Braid
loosely without pulling the dough.
Use a flip-flop motion rather than a
pulling motion. Then braid the other
half of the loaf.

Starting in the middle, braid one half;
secure ends. Braid the other half;
place on baking sheet. Repeat with
remaining dough, keeping space
between braids on baking sheet.
Cover with towel; let rise 25 to 30
minutes or until almost doubled in
size.
7 Combine 1 egg and 1 tablespoon
water. Brush over braids; sprinkle
with poppy seeds. Bake 30 minutes

or until golden brown and bread
sounds hollow when tapped on
bottom.

2 (24-slice) loaves

PER SLICE: 70 calories, 2.5 g total fat (.5 g saturated fat), 2 g
protein, 10.5 g carbohydrate, 20 mg cholesterol, 55 mg
sodium, .5 g fiber

Homemade Burger Buns

Toasted Garlic, Rosemary-Whole Wheat and Homemade Sesame Hamburger Buns

You don't need a membership in a gym to get great buns. You can achieve bun-perfection in your own kitchen in surprisingly little time, without even breaking a sweat. Then when those big, juicy burgers come off the grill, you can serve them in a bun they deserve. All too often, the bun is a disappointing after-thought, soft and squishy with no flavor, too big for the burger or too tough to chew.

The ideal bun is firm on the outside, with a pleasant crunch that complements the burger but doesn't overpower it. The inside should be delicate but not so soft that it falls apart when it meets a juicy patty and a ripe slice of tomato.

These buns can be made quickly. Fast-acting yeast cuts the rising time in half, and if you let your electric mixer do the work for you, there's no need for long and vigorous hand-kneading. Having great buns is easier than you think. Save your workout for backyard fun.

Tips for Perfect Buns

Use a stand mixer with a paddle or a hand mixer with a dough hook for these recipes. The dough also can be made by hand.

1. Mix the dough

Add enough bread flour to make a soft dough (it may feel sticky and may stick slightly to the sides of the bowl). Temperature and humidity affect how much flour is needed. Resist the temptation to add too much flour.

2. Shape into balls

After the dough rises, deflate it and divide it into 6 pieces. Gently form each piece into a ball, tucking under the cut edges at the bottom. Don't pull or stretch the dough too tightly trying to make perfectly shaped balls; the edges may separate as the dough bakes.

3. Rest and flatten

Let the balls rest 3 minutes to relax the gluten. Then flatten each one into a 3-inch round. If the balls are difficult to flatten, cover them and let rest another 5 minutes before trying again.

4. Add a little weight

Cover the buns with a towel; let them rise for 15 minutes. Then place a lightweight baking sheet on top of them. This keeps the tops from mounding and helps the buns stay evenly shaped.

5. Tap for doneness

Bake the buns until golden brown on top and bottom. To test for doneness, gently tap the bottom of the buns with your finger. They should sound slightly hollow, like tapping a partially empty box.

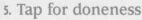

Toasted Garlic Hamburger Buns

1 cup warm water (110°F. to 115°F.), divided
½ teaspoon sugar
1 (¼-oz.) pkg. fast-acting dry yeast
2 tablespoons extra-virgin olive oil, divided
2 to 2½ cups bread flour, divided
1 teaspoon salt
3 large garlic cloves

1 Place ½ cup of the water, sugar and yeast in large bowl of stand mixer with paddle attachment. (Dough also can be made by hand.) Let stand 2 to 3 minutes or until yeast is dissolved. Add remaining ½ cup water, 1 tablespoon of the oil and 1 cup of the flour; beat at low speed until combined. Add salt. With mixer running, slowly add enough of the remaining flour to form a soft dough.
2 Beat at medium-low speed 5 minutes or until smooth and elastic. (If making by hand, knead 10 minutes.) Place in greased medium bowl; cover with plastic wrap and towel. Let rise in warm place 30 minutes or until doubled in size.
3 Gently punch down dough to deflate; place on lightly floured surface. Divide into 6 pieces. Form each piece into a ball; place on parchment paper-lined baking sheet. Cover with towel; let stand 3 minutes. Flatten into 3¾-inch rounds. Cover with towel; let rise 15 minutes.
4 Place another lightweight baking sheet or pan on top of towel covering buns. (This will act as a weight, making buns flatter and more even.) Let buns rise 25 minutes or until almost doubled in size (dough should hold slight indentation when gently pressed).
5 Meanwhile, heat oven to 375°F. With side of knife, mash garlic with dash of salt until fine paste forms (or use mini food processor). Place in small cup; stir in remaining 1 tablespoon oil. Brush tops of buns with garlic mixture. Bake 20 minutes or until golden brown and bottoms

sound hollow when gently tapped. Cool completely on wire rack.

6 buns

PER BUN: 215 calories, 5 g total fat (.5 g saturated fat), 5.5 g protein, 36 g carbohydrate, 0 mg cholesterol, 395 mg sodium, 1.5 g fiber

Homemade Sesame Hamburger Buns

- ½ cup warm water (110°F. to 115°F.)
- ½ teaspoon sugar
- 1 (¼-oz.) pkg. fast-acting dry yeast
- ½ cup warm milk (110°F. to 115°F.)
- 2 tablespoons butter, melted, cooled
- 2½ to 2¾ cups bread flour, divided
- 1 teaspoon salt
- 1 egg white, lightly beaten
- 2 tablespoons sesame seeds

1 Place water, sugar and yeast in large bowl of stand mixer with paddle attachment. (Dough also can be made by hand.) Let stand 2 to 3 minutes or until yeast is dissolved. Add milk, butter and 1 cup of the flour; beat at low speed until combined. Add salt; beat until combined. With mixer running, slowly add enough of the remaining flour to form a soft dough.

2 Beat at medium-low speed 5 minutes or until smooth and elastic. (If making by hand, knead 10 minutes.) Place in greased medium bowl; cover with plastic wrap and towel. Let rise in warm place 30 minutes or until doubled in size.

3 Gently punch down dough to deflate; place on lightly floured surface. Divide into 6 pieces. Form each piece into a ball; place on parchment paper-lined baking sheet. Cover with towel; let stand 3 minutes. Flatten into 3¾-inch rounds. Cover with towel; let rise 15 minutes.

4 Place another lightweight baking sheet or pan on top of towel covering buns. (This will act as a weight, making buns flatter and more even.) Let buns rise 25 minutes or until almost doubled in size (dough should hold slight indentation when gently pressed).

5 Meanwhile, heat oven to 375°F. Lightly brush top of buns with egg white; sprinkle with sesame seeds. Bake 20 minutes or until golden brown and bottoms sound hollow when gently tapped. Cool completely on wire rack.

6 buns

PER BUN: 280 calories, 6.5 g total fat (3 g saturated fat), 8.5 g protein, 46 g carbohydrate, 10 mg cholesterol, 440 mg sodium, 2.5 g fiber

Rosemary-Whole Wheat Hamburger Buns

- ½ cup warm water (110°F. to 115°F.)
- ½ teaspoon sugar
- 1 (¼-oz.) pkg. fast-acting dry yeast
- ½ cup warm milk (110°F. to 115°F.)
- 2 tablespoons butter, melted, cooled
- 1½ to 2 cups bread flour, divided
- 2 tablespoons chopped fresh rosemary
- 1 teaspoon salt
- ½ cup whole wheat flour
- 1 egg white, lightly beaten
- 6 tiny sprigs fresh rosemary

1 Place water, sugar and yeast in large bowl of stand mixer with paddle attachment. (Dough also can be made by hand.) Let stand 2 to 3 minutes or until yeast is dissolved. Add milk, butter and 1 cup of the bread flour; beat at low speed until combined. Add chopped rosemary and salt; beat until combined. With mixer running, slowly add whole wheat flour and enough of the remaining bread flour to form a soft dough.

2 Beat at medium-low speed 5 minutes or until smooth and elastic. (If making by hand, knead 10 minutes.) Place in greased medium bowl; cover with plastic wrap and towel. Let rise in warm place 30 minutes or until doubled in size.

3 Gently punch down dough to deflate; place on lightly floured surface. Divide into 6 pieces. Form each piece into a ball; place on parchment paper-lined baking sheet. Cover with towel; let stand 3 minutes. Flatten into 3¾-inch rounds. Cover with towel; let rise 15 minutes.

4 Place another lightweight baking sheet or pan on top of towel covering buns. (This will act as a weight, making buns flatter and more even.) Let buns rise 25 minutes or until almost doubled in size (dough should hold slight indentation when gently pressed).

5 Meanwhile, heat oven to 375°F. Lightly brush top of buns with egg white; lightly press rosemary sprig onto center of each bun. Bake 20 minutes or until golden brown and bottoms sound hollow when gently tapped. Cool completely on wire rack.

6 buns

PER BUN: 210 calories, 5 g total fat (3 g saturated fat), 6.5 g protein, 35.5 g carbohydrate, 10 mg cholesterol, 440 mg sodium, 2.5 g fiber

Scones Done Right

Christmas Scones

If you think of scones as dry, crumbly and tasteless, then you probably haven't eaten a real one. The scones sold in coffee shops and cafes across the United States often look enticing, but their taste is a disappointment. A true English scone is a delicious wonder, with a light, flaky texture and a delicate flavor. When served warm from the oven, it's something to be savored over a pot of tea or cup of coffee.

Making scones is perfectly easy. Any beginner can have success—the less you fuss, the better they are. In no more than 20 minutes, you can make the dough and get the scones in the oven. They also can be made ahead and baked the following morning. While the English have given us the perfect scone, there is an American innovation that greatly enhances them: adding a wide variety of flavors. Try these simple recipes with dried fruit, ginger or lemon, and you'll discover there's a lot to love about a real scone.

Easy Steps to Tender Scones

For the lightest, most delicate scones, follow these tips and serve them fresh from the oven:

- Use chilled butter and blend it into the flour mixture using a pastry blender or two knives. (If your hands tend to be cold, you can use your hands, as some pastry chefs do. Otherwise, use tools so the butter doesn't melt.)

- Work the butter into the flour mixture until it forms crumbs about the size of blueberries. As the scones bake, the butter slowly melts, creating pockets of air that make the scones flaky, light and tender.

- Use a fork to blend the liquid with the dry ingredients. Work quickly so that the dough will be soft, with little gluten. The more you mix the dough, the more gluten will develop, resulting in tougher scones.

- It's not necessary to knead this dough. Just quickly and gently press the dough with your hands until it holds together. To avoid developing gluten strands, which make the dough tough, don't overwork it or squeeze it.

- Pat the dough into a 1-inch-thick round, working on parchment paper for wedges or on a lightly floured surface for cutouts. Make sure the dough remains thick; if it's too thin, the scones will be drier inside.

- For wedges, cut the round into 8 pieces and separate the wedges slightly before baking. They'll come back together during baking, but they'll be easier to cut apart. For cutouts, leave enough room between the scones so they won't bake together and will have crisp edges.

- For a pretty finish, brush the tops of the scones with an egg wash (egg mixed with water) or cream, and sprinkle them with sugar. For a sparkly effect, use large crystallized sugar; or try granulated light brown raw sugar on Gingerbread Scones (pg. 105).

Blend cold butter into the flour mixture until the butter particles are blueberry-sized.

Add the liquid to the dry ingredients; then use a fork to evenly distribute the moisture.

Gently press the dough together with your hands, taking care not to overwork it.

Pat out the dough to 1-inch thickness before cutting it into wedges or making cutouts. Don't pat it too thin or the scones will be dry.

Slightly separate wedges on parchment paper to allow for expansion during baking. They'll be easier to cut when done.

Gingerbread Scones

- 2½ cups all-purpose flour
- ½ cup packed brown sugar
- 3 tablespoons sugar, divided
- 1 teaspoon baking powder
- ½ teaspoon baking soda
- ¼ teaspoon salt
- 2 teaspoons ground ginger
- ½ teaspoon ground cloves
- ½ teaspoon ground nutmeg
- ½ cup unsalted butter, chilled, cut up
- 2 eggs, divided
- ⅓ cup buttermilk
- 1 tablespoon molasses
- 1 tablespoon water
  Orange-Ginger Butter (recipe follows)

1 Heat oven to 400°F. Line baking sheet with parchment paper. In large bowl, whisk together flour, brown sugar, 2 tablespoons of the sugar, baking powder, baking soda and salt. Add ginger, cloves and nutmeg; whisk until well blended. With pastry blender or 2 knives, cut in butter until butter is size of blueberries.

2 In small bowl, whisk together 1 of the eggs, buttermilk and molasses until blended. Pour into flour mixture; stir with fork until evenly moistened. With hands, quickly and gently press together to form dough. Place on baking sheet; pat into 7-inch round 1 inch thick. Cut into 8 wedges; separate slightly.

3 In another small bowl, whisk together remaining 1 egg and water; lightly brush over top of scones. Sprinkle with remaining 1 tablespoon sugar. Bake 20 to 25 minutes or until toothpick inserted in center comes out clean. Cool on wire rack 10 minutes. Serve warm or at room temperature with Orange-Ginger Butter.

8 scones

PER SCONE: 430 calories, 22 g total fat (13.5 g saturated fat), 6 g protein, 52.5 g carbohydrate, 105 mg cholesterol, 250 mg sodium, 1.5 g fiber

Orange-Ginger Butter

- 6 tablespoons unsalted butter, softened
- 1 tablespoon powdered sugar
- 1 tablespoon grated orange peel
- ¼ teaspoon ground ginger

In small bowl, stir together all ingredients until well combined. (Butter can be prepared up to 2 days ahead. Cover and refrigerate.) Serve at room temperature.

Christmas Scones

- 2½ cups all-purpose flour
- ½ cup sugar
- 1 teaspoon baking powder
- ½ teaspoon baking soda
- ¼ teaspoon salt
- 1½ teaspoons ground cinnamon
- 1 teaspoon ground nutmeg
- 1 teaspoon ground allspice
- ¼ teaspoon ground cloves
- ½ cup dried cranberries
- ⅓ cup diced dried apricots
- ¼ cup finely chopped walnuts or pecans
- ½ cup unsalted butter, chilled, cut up
- 2 eggs, divided
- ¾ cup whipping cream
- 1 tablespoon water
- 1 tablespoon large crystallized sugar

1 Heat oven to 400°F. Line baking sheet with parchment paper. In large bowl, whisk together flour, sugar, baking powder, baking soda and salt. Add cinnamon, nutmeg, allspice and cloves; whisk until well blended. Stir in cranberries, apricots and walnuts until coated with flour. With pastry blender or 2 knives, cut in butter until butter is size of blueberries.

2 In small bowl, whisk together 1 of the eggs and cream until blended. Pour into flour mixture; stir with fork until evenly moistened. With hands, quickly and gently press together to form dough. Place on baking sheet; pat into 8-inch round 1 inch thick. Cut into 8 wedges; separate slightly.

3 In another small bowl, whisk together remaining 1 egg and water; lightly brush over top of scones. Sprinkle with crystallized sugar. Bake 20 to 25 minutes or until toothpick inserted in center comes out clean. Cool on wire rack 10 minutes. Serve warm or at room temperature.

8 scones

PER SCONE: 450 calories, 23 g total fat (12.5 g saturated fat), 7 g protein, 55.5 g carbohydrate, 110 mg cholesterol, 240 mg sodium, 2.5 g fiber

Garden Biscuits

Ricotta-Dill Buttermilk Biscuits

Picture an herb garden in full show. The basil, dill and lemon balm have matured but are still neat and trim in their allotted spaces. Later in the summer, a simple garden will have lost all form and design. Despite careful planning, the herbs will act like unruly children, running to every open space. But, when the herbs are still well behaved, you will be most inspired to wander the garden and create fresh uses for them.

So try simple homemade biscuits flavored with a variety of fresh herbs. Biscuits are light and fresh, can be made with a minimum of fuss, and they bake quickly without overheating the kitchen. Use a variety of herbs, from light lemon balm to hearty rosemary and sage. Lavender or nasturtium flowers perfume biscuits when mixed into the dough, while chopped or whole geranium leaves add a fragrant, decorative touch to biscuit tops. Bring the freshness of herbs into your kitchen with these delicate biscuits, the next best thing to having a table in the herb garden.

Creating Light Biscuits

Use a gentle hand and follow these tips to achieve light-as-air biscuits.

Low-protein flour The combination of all-purpose flour and cake flour creates dough with a lower protein content than dough made entirely with all-purpose flour. This results in light, airy, delicate biscuits. If you have access to low-protein, soft-wheat flour, also known as Southern flour (White Lily is one brand), you can use that in place of the all-purpose flour and cake flour combination.

Cutting in the butter Mix the chilled butter into the flour using a pastry blender or two knives. Use a cutting

Pieces should be the size of blueberries.

motion to blend and distribute the butter until the pieces are about the size of blueberries. These bits of butter will melt during baking, creating pockets of flakiness.

Wet, sticky dough Stir the wet ingredients into the flour mixture with a fork, mixing just until the dry ingredients are moistened. The dough will be very wet and sticky, and you may think you have measured wrong. You haven't; biscuit dough should be fairly wet because the moisture in the dough creates steam during baking, thereby creating light, airy bread.

Patting and cutting To shape the biscuits, place the dough on a floured work surface and sprinkle it with flour. Pat out the dough with floured hands to about ¾-inch thickness. (It is not necessary to roll the dough with a rolling pin.) Using a floured knife or biscuit cutter, cut the dough into shapes; use a spatula to transfer the biscuits to a baking sheet. If the biscuits are misshapen, that's okay; they will still bake just fine. You can flour the outside of the biscuits so they aren't too sticky to work with, but shake off any excess flour. Avoid incorporating too much flour into the dough because the biscuits will turn out heavy.

The dough will be wet and sticky.

Pat out the dough.

Cut the dough.

Lavender Biscuits with Apricot Cream

BISCUITS
- 1 cup all-purpose flour
- 1 cup cake flour
- 1 tablespoon baking powder
- 2 tablespoons chopped fresh lavender or 2 teaspoons dried
- ¼ teaspoon salt
- 6 tablespoons unsalted butter, chilled, cut up
- 1 egg, beaten
- ⅔ cup whole milk
- 1 tablespoon sugar

APRICOT CREAM
- 2 ripe apricots, finely chopped
- 1 tablespoon sugar
- ½ cup whipping cream

1 Heat oven to 425°F. Lightly grease baking sheet or line with parchment paper. In large bowl, combine all-purpose flour, cake flour, baking powder, lavender and salt. With pastry blender, cut in butter until butter is size of blueberries.

2 In small bowl, whisk together egg and milk. Add to flour mixture, mixing just until soft dough forms. (Dough will be very moist and sticky.)

3 On floured surface with well-floured hands, knead dough 2 to 3 times to combine. Pat dough to form ¾-inch-thick square. Cut into 8 rectangles. Place on baking sheet. Sprinkle with 1 tablespoon sugar.

4 Bake 15 minutes or until pale brown.

5 Meanwhile, in medium bowl, stir together apricots and 1 tablespoon sugar; let stand until sugar dissolves. In medium bowl, beat cream at medium-high speed until soft peaks form. Fold into apricot mixture. Serve apricot cream with warm biscuits. Refrigerate leftover cream.

8 servings

PER SERVING: 280 calories, 15 g total fat (9 g saturated fat), 5 g protein, 31.5 g carbohydrate, 70 mg cholesterol, 280 mg sodium, 1 g fiber

Lemon Herb Biscuits with Nasturtium Butter

BISCUITS
- 1 cup all-purpose flour
- 1 cup cake flour
- 3 tablespoons chopped fresh lemon herbs (lemon thyme, lemon verbena, lemon balm or lemon basil)
- 1 tablespoon baking powder
- ¼ teaspoon salt
- 6 tablespoons unsalted butter, chilled, cut up
- ¾ cup whipping cream

BUTTER
- ¼ cup unsalted butter, softened
- 2 tablespoons chopped nasturtium flowers

1 Heat oven to 425°F. Grease 8-inch round pan. In large bowl, combine all-purpose flour, cake flour, herbs, baking powder and salt. With pastry blender, cut in 6 tablespoons butter until butter is size of blueberries. Stir in cream, mixing just until soft dough forms. (Dough will be very soft and moist.)
2 On floured surface with well-floured hands, knead dough 2 to 3 times to combine. Pat dough to form ¾-inch-thick round. Cut with 2½-inch round cutter into 8 biscuits, gently pressing together dough scraps as necessary. Place in pan.
3 Bake 20 minutes or until light golden brown.
4 Meanwhile, in small bowl, stir together ¼ cup butter and nasturtium flowers. Serve butter with warm biscuits.

8 servings

PER SERVING: 315 calories, 21.5 g total fat (13.5 g saturated fat), 3.5 g protein, 26.5 g carbohydrate, 65 mg cholesterol, 265 mg sodium, 1 g fiber

Rosemary-Sage Biscuits

- 1 cup cake flour
- ¾ cup all-purpose flour
- ¼ cup whole wheat flour
- 1 tablespoon baking powder
- 2 teaspoons chopped fresh rosemary
- ¼ teaspoon salt
- 6 tablespoons unsalted butter, chilled, cut up
- 1 egg, beaten
- ⅔ cup whole milk
- 6 fresh sage leaves

1 Heat oven to 425°F. Lightly grease baking sheet or line with parchment paper. In large bowl, combine cake flour, all-purpose flour, whole wheat flour, baking powder, rosemary and salt. With pastry blender, cut in butter until butter is size of blueberries.
2 In small bowl, whisk together egg and milk. Add to flour mixture, mixing just until soft dough forms. (Dough will be very moist and sticky.)
3 On floured surface with well-floured hands, knead dough 2 to 3 times to combine. Pat dough to form ¾-inch-thick round. Cut into 6 wedges. Press sage leaf onto top of each wedge. Place on baking sheet.
4 Bake 15 minutes or until light golden brown. Serve warm.

6 servings

PER SERVING: 290 calories, 14 g total fat (8 g saturated fat), 6 g protein, 35.5 g carbohydrate, 70 mg cholesterol, 370 mg sodium, 1.5 g fiber

Ricotta-Dill Buttermilk Biscuits

FILLING
- ¼ cup thinly sliced green onions
- ¼ cup ricotta cheese
- 1 tablespoon chopped fresh dill
- 1 tablespoon butter, softened
- ⅛ teaspoon salt
  Dash freshly ground pepper

BISCUITS
- 1½ cups all-purpose flour
- ½ cup cake flour
- 1½ teaspoons baking powder
- ¼ teaspoon baking soda
- ¼ teaspoon salt
- ⅓ cup unsalted butter, chilled, cut up
- 1 egg, beaten
- ½ cup buttermilk

1 Heat oven to 425°F. Lightly grease baking sheet or line with parchment paper. In small bowl, stir together all filling ingredients.
2 In large bowl, combine all-purpose flour, cake flour, baking powder, baking soda and salt. With pastry blender, cut in ⅓ cup butter until butter is size of blueberries.
3 In another small bowl, whisk together egg and buttermilk. Add to flour mixture, mixing just until soft dough forms. (Dough will be moist and sticky.)
4 On floured surface with well-floured hands, knead dough 2 to 3 times to combine. Pat dough to form ⅜-inch-thick square. With floured knife, cut into 6 rectangles. Press each piece lightly to flatten.
5 Spoon filling onto center of each dough piece. With well-floured hands, fold dough around filling; shape into round and flatten to about ¾-inch thickness. Place on baking sheet.
6 Bake 15 minutes or until light golden brown. Serve warm.

6 servings

PER SERVING: 305 calories, 15 g total fat (9 g saturated fat), 7.5 g protein, 35 g carbohydrate, 75 mg cholesterol, 380 mg sodium, 1 g fiber

Prized for the Rise

**Almond-Cardamom
Popovers**

Popovers belong in the unique category of special-effects cooking. From a simple batter of flour, milk and eggs emerge large golden puffs, crispy on the outside, moist and tender on the inside, and nearly weightless. And they look spectacular, making them a favorite for special occasions. Yet popovers are deceptively easy to make, so you can serve them any time you're looking for a quick, light bread for breakfast, lunch or dinner.

Popovers don't rely on leavening agents as most quick breads do; instead, steam produced from the batter while they bake causes them to rise. To ensure a high-rising bread, pay attention to ingredients, pans and baking techniques.

Perfect Popovers

Ingredients The combination of a whole egg and egg whites contributes to the unique texture of popovers. The whole egg provides structure as the popover rises and fat for tenderness and taste. Egg whites have a drying effect, creating the crisp, crunchy outside and soft, tender interior.

All-purpose flour is best for most popovers because it contains the proper amount of gluten needed for rising. If you use cake flour, which has less gluten, the popovers may split open, as though they have exploded. Bread flour has too much gluten, resulting in tough popovers. (When using other grains, however, such as cornmeal in Cheddar Cornmeal Popovers, the bread flour's additional gluten makes up for the lack of gluten in the cornmeal.)

Method Popovers are best when the batter rests about 30 minutes before baking. The gluten has a chance to relax and the resulting popovers are very tender. As with any quick bread, the less you handle the batter, the more tender the popovers will be.

Pans You can bake popovers in muffin cups, popover tins, custard cups or old-fashioned cast-iron tins, but popovers rise the highest when heat penetrates all sides of the pan. For that reason, popover tins (with six individual cups linked together by thin metal rods) or individual custard cups work best. Fill the tins three-quarters full for the highest rise. In my pan, this gives me five popovers. If you divide the batter among all six cups, your popovers won't rise as high because each tin will have less batter.

Heat Popovers require a high temperature to rise and a lower temperature to bake completely. There are two ways to achieve this: Bake them in a high-temperature oven and then lower the temperature, or bake them in a low-temperature oven and then raise the temperature. I use a combination of the two methods to get the best results: Bake the popovers in the lower third of the oven to provide full heat at the bottom of the pan. Preheat the oven at a lower temperature, increase the heat when you put the tins in the oven and then reduce the heat for the last 20 minutes. The result is popovers that rise fully, yet bake to an even, dry finish. If your popovers are baking lopsided, your oven may not be heating evenly.

You must cut a slit in the side of the popovers during the final minutes of baking to allow the steam to escape and help the drying process. If you don't do this, the inside texture will be gummy instead of soft and moist.

Almond Cardamom Popovers

POPOVERS
- 1 cup whole milk
- ¼ Teaspoon cardamon
- Dash salt
- 1 teaspoon almond extract
- 1 egg
- 2 egg whites
- 1 tablespoon unsalted butter, melted
- 1 cup all-purpose flour

TOPPING
- 1 tablespoon unsalted butter, melted
- 1 tablespoon sugar

1 In large bowl, combine milk, cardamom, salt, almond extract, egg and egg whites; mix with wire whisk until combined. Whisk in 1 tablespoon melted butter. Add flour; whisk just until smooth. Do not overbeat. Let batter rest 30 minutes.

2 Meanwhile, place oven rack in lower third of oven; heat to 325°F. Spray 5 cups in popover pan with nonstick cooking spray. Pour batter into sprayed cups.

3 Place on rack in lower third of oven; immediately increase oven temperature to 425°F. Bake 20 minutes.

4 Reduce oven temperature to 325°F.; bake an additional 20 minutes or until golden brown and firm. Make 1-inch slit in side of each popover with sharp knife; bake an additional 5 minutes.

5 Remove from oven; immediately brush tops with 1 tablespoon melted butter. Sprinkle with sugar. Serve warm.

5 popovers

PER POPOVER: 190 calories, 7 g total fat (4 g saturated fat), 60 mg cholesterol, 115 mg sodium, 1 g fiber

Caramel Dreams

Buttery Soft, Chocolate Swirl, Ginger Cream and Toasted Pecan Caramels

Everybody loves soft, gooey, stick-to-your-teeth caramels. But good caramels aren't easy to find. Now, each year as the holiday season approaches, you can make a variety to share with family and friends. Everyone has their favorites, from Buttery Soft Caramels, which taste like the topping of a double-dipped caramel apple, to Ginger Cream Caramels, which leave the tangy bite of fresh ginger lingering long after the caramel is gone. Silky smooth and soft, these caramels will disappear almost as quickly as you can make them.

Basic caramels are made from a few simple ingredients: butter, sugar, cream and corn syrup. The way the ingredients are combined and the temperature they're cooked at create the vast variety of caramel textures and flavors. With a watchful eye and the right equipment, they're easy to make.

Stages Of Cooking Caramels

Cooking caramels requires patience and a watchful eye. The caramel should cook steadily, but slowly, to develop deep flavor. It takes 20 to 30 minutes for the candy to cook. During that time, the caramel should boil steadily at a medium boil. The entire surface of the mixture must be boiling for the caramel to cook evenly. As it cooks, watch the thermometer because the temperature can change quickly. Always check the temperature at eye level to get an accurate reading. Begin cooking the mixture slowly to dissolve the sugar. Here are the stages of cooking:

1. Attach the candy thermometer to the side of the pan and monitor the temperature of the mixture. It will rise quickly to 220°F., but the color doesn't change much.

2. By 230°F., the mixture is light brown in color. It's important to begin stirring constantly at this point. As the caramel reaches 240°F. to 245°F., the caramel begins to deepen in color, the bubbles get larger, and the mixture thickens. Keep stirring, especially into the edges of the pan.

3. As the caramel reaches final temperature, the color deepens to a golden brown, the mixture thickens and the bottom of the saucepan begins to appear while stirring. When the final temperature is reached, immediately pour the caramel into a prepared pan. Don't scrape the caramel from the bottom of the saucepan into the prepared pan; it may be overcooked. Instead, pour it into a small bowl—it makes a nice little treat for the cook!

Buttery Soft Caramels

½ cup unsalted butter
2 cups sugar
1½ cups whipping cream
1 cup light corn syrup

1 Line 8-inch square pan with foil; spray with nonstick cooking spray. Melt butter in Dutch oven or heavy, large (4½- to 6-quart) saucepan over low heat. Add sugar, cream and corn syrup; stir to mix. Increase heat to medium; bring to a boil, stirring frequently.

2 Insert candy thermometer into mixture and attach to side of Dutch oven. Cook, stirring frequently, until thermometer registers 230°F. At this point, it is important to watch mixture carefully. Begin stirring constantly until thermometer registers 248°F. (firm-ball stage).

3 Immediately pour caramel mixture into pan; do not scrape Dutch oven. Let stand 6 to 8 hours or until cool and set.

4 Remove caramel from pan by lifting foil. Remove foil. With large knife, cut caramel into 64 pieces. Wrap each piece individually.

64 caramels

PER CARAMEL: 65 calories, 3 g total fat (2 g saturated fat), 0 g protein, 10 g carbohydrate, 10 mg cholesterol, 5 mg sodium, 0 g fiber

Chocolate Swirl Caramels

½ cup unsalted butter
2 cups sugar
1½ cups whipping cream
1 cup light corn syrup
2 oz. bittersweet chocolate, finely chopped

1 Line 8-inch square pan with foil; spray with nonstick cooking spray. Melt butter in Dutch oven or heavy, large (4½- to 6-quart) saucepan over low heat. Add sugar, cream and corn syrup; stir to mix. Increase heat to medium; bring to a boil, stirring frequently.

2 Insert candy thermometer into mixture and attach to side of Dutch oven. Cook, stirring frequently, until thermometer registers 230°F. At this point, it is important to watch mixture carefully. Begin stirring constantly until thermometer registers 248°F. (firm-ball stage).

3 Immediately pour half of caramel mixture into pan. Sprinkle with half of chocolate. Pour remaining caramel mixture over chocolate; do not scrape Dutch oven. Sprinkle with remaining chocolate; let stand 2 to 3 minutes or until chocolate is melted. Run knife once through mixture to swirl. Let stand 6 to 8 hours or until cool and set.

4 Remove caramel from pan by lifting foil. Remove foil. With large knife, cut caramel into 64 pieces. Wrap each piece individually.

64 caramels

PER CARAMEL: 70 calories, 3.5 g total fat (2 g saturated fat), 0 g protein, 10.5 g carbohydrate, 10 mg cholesterol, 5 mg sodium, 0 g fiber

Ginger Cream Caramels

    2 cups sugar
    2 cups whipping cream
    1 cup light corn syrup
    1 tablespoon finely grated
         fresh ginger

1 Line 8-inch square pan with foil; spray with nonstick cooking spray. Place all ingredients in Dutch oven or heavy, large (4½- to 6-quart) saucepan. Bring to a boil over medium heat, stirring frequently.

2 Insert candy thermometer into mixture and attach to side of Dutch oven. Cook, stirring frequently, until thermometer registers 230°F. At this point, it is important to watch mixture carefully. Begin stirring constantly until thermometer registers 245°F. (firm-ball stage).

3 Immediately pour caramel mixture into pan; do not scrape Dutch oven. Let stand 6 to 8 hours or until cool and set.

4 Remove caramel from pan by

lifting foil. Remove foil. With large knife, cut caramel into 64 pieces. Wrap each piece individually.

64 caramels

PER CARAMEL: 60 calories, 2.5 g total fat (1.5 g saturated fat), 0 g protein, 10 g carbohydrate, 10 mg cholesterol, 5 mg sodium, 0 g fiber

Toasted Pecan Caramels

    2½ cups pecan halves
    ½ cup butter
    2 cups sugar
    1½ cups whipping cream
    1 cup light corn syrup

1 Heat oven to 375°F. Line 8-inch square pan with foil; spray with nonstick cooking spray. Place pecans on baking sheet; bake 5 to 10 minutes or until lightly toasted. Set aside ½ cup pecans. Place remaining pecans in foil-lined pan.

2 Melt butter in Dutch oven or large (4½- to 6-quart) heavy saucepan over low heat. Add sugar, cream and corn syrup; stir to mix. Increase heat to medium; bring to a boil, stirring frequently.

3 Insert candy thermometer into mixture; attach to side of Dutch oven. Cook, stirring frequently, until thermometer registers 230°F. At this point, it is important to watch mixture carefully. Begin stirring constantly until thermometer registers 248°F. (firm-ball stage).

4 Immediately pour caramel mixture into pan; do not scrape Dutch oven. Sprinkle with reserved ½ cup pecans. Let stand 6 to 8 hours or until cool and set.

5 Remove caramel from pan by lifting foil. Remove foil. With large knife, cut caramel into 64 pieces. Wrap each piece individually.

64 caramels

PER CARAMEL: 95 calories, 6 g total fat (2 g saturated fat), .5 g protein, 11 g carbohydrate, 10 mg cholesterol, 15 mg sodium, .5 g fiber

Caramel Equipment

Success when making caramels depends in part on having the right tools. Here's what you need:

Large, heavy pot Use a 4½- to 6-quart Dutch oven or saucepan. The pan must be large enough to accommodate the mixture as it rises during boiling so it doesn't boil over. A heavy pot decreases the chance of scorching or burning.

Candy thermometer This is necessary to accurately monitor the temperature of the mixture. The higher the temperature, the firmer the caramel will be. The thermometer should clip onto the side of the pan, and it should have markings every 2 degrees. Markings every 5 degrees are not accurate enough for candy.

Wooden spoon Because the mixture gets very hot, use a wooden spoon for stirring rather than a metal one, which conducts heat. You can also use a rubber spatula, if it is rated heat resistant.

The Ultimate Cookie

(From Top)
Lemon Glitter Cookies,
Chocolate-Pistachio Cookies,
Coconut-Lime Snowballs,
Double-Dip Chocolate-Orange Cookies,
Cardamom-Ginger Cookies,
Raspberry-Almond Paste Gems

Who doesn't love baked cookies during the holidays? But who has time to make dozens of different kinds? Instead, make just one cookie: the ultimate sugar cookie. Tender and rich with a creamy, buttery taste that is accented with a hint of lemon, this cookie is the perfect holiday sweet. While delicious unadorned, the real magic in this cookie is the fact that it can be decorated to make six entirely different, unique-tasting cookies.

This recipe easily fits into hectic schedules. The dough can be made a day ahead, and the cookies can be baked, cooled and frozen several weeks ahead, if you like. (Freeze them before decorating; then thaw them when you need them and decorate as desired.) You can decorate the cookies all at once or decorate only as many as you plan to serve. Make each of the variations, or only one or two—it's your choice. The toppings can easily be doubled or tripled to make several dozen, too.

1½ cups unsalted butter, softened
1 cup sugar
1 egg
1 egg yolk
2 teaspoons grated lemon peel
2½ cups all-purpose flour
1 teaspoon baking powder
½ teaspoon salt

1 In large bowl, beat butter at medium speed until smooth and creamy. Slowly add sugar; beat until well blended. Add egg, egg yolk and lemon peel; beat until thoroughly mixed.

2 In medium bowl, stir together flour, baking powder and salt. Slowly add flour mixture to butter mixture, beating at low speed just until combined.

3 Divide dough into thirds. Shape each third into flat round; wrap in plastic wrap. Refrigerate at least 2 hours or overnight. (Dough can be made up to 1 day ahead.)

4 Heat oven to 375°F. Sprinkle surface with flour. Roll out 1 dough round to ⅛-inch thickness. Using 2½-inch cookie cutters, cut into desired shapes. Place at least 1 inch apart on ungreased baking sheets. Bake 8 to 10 minutes or until light brown around edges. Cool on wire rack. Repeat with remaining dough and dough scraps. Store in airtight container or freeze up to 1 month.

About 7½ dozen (2½-inch) cookies

PER COOKIE: 55 calories, 3 g total fat (2 g saturated fat), .5 g protein, 6 g carbohydrate, 15 mg cholesterol, 20 mg sodium, 0 g fiber

Cookie Pointers

COOKIE DOUGH

• Soften the butter, but don't let it get too soft. Press your thumb gently into the butter; it should leave an indent but not be squishy. If the butter is too soft, the cookies will spread too much during baking.

• Slowly add the sugar to the butter and beat the mixture until it's smooth and creamy, not fluffy. Although it is important for cakes, it is not necessary to beat air into the butter mixture for cookies.

• For tender cookies, mix in the flour only until it is blended, no more. If you continue mixing the dough after the flour has been blended, gluten will develop, resulting in tough cookies.

• Give the dough ample time to chill; don't rush the process. The dough needs time to relax and let the flour absorb the moisture for easier rolling.

COOKIE CUT-OUTS

• To make sure the cookies bake uniformly, roll the dough to an even thickness. Measure the thickness of the dough in several places using a ruler that measures right to the surface.

• To add variety, make each type of cookie a different shape.

• Press, but do not twist, cookie cutters. Remove excess dough around the cut-out, then lift the cookie with a spatula.

• Keep the cookie dough well chilled. If it's warm in the kitchen, refrigerate the cut-outs before baking.

COOKIE BAKING

• Invest in several heavy, rimless baking sheets so you don't need to wait for baking sheets to cool between batches.

• Watch the first pan carefully; 1 to 2 minutes can make a difference. Use the visual doneness test (bake until light brown around the edges), not just the time.

Chocolate reflects the surface on which it is cooled; use shiny foil for a shiny look.

Baby spoons come in handy for spooning on small amounts.

Small, offset spatulas easily spread icing.

Small brushes work best for painting on glaze.

Lemon Glitter Cookies

3 tablespoons powdered sugar
1 teaspoon fresh lemon juice
1 teaspoon light corn syrup
½ teaspoon finely grated
     lemon peel
12 cooled baked Sugar Cookies
     Edible glitter or sparkling
     sugar for sprinkling

In small bowl, stir together powdered sugar, lemon juice, corn syrup and lemon peel. Using pastry brush, brush lemon mixture over cookies; sprinkle with edible glitter.

1 dozen cookies

Cardamom-Ginger Cookies

1 tablespoon sugar (sparkling
     sugar preferred)
¼ teaspoon ground cardamom
¼ teaspoon ground ginger
12 cooled baked Sugar Cookies
1 teaspoon unsalted butter, melted

In small cup, stir together sugar, cardamom and ginger. Lightly brush cookies with melted butter; sprinkle with sugar mixture.

1 dozen cookies

Coconut-Lime Snowballs

¼ cup powdered sugar
1 teaspoon corn syrup
1 teaspoon fresh lime juice
12 cooled baked Sugar Cookies
½ cup flaked coconut

In small bowl, stir together powdered sugar, corn syrup and lime juice until smooth. Spread frosting over cookies; top with coconut.

1 dozen cookies

Chocolate-Pistachio Cookies

¼ cup finely chopped pistachios
2 oz. bittersweet chocolate,
     finely chopped
12 cooled baked Sugar Cookies

Line baking sheet with foil, shiny side up. Place pistachios in small bowl. Heat chocolate in small microwave-safe bowl 40 to 60 seconds or until melted, stirring occasionally. Dip edges of cookies in chocolate, then in pistachios; place on baking sheet. Let stand until chocolate is set.

1 dozen cookies

Double-Dip Chocolate-Orange Cookies

4 oz. semisweet chocolate,
     finely chopped
     Scant ½ teaspoon orange
     oil, divided
12 cooled baked Sugar
     Cookies
4 oz. white chocolate, finely
     chopped

1 Line baking sheet with foil, shiny side up. Heat semisweet chocolate and scant ¼ teaspoon of the orange oil in small microwave-safe bowl 40 to 60 seconds or until melted, stirring occasionally. Dip half of each cookie in semisweet chocolate; place on baking sheet. Let stand or refrigerate until chocolate is set.
2 Heat white chocolate and remaining scant ¼ teaspoon orange oil in small microwave-safe bowl 20 to 40 seconds or until chocolate is melted, stirring occasionally. Dip half of each cookie in white chocolate, partly overlapping semisweet chocolate; place on baking sheet. Let stand or refrigerate until chocolate is set.

1 dozen cookies

Raspberry-Almond Paste Gems

2 tablespoons almond paste
1 tablespoon unsalted butter,
     softened
12 cooled baked Sugar Cookies
¼ cup raspberry preserves
¼ cup sliced almonds
     Powdered sugar for sprinkling

In small bowl, stir together almond paste and butter using back of spoon to create smooth paste. Spread about ½ teaspoon almond paste mixture over each cookie; spread with ½ teaspoon raspberry preserves. Garnish each cookie with 4 sliced almonds; sprinkle with powdered sugar.

1 dozen cookies

Heavenly Cakes

Chocolate Angel Food Cake with Triple-Chocolate Glaze

The delicate nuances of an angel food cake suit the season's cravings for lighter fare. Yet many cooks seem hesitant to make one. Perhaps it's the towering heights to which these cakes rise that bring out the jitters, or maybe it's the seemingly odd idea of cooling a cake by hanging it upside down on a bottle.

Set your fears aside. Angel food cakes are surprisingly easy to make. If you can whip egg whites, you can handle this dessert. As for equipment, while you do need an angel food cake pan, it's not expensive. And once you find out just how easy these cakes are to make, you'll get plenty of return on that minor investment.

Tips for Success

The impressive height and airy texture of angel food cake come from beaten egg whites. Follow these tips to get the most volume without sacrificing tenderness.

EQUIPMENT

Fat-free Make sure all your utensils, including your hands, are free of grease. Any trace of grease—or yolk—on the beaters or in the mixing bowl could prevent the eggs from developing the volume you need. In addition, don't grease the pan because the batter must be able to cling to the sides and climb as the cake bakes.

Pan options These recipes require angel food cake pans—straight-sided tube pans. There are several types that work. Those with removable bottoms are the easiest to unmold. Pans with nonremovable bottoms also can be used, but for easy removal after baking, line the bottom with parchment paper before adding the batter. Nonstick pans work fine, too. The cake clings to the nonstick surface and won't slip out of the pan, even when it's upside down, although the surface of the cake will be a little darker.

INGREDIENTS

Eggs They should be at cool room temperature. Warm egg whites whip up quickly but lack the structure to hold during baking, while cold egg whites don't whip up to their full potential. To quickly bring cold eggs to cool room temperature, place the egg whites in a large bowl. Place the bowl in a sink filled with 2 to 3 inches of hot tap water, and let it stand 1 to 3 minutes, stirring occasionally.

Sugars Two sugars are used for best results. Superfine sugar dissolves easily in the egg whites, creating a stable foam, while powdered sugar blends easily with the flour during folding. You can buy superfine sugar or make your own by pulsing granulated sugar in a food processor until finely ground.

METHOD

Sift three times To thoroughly combine the dry ingredients and aerate the flour, sift three times. Use a large, fine strainer, and sift onto a large piece of waxed paper or parchment paper.

Beat egg whites The egg whites should be beaten until they are glossy. The tips should bend slightly and look smooth, not firm with clumps.

Fold gently Add the flour mixture to the egg whites and fold in three batches. This helps to keep the air in the egg whites so they provide maximum rise when baking. Use a large rubber spatula, which can be purchased in a kitchen or restaurant supply store.

Cool upside down The cake is so light that if you don't invert it to cool, gravity pulls it down, collapsing the fragile air cells. When the cake is done baking, invert the pan and place it on the neck of a bottle. If the pan has feet, you can invert the pan and rest it on them.

When cool, the cake is less fragile and the pan can be turned right-side up. To remove the cake, run a thin knife or spatula around its outer and inner edges. Use a serrated knife to slice it.

For a light, airy cake, sift the flour three times.

Use an extra-large spatula to gently fold the flour into the egg whites.

After adding the sugar, beat the egg whites until glossy and peaks bend slightly.

Invert the cake pan and cool completely.

Chocolate Angel Food Cake with Triple-Chocolate Glaze

CAKE
- ¼ cup Dutch-processed cocoa
- ¼ cup hot water
- ¾ cup all-purpose flour
- ½ cup powdered sugar
- ¼ teaspoon salt
- 1½ cups egg whites (10 to 12 large), cool room temperature
- 1½ teaspoons cream of tartar
- 1 teaspoon vanilla extract
- 1¼ cups superfine sugar

SEMISWEET CHOCOLATE GLAZE
- 4 oz. semisweet chocolate, chopped
- 4 tablespoons unsalted butter, softened, cut up
- 1 tablespoon light corn syrup

MILK CHOCOLATE GLAZE
- 2 oz. milk chocolate, chopped
- 2 tablespoons unsalted butter, softened, cut up
- 1½ teaspoons corn syrup

WHITE CHOCOLATE GLAZE
- 2 oz. white chocolate, chopped
- 2 tablespoons unsalted butter, softened, cut up
- 2 teaspoons whipping cream
- 1½ teaspoons corn syrup

1 Heat oven to 350°F. In small bowl, stir together cocoa and hot water until cocoa is dissolved.

2 Place flour, powdered sugar and salt in medium bowl. Sift 3 times to evenly distribute ingredients.

3 Place egg whites in large bowl; beat at medium-low speed until loose and foamy. Add cream of tartar and vanilla; beat at medium-high speed until soft peaks just begin to form. With mixer running, slowly add superfine sugar in steady stream, beating just until egg whites are glossy and hold peaks that slightly bend at the tip. (Do not overbeat; peaks should not be dry and stiff.) Place about 1 cup of the egg white mixture in small bowl. Add cocoa mixture; stir until thoroughly combined.

4 Place chocolate mixture over remaining egg white mixture. Immediately sift one-third of the flour mixture over chocolate mixture; gently fold to incorporate. Repeat with remaining flour mixture, making sure no lumps of flour remain but being careful egg whites do not deflate. Gently spoon mixture into ungreased 10-inch tube pan with removable bottom. Run long narrow spatula through cake to eliminate any large air bubbles; gently smooth top.

5 Bake 35 to 40 minutes or until cake springs back when gently touched and skewer inserted in center comes out clean. (Top may crack as it bakes.) Invert cake onto neck of bottle or funnel, or let stand upside-down on feet attached to tube pan. Cool completely in pan 2 to 3 hours.

6 To remove cake from pan, slide thin narrow knife or spatula around edges of pan and tube. Lift tube out of pan; invert cake onto serving platter.

7 Place all semisweet chocolate glaze ingredients in small saucepan. Heat over low heat, stirring constantly, until chocolate is melted and smooth. Remove from heat; let stand until slightly thickened. Drizzle over cake.

8 Place all milk chocolate glaze ingredients in small saucepan. Heat over low heat, stirring constantly, until chocolate is melted and smooth. Remove from heat; let stand until slightly thickened. Drizzle over cake.

9 Place all white chocolate glaze ingredients in small saucepan. Heat over low heat, stirring constantly, until chocolate is partially melted. Remove from heat; continue stirring until chocolate is melted and smooth. Let stand until slightly thickened; drizzle over cake.

12 servings

PER SERVING: 325 calories, 14 g total fat (8.5 g saturated fat), 5.5 g protein, 47.5 g carbohydrate, 25 mg cholesterol, 115 mg sodium, 1.5 g fiber

Nutmeg Angel Food Cake with Caramel Drizzle

CAKE
- 1 cup all-purpose flour
- ½ cup powdered sugar
- ½ teaspoon freshly grated nutmeg
- ¼ teaspoon salt
- 1½ cups egg whites (10 to 12 large), cool room temperature
- 1½ teaspoons cream of tartar
- 1 teaspoon vanilla extract
- 1 cup superfine sugar

CARAMEL
- ¼ cup unsalted butter
- ½ cup packed light brown sugar
- 1 cup whipping cream

1 Heat oven to 350°F. Place flour, powdered sugar, nutmeg and salt in medium bowl. Sift 3 times to evenly distribute ingredients.

2 Place egg whites in large bowl; beat at medium-low speed until loose and foamy. Add cream of tartar and vanilla; beat at medium-high speed until soft peaks just begin to form. With mixer running, slowly add superfine sugar in steady stream, beating just until egg whites are glossy and hold peaks that slightly bend. (Do not overbeat; peaks should not be dry and stiff.)

3 Sift one-third of the flour mixture over egg white mixture; gently fold to incorporate. Repeat with remaining flour mixture, making sure no lumps of flour remain but being careful egg whites do not deflate. Gently spoon mixture into ungreased 10-inch tube pan with removable bottom. Run long narrow spatula through cake to eliminate any large air bubbles; gently smooth top.

4 Bake 35 to 40 minutes or until cake is golden brown, springs back when gently touched and skewer inserted in center comes out clean. (Top may crack as it bakes.) Invert cake onto neck of bottle or funnel, or let stand upside-down on feet attached to tube pan. Cool completely in pan 2 to 3 hours.

5 Meanwhile, to make sauce, melt butter in medium saucepan over medium heat. Add brown sugar; cook and stir 1 to 2 minutes or until sugar is dissolved. Add cream; bring to a boil. Boil 5 to 6 minutes until slightly thickened; cool to glaze consistency.

6 To remove cake from pan, slide thin narrow knife or spatula around edges of pan and tube. Lift tube out of pan; invert cake onto serving platter. Spoon caramel onto cake, allowing some to drizzle down side; let stand until caramel is firm. Slice with serrated knife.

12 servings

PER SERVING: 265 calories, 10 g total fat (6.5 g saturated fat), 5 g protein, 39.5 g carbohydrate, 32.5 mg cholesterol, 110 mg sodium, .5 g fiber

Vanilla Bean Angel Food Cake with Fresh Berries

CAKE
2 vanilla beans, halved lengthwise
8 tablespoons powdered sugar, divided
1 cup all-purpose flour
¼ teaspoon salt
1½ cups egg whites (10 to 12 large), cool room temperature
1½ teaspoons cream of tartar
2 teaspoons vanilla extract
½ teaspoon almond extract
1 cup superfine sugar

BERRIES
3 cups assorted fresh berries, such as raspberries, blackberries and strawberries
2 tablespoons superfine sugar
¼ teaspoon vanilla extract

1 Heat oven to 350°F. On cutting board, scrape inside of vanilla beans with tip of small knife to remove seeds. Sprinkle seeds with 1 tablespoon of the powdered sugar; using side of knife, combine to disperse seeds throughout sugar. Place seeds with sugar in medium bowl; add remaining 7 tablespoons powdered sugar, flour and salt. Sift 3 times to evenly distribute ingredients.

2 Place egg whites in large bowl; beat at medium-low speed until loose and foamy. Add cream of tartar, vanilla and almond extract; beat at medium-high speed until soft peaks just begin to form. With mixer running, slowly add 1 cup superfine sugar in steady stream, beating just until egg whites are glossy and hold peaks that slightly bend. (Peaks should not be dry and stiff.)

3 Sift one-third of the flour mixture over egg white mixture; gently fold to incorporate. Repeat with remaining flour mixture, making sure no lumps of flour remain but being careful egg whites do not deflate. Gently spoon mixture into ungreased 10-inch tube pan with removable bottom. Run long narrow spatula through cake to eliminate any large air bubbles; gently smooth top.

4 Bake 35 to 40 minutes or until cake is golden brown, springs back when gently touched and skewer inserted in center comes out clean. (Top may crack as it bakes.) Invert cake onto neck of bottle or funnel, or let stand upside-down on feet attached to tube pan. Cool completely in pan 2 to 3 hours.

5 Meanwhile, combine all berry ingredients in medium bowl. Let stand 20 to 30 minutes or until sugar is dissolved and juices have formed.

6 To remove cake from pan, slide thin narrow knife or spatula around edges of pan and tube. Lift tube out of pan; invert cake onto serving platter. Slice with serrated knife; serve with berry mixture.

12 servings

PER SERVING: 160 calories, .5 g total fat (0 g saturated fat), 4.5 g protein, 35.5 g carbohydrate, 0 mg cholesterol, 100 mg sodium, 2 g fiber

Temptation of the Tart

Almond-Pear Tarte Tatin

The classic French apple dessert, tarte Tatin (pronounced tah-TAN), is a country-style pie that's baked upside down. What makes this dessert so extraordinary is the technique of slowly cooking the apples in sugar syrup until the sugar caramelizes and saturates the fruit. The pie is baked with a crisp, puffy crust covering the apples, then served upside down with the caramel-drenched apples displayed on top.

The pie is cooked in two stages. First the fruit is cooked on top of the stove until tender and caramelized. Then it's draped with a simple pastry and baked until crisp and golden. We offer two variations of the classic recipe: The first substitutes pears for the apples; the second adds a hint of fresh ginger to the apple. Although their methods are different from a traditional pie, these recipes are very easy and the results always spectacular.

Tarte Tatin Tips

During testing, we experimented with eliminating the two-step cooking process, but the results were disappointing. The fruit must be cooked on the stovetop so the excess juices evaporate and the caramel can be watched carefully.

Pan Several companies make Tarte Tatin pans. They're wider and deeper than a normal pie pan and can go from the stovetop to the oven. However, a special pan isn't necessary. You can use a large ovenproof skillet (10- to 12-inch diameter), preferably with sloping sides to help excess juices evaporate quickly. Go to cookingclub.com and click on Featured Links for Tarte Tatin pan sources.

Fruit Choose fruit that is ripe but firm. Apples should hold their shape during cooking. Rome, Fuji, Golden Delicious, Braeburn and Gala all work well. For pears, Anjous work best, but be sure they're not soft or they will be too juicy. Cut the fruit into large wedges; smaller pieces turn mushy while caramelizing.

Caramelizing Arrange the fruit over the sugar in the pan, packing it tightly because it shrinks during cooking. As the sugar melts and the fruit juices mingle with it, the resulting syrup begins to boil around the fruit. Cook the fruit slowly; don't rush the process. The fruit should be tender by the time a rich caramel forms. Use a spatula to gently press the fruit into the syrup. The juiciness of fruit varies, so adjust heat and cooking time if necessary.

The caramel should be golden brown and slightly thickened when ready.

Pastry Any pastry can be used for this dessert, from a simple pie crust to ready-made puff pastry. Cut the pastry to fit the pan and refrigerate the cut piece to keep it cold. When the fruit is ready, gently drape the pastry over the fruit, tucking the edges inside the pan. It's fine if it looks rustic.

The pastry should be golden brown and slightly puffed when removed from the oven. Carefully turn the pie upside down onto a serving platter that's large enough to catch the caramel juices that flow from the pie.

1. Place large wedges of fruit over the sugar in the bottom of the pan.

2. As the fruit cooks, gently press the wedges into the syrup with a spatula.

3. Keep the pastry cold until you're ready for it. Then place it over the fruit.

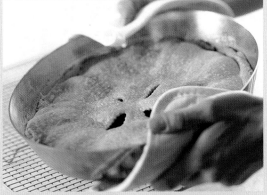

4. When the tart has finished baking, turn it upside down onto a platter.

Almond-Pear Tarte Tatin

1 sheet frozen puff pastry (from 17.3-oz. pkg.)
3 tablespoons unsalted butter, cut up, divided
½ cup plus 1 tablespoon sugar, divided
4 medium firm but ripe Anjou pears, peeled, each cut into 6 wedges
¼ teaspoon almond extract
6 tablespoons sliced almonds, divided

1 Thaw pastry according to package directions. On lightly floured surface, roll pastry into 10-inch square; cut into 10-inch round. Place on baking sheet. With small knife, make 4 slits in center of pastry for steam to escape. Refrigerate until ready to use.
2 Place oven rack in bottom rack position. Heat oven to 400°F. Melt 2 tablespoons of the butter in large (10-inch) skillet over medium heat. Remove from heat. Sprinkle with ½ cup of the sugar. Arrange pears over sugar mixture.
3 Cook over medium heat 20 to 25 minutes or until sugar is deep golden brown, thick and syrupy. (Occasionally press pears into sugar syrup with spatula during cooking.) Remove from heat; sprinkle with almond extract and 2 tablespoons of the sliced almonds.
4 Melt remaining 1 tablespoon butter in microwave-safe bowl. Place pastry over pears, tucking edge inside skillet. Brush pastry with melted butter; sprinkle with remaining 4 tablespoons sliced almonds and remaining 1 tablespoon sugar.
5 Bake 25 to 30 minutes or until pastry is golden brown and pears are tender. (Tart can be made up to 4 hours ahead. To reheat, place in 350°F. oven 10 to 15 minutes or until warm.) Let stand 10 minutes; invert onto serving platter. Serve warm or at room temperature.

8 servings

PER SERVING: 315 calories, 17 g total fat (6.5 g saturated fat), 3 g protein, 39.5 g carbohydrate, 40 mg cholesterol, 65 mg sodium, 3.5 g fiber

Apple-Ginger Tarte Tatin

CRUST
1 cup all-purpose flour
1 tablespoon sugar
⅛ teaspoon salt
¼ cup unsalted butter, chilled, cut up
2 tablespoons shortening
2 to 3 tablespoons ice water

FILLING
6 Rome apples, peeled, each cut into 6 wedges
2 teaspoons grated fresh ginger
1 teaspoon ground cinnamon
¼ cup unsalted butter
¾ cup sugar

1 In medium bowl, stir together flour, 1 tablespoon sugar and salt. With pastry blender or two knives, cut in butter and shortening until mixture resembles coarse crumbs with some pea-sized pieces. Add 2 tablespoons of the water; stir until dough begins to form, adding additional water 1 teaspoon at a time if necessary. Shape into flat round; cover. Refrigerate 1 hour.
2 Place oven rack in bottom rack position. Heat oven to 400°F. In large bowl, combine apples, ginger and cinnamon. In large (10-inch) skillet, melt ¼ cup butter over medium heat. Remove from heat. Sprinkle with ¾ cup sugar. Arrange apples over sugar mixture.
3 Cook over medium heat 20 to 25 minutes or until sugar is deep golden brown, thick and syrupy. Remove from heat.
4 Meanwhile, roll dough into 11-inch round, about ⅛ inch thick. Cut dough into 10-inch round. With small knife, make 4 slits in center of pastry for steam to escape. Place pastry over apples; tuck edges inside pan.
5 Bake 30 to 35 minutes or until pastry is golden brown and apples are tender. Cool on wire rack 10 minutes; invert onto serving platter. Serve warm or at room temperature.

8 servings

PER SERVING: 320 calories, 15 g total fat (8 g saturated fat), 2 g protein, 47 g carbohydrate, 30 mg cholesterol, 40 mg sodium, 2.5 g fiber

Summer's Best Tarts

Mixed Berry Tart with Raspberry Glaze

The luscious fruit so abundant right now requires only the simplest treatment to transform it into dessert. One favorite way is to serve it in a tart. Pile uncooked fruit in a delicious crust and top it with a lightly flavored glaze. To showcase the fruit properly, and make this a winning dessert, it's important to choose the right crust and glaze.

The crust is a classic cookie dough version with a sweet, buttery taste that complements but doesn't overpower the fruit. It remains crisp to the bite beneath juicy berries and tree fruit. And it's easy to make because you simply press it into the pan rather than roll it. The glaze is delicate, not gloppy. It's a light topping, with orange, lemon or raspberry notes, which coats the fruit and enhances its natural flavors.

To make it easier for entertaining, the tarts can be made several hours before serving. Now is the perfect time, when there's so much fruit to enjoy, to learn the technique for making this summery treat.

Kitchen Tips for Fruit Tarts

These luscious tarts require a few steps of preparation, but none are difficult. The fruit, of course, should be in its prime, at the peak of ripeness, but not overly ripe. The crust and glaze can be made ahead, and the tart can be assembled a couple of hours in advance.

CRUST

The crust for these tarts is made from sweet dough that's similar to cookie dough. It can be mixed in a food processor or stand mixer, or by hand. To keep the crust tender, don't overmix it. After the egg is added and the dough becomes moist and crumbly, simply press the dough together into a flat disk. If you continue to mix the dough until it forms a ball, it will be less tender.

Once the dough is made, transfer it to a tart pan. This procedure is different from most pastry crusts. Rather than first chilling it and then rolling it, you immediately press the dough into the tart pan using your fingers. This technique pushes the butter into the flour, creating a short pastry—one that's tender, but not flaky—with a consistency similar to shortbread cookies. This pastry is best for tarts with juicy fillings because it will hold the juicy fruit without becoming soggy.

The crust is baked without any filling. After pressing the dough into the pan, prick it all over with a fork and chill it until it's cold. When you're ready to bake it, line the dough with foil, making sure you press the foil onto all surfaces of the dough, especially along the bottom edge. Some recipes call for using dried beans or pie weights to weigh down the dough; that isn't necessary for this recipe. The foil and the fork pricks prevent the dough from puffing during baking. Bake the crust until it's partially cooked and set. Remove the foil and continue baking until the crust is golden brown. After it's cooled, spread some of the glaze over the bottom of the crust before adding the fruit. This helps keep the crust crisp by shielding it from the fruit's juices. The remaining glaze can be spooned over the fruit.

GLAZE

There are three glaze options for the fruit tarts: a brilliantly colored raspberry, a sweet-tart lemon and a delicate honey-orange. They offer delicious alternatives to the overly sweet and thick glazes often sold in supermarkets. Rather than masking the fruit flavor, these glazes enhance its natural taste. Each glaze can be paired with a variety of fruits and crusts or used as a topping for fresh fruit or ice cream.

This is a no-roll crust. Simply press it into the pan's bottom and sides.

Foil prevents the crust from puffing. After partial baking, remove the foil to allow the crust to get crispy.

Spreading glaze over the baked crust shields it from the fruit's juices and helps it stay crisp.

Choose from three lightly sweet glazes that complement fresh fruit.

Mixed Berry Tart with Raspberry Glaze

CRUST
- 5 tablespoons sliced almonds, toasted
- 1 cup all-purpose flour
- ¼ cup sugar
- ⅛ teaspoon salt
- 6 tablespoons unsalted butter, chilled, cut up
- 1 egg
- ¼ teaspoon almond extract

GLAZE
- 1 (10-oz.) pkg. frozen raspberries in syrup, thawed
- 3 tablespoons sugar

FILLING
- 2 cups strawberries, quartered
- 1 cup blueberries
- 1 cup raspberries

1 Reserve 2 tablespoons of the toasted almonds for garnish. Pulse remaining 3 tablespoons toasted almonds in food processor until ground. Add flour, ¼ cup sugar and salt; pulse to mix. Add butter; pulse until butter is size of small peas. In small bowl, whisk together egg and almond extract; add to flour mixture. Pulse until dough is moist and crumbly. (Dough also can be made in bowl using pastry blender or two knives.) Shape dough into flat round. With lightly floured hands, press dough evenly into bottom and up sides of 9-inch tart pan with removable bottom. Pierce dough all over with fork. Refrigerate 30 minutes or until cold.

2 Meanwhile, heat oven to 400°F. Line dough with foil sprayed with nonstick cooking spray; bake 15 minutes. Remove foil; if crust is puffed, prick several times with fork. Bake an additional 10 to 15 minutes or until golden brown; cool completely on wire rack. (Crust can be made up to 1 day ahead. Cover and store at room temperature.)

3 Meanwhile, place thawed raspberries with syrup in blender; blend until smooth. Strain to remove seeds. Place strained raspberry juice and 3 tablespoons sugar in large skillet. Bring to a boil over high heat; boil 4 minutes or until slightly thickened and reduced to ½ cup. Cool to room temperature. (Glaze can be made up to 1 day ahead. Cover and refrigerate.)

4 To assemble tart, brush bottom of crust with glaze. Arrange strawberries over glaze. Place blueberries over strawberries; top with raspberries. Brush remaining glaze over fruit. Garnish with sliced almonds. (Tart can be assembled up to 2 hours ahead.) Store in refrigerator.

8 servings

PER SERVING: 275 calories, 11.5 g total fat (6 g saturated fat), 4 g protein, 40 g carbohydrate, 50 mg cholesterol, 45 mg sodium, 4 g fiber

Fresh Peach Tart with Honey-Orange Glaze

CRUST
- 1 cup plus 3 tablespoons all-purpose flour
- ¼ cup sugar
- ½ teaspoon ground nutmeg
- ⅛ teaspoon salt
- 6 tablespoons unsalted butter, chilled, cut up
- 1 egg
- ½ teaspoon vanilla extract

GLAZE
- ¾ cup orange marmalade
- 3 tablespoons orange blossom or other floral honey
- 1 tablespoon orange juice
- 1 tablespoon packed light brown sugar

FILLING
- 1 cup whipping cream
- 1 tablespoon packed light brown sugar
- 5 peaches, peeled, sliced (½ inch)

1 Heat oven to 400°F. Place flour, sugar, nutmeg and salt in food processor; pulse to mix. Add butter; pulse until butter is size of small peas. In small bowl, whisk together egg and vanilla; add to flour mixture. Pulse until dough is moist and crumbly. (Dough also can be made in bowl using pastry blender or two knives.) Shape dough into flat round. With lightly floured hands, press dough evenly into bottom and up sides of 10-inch tart pan with removable bottom. Pierce dough all over with fork. Refrigerate 30 minutes or until cold.

2 Line dough with foil sprayed with nonstick cooking spray; bake 15 minutes. Remove foil; if crust is puffed, prick several times with fork. Bake an additional 10 to 15 minutes or until golden brown; cool completely on wire rack. (Crust can be made up to 1 day ahead. Cover and store at room temperature.)

3 Meanwhile, in medium microwave-safe bowl, whisk together all glaze ingredients. Microwave on high 30 to 60 seconds or until marmalade has melted. Strain through sieve; cool to room temperature. (Glaze can be made up to 1 day ahead. Cover and refrigerate. Bring to room temperature before using.)

4 In large bowl, beat cream and brown sugar at medium-high speed until soft peaks form.

5 To assemble tart, brush bottom of crust generously with glaze. Reserve ½ cup whipped cream for garnish; spread remaining whipped cream over bottom of crust. In another large bowl, toss peaches with remaining glaze. Place peaches over whipped cream. Garnish with reserved ½ cup whipped cream. Serve immediately. Refrigerate leftovers.

8 servings

PER SERVING: 415 calories, 19 g total fat (11.5 g saturated fat), 4 g protein, 59 g carbohydrate, 85 mg cholesterol, 65 mg sodium, 2 g fiber

Lemon-Glazed Blueberry Tart

CRUST
1 cup plus 3 tablespoons all-purpose flour
¼ cup sugar
1 tablespoon poppy seeds
⅛ teaspoon salt
6 tablespoons unsalted butter, chilled, cut up
1 egg
½ teaspoon vanilla extract

GLAZE
½ cup sugar
1½ tablespoons cornstarch
Dash salt
½ cup whipping cream
3 egg yolks
3 tablespoons fresh lemon juice
1 teaspoon grated lemon peel

BERRIES
3 cups fresh blueberries, divided

1 Heat oven to 400°F. Place flour, ¼ cup sugar, poppy seeds and ⅛ teaspoon salt in food processor; pulse to mix. Add butter; pulse until butter is size of small peas. In small bowl, whisk together egg and vanilla; add to flour mixture. Pulse until dough is moist and crumbly. (Dough also can be made in bowl using pastry blender or two knives.) Shape dough into flat round. With lightly floured hands, press dough evenly into bottom and up sides of 9-inch tart pan with removable bottom. Pierce dough all over with fork. Refrigerate 30 minutes or until cold.

2 Line dough with foil sprayed with nonstick cooking spray; bake 15 minutes. Remove foil; if crust is puffed, prick several times with fork. Bake an additional 10 to 15 minutes or until golden brown; cool completely on wire rack. (Crust can be made up to 1 day ahead. Cover and store at room temperature.)

3 In medium saucepan, stir together ½ cup sugar, cornstarch and dash salt. Whisk in cream. Bring to a boil over medium heat, stirring occasionally; boil 1 to 3 minutes or until thickened.

Place egg yolks in small bowl; slowly whisk in half of the hot cream mixture. Return mixture to saucepan; cook over medium to medium-low heat until mixture just begins to thicken, stirring occasionally. Do not let boil. Remove from heat; stir in lemon juice and lemon peel.

4 To assemble tart, spoon ¼ cup glaze over bottom of crust. Arrange 1½ cups of the blueberries in crust; pour remaining glaze over blueberries. Top with remaining 1½ cups blueberries. Store in refrigerator. (Tart can be assembled up to 8 hours ahead.)

8 servings

PER SERVING: 335 calories, 16.5 g total fat (9 g saturated fat), 5 g protein, 43.5 g carbohydrate, 145 mg cholesterol, 95 mg sodium, 2 g fiber

Sweets

Fudge for Everyone

Espresso Pecan Fudge

Fudge is the classic American candy: plain and simple on the outside, delightfully rich on the inside. And for the holidays, it's the candy of choice. If you've never made a batch of fudge, it's easy to make at home, doesn't require any unusual ingredients, and the only special equipment you need is a candy thermometer (and that's only for certain types of fudge).

There are many different kinds of fudge. They vary in flavor, texture and how they're made. These chocolate-intensive recipes are made in two different styles.

Classic fudge begins with a sugar syrup made by boiling sugar, cream and chocolate to the soft-ball stage. After it's cool, the fudge is beaten until thickened. It's the trickiest fudge to make, but I've discovered some secrets so the fudge will turn out perfect every time you make it.

Recipes containing marshmallows and evaporated milk utilize modern shortcuts and take the guesswork out of making this candy. They're still based on a sugar syrup, but the marshmallows, made with sugar syrup, gelatin and egg whites, combine to keep the sugar crystals small and the fudge extra creamy. Whatever your preference, these recipes should satisfy anyone who loves fudge.

Steps to Perfect Old-Fashioned Fudge

Old-fashioned fudge takes more care because it's made with a sugar syrup, but the results are outstanding.

- The quality of your fudge depends on the chocolate you use and following the recipe instructions carefully. For best results, use high-quality chocolate bars, never chocolate chips.

- Use a heavy, large pot to accommodate the hot cooking temperature and to provide plenty of room; the mixture bubbles and rises considerably during boiling.

- You'll need a candy thermometer for the sugar syrup; it must be cooked to the soft-ball stage (when a drop of syrup forms a soft ball when dropped into cold water).

When making the sugar syrup, brush the sides of the pan with a pastry brush dipped in water. This dissolves sugar crystals that form on the sides. Repeat the procedure after adding the chocolate.

Bring the chocolate mixture to the soft-ball stage without stirring, and do not scrape the pot when pouring the mixture into the bowl. Any stirring or scraping during this time causes crystallization.

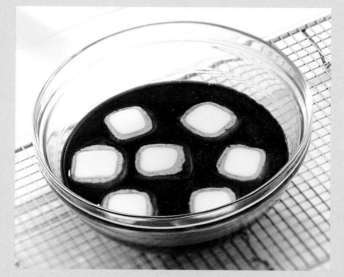

Let the butter melt on top of the chocolate while the chocolate mixture begins to cool. To keep the fudge from becoming grainy, do not stir the mixture until the temperature of the fudge drops to 110°F. (about 1 hour).

Once the mixture has cooled, beat it until thickened. The sugar crystals will be very small and evenly distributed, creating a smooth and creamy fudge. Use an electric mixer unless your arms are strong.

Old-Fashioned Mixed Nut Fudge

2 cups sugar
¾ cup heavy whipping cream
¼ cup light corn syrup
12 oz. semisweet chocolate, chopped
¼ cup unsalted butter, cut up
1 cup coarsely chopped mixed nuts
2 teaspoons vanilla extract

1 Place sugar, cream and corn syrup in heavy large saucepan; stir until well blended. Heat over medium-high heat, stirring constantly, until sugar dissolves and mixture just begins to come to a boil, 3 to 5 minutes. Remove from heat. With pastry brush dipped in water, wash down sides of pan to remove any sugar crystals.
2 Add chocolate; let stand 1 to 2 minutes or until chocolate is soft. Stir gently until chocolate is melted. Repeat brushing sides of pan with water to eliminate any sugar crystals.
3 Return saucepan to medium heat. Attach candy thermometer to side of pan. Cook, without stirring, 6 to 8 minutes or until mixture reaches 238°F. (soft-ball stage). Pour into large bowl (do not scrape bottom of pan). Place butter on top of chocolate mixture (do not stir butter into mixture).
4 Carefully place bowl on wire rack. Place clean candy thermometer in bowl. Let stand, undisturbed, until candy thermometer reaches 110°F., about 1 hour. Meanwhile, line 8-inch square pan with foil; spray with nonstick cooking spray.
5 Beat chocolate mixture at medium to medium-low speed 5 to 10 minutes or until fudge loses sheen and begins to thicken to the consistency of frosting. Stir in nuts and vanilla. Spread in pan; refrigerate 1 hour or until firm. Cover and store in refrigerator up to 3 weeks.

64 pieces

PER PIECE: 80 calories, 4.5 g total fat (2 g saturated fat), .5 g protein, 11 g carbohydrate, 5 mg cholesterol, 20 mg sodium, .5 g fiber

Chocolate-Orange Truffle Fudge

12 oz. semisweet chocolate, chopped
4 oz. unsweetened chocolate, chopped
3 cups miniature marshmallows
2 cups sugar
1 (12-oz.) can evaporated milk
½ cup unsalted butter, cut up
1½ teaspoons grated orange peel

1 Line 8-inch square pan with foil; spray with nonstick cooking spray. Place semisweet chocolate, unsweetened chocolate and marshmallows in large bowl. In heavy large saucepan, stir together sugar, evaporated milk and butter. Bring to a rolling boil over medium heat, stirring occasionally; boil 6 minutes.
2 Pour hot milk mixture over chocolate mixture. With clean spoon, stir gently until combined. Let stand 3 minutes or until marshmallows are soft; stir until smooth. Stir in orange peel. Pour into pan; refrigerate 3 to 4 hours or until firm. Cover tightly and store in refrigerator up to 3 weeks.

64 pieces

PER PIECE: 85 calories, 4.5 g total fat (2.5 g saturated fat), 1 g protein, 12.5 g carbohydrate, 5 mg cholesterol, 10 mg sodium, .5 g fiber

Espresso-Pecan Fudge

16 oz. semisweet chocolate, chopped
3 cups miniature marshmallows
3 tablespoons instant espresso coffee powder
2 cups sugar
1 (12-oz.) can evaporated milk
½ cup unsalted butter, cut up
2 cups toasted pecan halves, coarsely chopped

1 Line 8-inch square pan with foil; spray with nonstick cooking spray. Place chocolate, marshmallows and espresso coffee powder in large bowl. In heavy large saucepan, stir together sugar, evaporated milk and butter. Bring to a rolling boil over medium heat, stirring occasionally; boil 6 minutes.
2 Pour hot milk mixture over chocolate mixture. With clean spoon, stir gently until combined. Let stand 3 minutes or until marshmallows are soft; stir until smooth. Stir in pecans. Pour into pan; refrigerate 3 to 4 hours or until firm. Cover tightly and store in refrigerator up to 3 weeks.

64 pieces

PER PIECE: 105 calories, 6 g total fat (2.5 g saturated fat), 1 g protein, 13.5 g carbohydrate, 5 mg cholesterol, 10 mg sodium, .5 g fiber

Cool and Creamy

**Double Vanilla Cream
Panna Cotta with Strawberries**

Panna cotta (cooked cream) is an Italian star that has won the hearts of many Americans. Traditionally made with fresh cream, sugar and vanilla or almond flavoring, the cream is not really cooked as much as warmed. It's a snap to make and perfect for entertaining because it must be done ahead. While delicious on its own, it's often accompanied by a sauce or, as in Italy, just-picked summer fruit.

Panna cotta is similar to custard desserts such as crème brûlée, crème caramel or flan, but it's technically not a custard because it doesn't use eggs for thickening. Instead, it's thickened with a small amount of gelatin, lending this dessert a lighter texture and taste. The key to a successful panna cotta is the amount of gelatin. These recipes use the smallest amount possible—just enough so they can be unmolded, but not enough to remind you of a Jell-O dessert. The result is a creamy, melt-in-your-mouth sweet that's great for guests—or an everyday treat.

Making Panna Cotta

Adding Flavor Panna cotta can be made in many different flavors, but the key is to add flavor without altering the creamy texture. The best way to do this is to

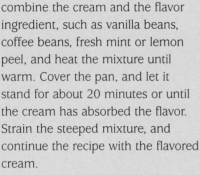

combine the cream and the flavor ingredient, such as vanilla beans, coffee beans, fresh mint or lemon peel, and heat the mixture until warm. Cover the pan, and let it stand for about 20 minutes or until the cream has absorbed the flavor. Strain the steeped mixture, and continue the recipe with the flavored cream.

Working with Gelatin

Unflavored gelatin comes in two forms: powdered (or granulated) and sheets (or leaves). Although chefs prefer sheet gelatin, powdered gelatin is the form most available to home cooks and the easiest one for them to use. These recipes are written using powdered gelatin. Follow these tips for success:

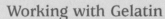

- We found that the amount of gelatin in a ¼-ounce package varies. A small change in the amount of gelatin can have a big effect on the texture. For accuracy, carefully measure gelatin with a measuring spoon instead of relying on amounts indicated on the package.

- Gelatin needs to be softened in cold liquid before use. Place the water or other cold liquid in a small heatproof bowl, and sprinkle it with gelatin. Let the gelatin stand 2 to 3 minutes or until it has softened and swelled. Sometimes, the liquid will set; this is okay.

- After the gelatin has softened, it needs to be dissolved. Place the softened gelatin mixture (in the heatproof bowl) in a small pan of simmering water; stir until all of the gelatin is dissolved. The mixture should turn to liquid and feel completely smooth, with no graininess. Do not let the gelatin boil. Also, if the gelatin is not completely dissolved, lumps will appear.

Cooling Before pouring the panna cotta into ramekins, stir and cool the mixture in a bowl of ice water until it's slightly thickened. Pouring the hot gelatin mixture into ramekins and refrigerating it immediately can cause it to separate during cooling.

Unmolding Panna cotta can be served in individual ramekins or, unmolded and served on dessert plates.

To unmold the panna cottas, run a thin knife around the outside edge of the ramekins, and invert them onto serving plates. If needed, a warm towel can be placed around the ramekins briefly to help them release. Be careful about applying too much heat because the panna cotta could melt. You might find it helpful to lightly dampen the plate first. This allows you to move the panna cotta around the plate, if necessary. Once it's positioned, wipe the plate dry.

Lemon-Mint Panna Cotta

CUSTARD
- 1¼ cups heavy whipping cream
- 1 cup half-and-half, divided
- 1½ tablespoons chopped fresh mint
- ½ medium lemon
- 2½ teaspoons unflavored gelatin
- ⅓ cup sugar

GARNISH
- 1 tablespoon powdered meringue or powdered egg white
- 1 tablespoon water
- Mint leaves
- Sugar

1 Place heavy cream, ¾ cup of the half-and-half and mint in medium saucepan. With vegetable peeler, remove lemon peel, avoiding bitter white pith below peel; add to cream. Cook over medium heat 3 to 4 minutes or until small bubbles form around edge of pan, stirring occasionally. Do not boil. Cover; remove from heat. Let stand 20 minutes.

2 Meanwhile, lightly spray 4 (6-oz.) ramekins or custard cups with nonstick cooking spray; place on baking sheet. Place remaining ¼ cup half-and-half in small heatproof cup or bowl. Stir in gelatin; let stand 2 to 3 minutes or until softened. Place cup in small skillet of simmering water; stir until gelatin is dissolved.

3 Strain cream mixture into medium bowl; discard mint and lemon peel. Return mixture to saucepan; stir in ⅓ cup sugar. Cook over medium heat 1 to 2 minutes or until sugar dissolves, stirring constantly. Do not let boil. Remove from heat. Stir in gelatin mixture.

4 Pour mixture into same medium bowl; place over large bowl of ice water. Cool, stirring constantly, 6 to 8 minutes or until slightly thickened. Pour into ramekins.

5 Cover and refrigerate 2 hours or overnight, until set. (Panna cotta can be made up to 1 day ahead. Cover and refrigerate.)

6 To make sugared mint leaves, in small bowl, whisk together meringue powder and water until well mixed and frothy. Using small brush, paint mixture on both sides of mint leaves; sprinkle with sugar. Let stand 2 hours or until dry. Store in airtight container. (Sugared mint leaves can be made up to 1 day ahead.)

7 To serve, run knife around edge of ramekins; invert onto serving plates. Garnish with sugared mint leaves.

4 servings

PER SERVING: 420 calories, 34.5 g total fat (21.5 g saturated fat), 6 g protein, 23.5 g carbohydrate, 125 mg cholesterol, 75 mg sodium, 0 g fiber

Double Vanilla Cream Panna Cotta with Strawberries

CREAM
- 1¼ cups heavy whipping cream
- 1 cup half-and-half, divided
- 1 vanilla bean, halved lengthwise
- 5 tablespoons sugar, divided
- 2½ teaspoons unflavored gelatin
- 1 teaspoon vanilla extract

STRAWBERRIES
- 2 cups sliced fresh strawberries
- ¼ cup sugar
- 1 tablespoon raspberry vinegar
- 1 teaspoon grated orange peel
- 1 teaspoon vanilla extract

1 Place cream and ¾ cup of the half-and-half in medium saucepan. Scrape seeds from vanilla bean onto cutting board; sprinkle 1 tablespoon of the sugar over seeds. Scrape seeds and sugar together until evenly combined. Add scraped bean, vanilla seeds with sugar and remaining 4 tablespoons sugar to cream mixture; stir to combine. Cook over medium heat 3 to 4 minutes or until small bubbles form around edge of pan and sugar dissolves, stirring occasionally. Do not boil. Cover; remove from heat. Let stand 20 minutes.

2 Lightly spray 4 (6-oz.) ramekins or custard cups with nonstick cooking spray; place on baking sheet. Place remaining ¼ cup half-and-half in small heatproof cup or bowl. Stir in gelatin; let stand 2 to 3 minutes or until set. Place cup in small skillet of simmering water; stir until gelatin is dissolved. Stir gelatin mixture and 1 teaspoon vanilla extract into cream mixture.

3 Strain into medium bowl. Place in large bowl filled with ice water; cool, stirring constantly, 6 to 8 minutes or until slightly thickened and vanilla seeds are suspended. Pour into ramekins. Cover and refrigerate 2 hours or overnight, until set. (Panna cotta can be made up to 1 day ahead. Cover and refrigerate.)

4 To prepare strawberries, in medium bowl, stir together all strawberry ingredients. Let stand 30 to 60 minutes, stirring occasionally, or until sugar dissolves and juices form. (Strawberries can be prepared up to 1 day ahead. Cover and refrigerate.)

5 To serve, run knife around edge of ramekins; invert onto serving plate. Top with strawberries.

4 servings

PER SERVING: 480 calories, 35 g total fat (21.5 g saturated fat), 5 g protein, 39 g carbohydrate, 125 mg cholesterol, 55 mg sodium, 2 g fiber

Baklava Revealed

Chocolate Almond Baklava

With its tissue-thin layers of pastry stuffed with rich nuts and dripping with honey syrup, baklava is a food that looks intimidating and could best be enjoyed at a good Greek restaurant. But baklava looks more difficult than it really is. The filling is simple enough, and with a few tips, it's easy to build your confidence in handling phyllo dough.

Working with Phyllo

Working with phyllo dough is not difficult; just relax, be confident and wield a large pastry brush.

Buying Most phyllo dough is sold frozen in grocery stores or ethnic markets. How the phyllo has been stored at the market plays a role in how easy it is to handle at home. If the dough has been handled correctly, the phyllo sheets will not stick together once they have thawed. If they do stick together, it's an indication that the dough may have begun to thaw improperly at some point and was later refrozen. To ensure you get dough that's been handled properly, purchase phyllo from stores that have a large turnover. Choose a package from the middle of the freezer case because boxes sitting near the door occasionally can be subject to thaw-freeze cycles.

Thawing Phyllo dough must be thawed correctly. It requires planning, and the process cannot be rushed. Place frozen phyllo, in its package, in the refrigerator, and let it stand 8 hours or overnight until thawed. Phyllo cannot be thawed on the countertop because condensation will form and cause the dough to stick. It also cannot be thawed in the microwave or oven. If properly stored and thawed, the sheets of dough should be dry but pliable and separate easily without sticking.

Handling It's best to have all ingredients and equipment ready to go before taking out the phyllo. Then work quickly and steadily. Because the dough dries out fast, it's important to keep it covered at all times. The simplest and best method is to unroll thawed phyllo on the counter and cover it with a clean, dry kitchen towel. It's often suggested that a damp towel be used; water causes phyllo dough to stick together, however, so this method can be counterproductive. Properly thawed, unused phyllo can be rolled up and placed in the original package, then in a resealable freezer bag and frozen again for another use.

Butter The characteristic flakiness of phyllo dough is created by layering sheets of dough and brushing each one with butter. Every sheet must be completely covered with butter to prevent drying out and to create the delicate flakiness of this pastry. Any edges that are not brushed with butter will quickly dry and crack. Use a soft, wide pastry brush for applying the butter; a large brush makes the job faster and easier. For fluffier, crisper and nicely browned dough, our recipes use clarified, unsalted butter. It's pure butterfat without added water and salt.

Troubleshooting Phyllo dough is very forgiving, so don't worry if there are wrinkles or tears. Each layer of pastry covers any wrinkles that occur, and butter can be used

Completely brush each sheet of phyllo with butter.

Cut the baklava before baking.

Pour the syrup over the baklava as soon as it is out of the oven.

effectively to patch any tears. Just work quickly, and thaw a few extra sheets of phyllo dough so you can discard any sheets that are causing problems.

Cutting Baklava must be cut before baking to ensure even edges. Cut all the way to the bottom and go back over each cut to make sure it is cut through.

Syrup The honey syrup poured over baklava after baking is what gives this dessert its unique flavor and sweetness. To ensure crisp baklava, make sure the syrup is at a cool room temperature and is poured over the hot baklava as it emerges from the oven. The pastry and filling will absorb the syrup, melding the flavors together. If the syrup is poured over cooled baklava, the syrup sits on the outside of the pastry, creating sticky baklava with uneven flavor.

Chocolate-Almond Baklava

SYRUP
1 cup sugar
½ cup water
¼ cup honey
¾ teaspoon almond extract

FILLING
1½ cups toasted whole blanched almonds
¼ cup sugar
3 oz. bittersweet chocolate, finely chopped

PHYLLO
1 cup unsalted butter, cut up
½ teaspoon almond extract
24 sheets frozen phyllo dough, thawed

1 Combine all syrup ingredients in medium saucepan. Bring to a boil over medium-high heat. Reduce heat to medium or medium low; gently boil 5 minutes or until slightly thickened. Cool. (Syrup will thicken as it cools.)
2 Place half of the almonds in food processor; process until finely chopped. Repeat with remaining almonds. In medium bowl, stir together all filling ingredients.
3 Heat butter in microwave-safe measuring cup in microwave on high 40 to 60 seconds or until melted; skim and discard foam off top. Pour clear butter into small cup; discard remaining milky substance at bottom. Stir in ½ teaspoon almond extract.
4 Heat oven to 350°F. Butter 13x9-inch pan. Unroll phyllo onto cutting board; cut to 13x9 inches. Discard excess phyllo, or reserve for another use. Cover phyllo with large dry towel. Lay 1 phyllo sheet in bottom of pan; brush with butter mixture. Repeat, using 12 phyllo sheets. Evenly sprinkle filling over phyllo. Top with remaining 12 phyllo sheets, brushing each layer with butter mixture.
5 Cut baklava crosswise into 1½-inch strips, cutting all the way to bottom. Cut diagonally to create diamond shapes, or cut into squares. Bake 25 to 30 minutes or until slightly puffed and light golden brown. Place on wire rack; immediately pour cooled syrup over baklava. Cool completely.

About 4 dozen

PER PIECE: 105 calories, 6.5 g total fat (3 g saturated fat), 1.5 g protein, 11.5 g carbohydrate, 10 mg cholesterol, 15 mg sodium, 1 g fiber

Spiced Cranberry-Nut Baklava

SYRUP
1 cup sugar
½ cup water
1 tablespoon honey (preferably orange blossom)
3 strips orange peel (each about 4x1 inch)
½ teaspoon ground cinnamon
¼ teaspoon ground allspice
⅛ teaspoon ground cloves

FILLING
¾ cup walnuts, toasted
¾ cup pecans, toasted
⅔ cup finely chopped dried cranberries
¼ cup sugar
1½ teaspoons grated orange peel
2 teaspoons ground cinnamon
½ teaspoon ground nutmeg
¼ teaspoon ground allspice
⅛ teaspoon ground cloves

PHYLLO
1 cup unsalted butter, cut up
24 sheets frozen phyllo dough, thawed

1 Combine all syrup ingredients in medium saucepan. Bring to a boil over medium-high heat. Reduce heat to medium or medium low; gently boil 5 minutes or until slightly reduced. Strain into small bowl; cool. (Syrup will thicken as it cools.)
2 Place walnuts in food processor; pulse until finely chopped. Place in medium bowl. Repeat with pecans. Stir in all remaining filling ingredients.
3 Heat butter in microwave-safe measuring cup in microwave on high 40 to 60 seconds or until melted; skim and discard foam off top. Pour clear butter into small cup; discard remaining milky substance at bottom.
4 Heat oven to 350°F. Butter 13x9-inch pan. Unroll phyllo onto cutting board; cut to 13x9 inches. Discard excess phyllo, or reserve for another use. Cover phyllo with large dry towel. Lay 1 phyllo sheet in bottom of pan; brush with butter. Repeat, using 12 phyllo sheets. Spread filling over phyllo. Top with remaining 12 phyllo sheets, brushing each layer with butter.
5 Cut baklava crosswise into 1½-inch strips, cutting all the way to bottom. Cut diagonally to create diamond shapes, or cut into squares. Bake 25 to 30 minutes or until slightly puffed and light golden brown. Place on wire rack; immediately pour cooled syrup over baklava. Cool completely.

About 4 dozen

PER PIECE: 90 calories, 5.5 g total fat (2.5 g saturated fat), 1 g protein, 10.5 g carbohydrate, 10 mg cholesterol, 15 mg sodium, .5 g fiber

Standout Dessert Sauce

**Cranberry Upside-Down Tart with
Vanilla Bean Crème Anglaise**

Crème anglaise has the consistency of heavy whipping cream. It's made with just sugar, milk or cream, and egg yolks; it contains no flour or starch of any kind. The classic crème anglaise is made with fresh vanilla beans, but other flavors—such as ginger, espresso, maple, almond or chocolate—add to its versatility. Serve it as a simple sauce alongside cakes, pies and fruits; layer it in trifles; freeze it to make ice cream; or mold it into shimmering Bavarian cream. For a dramatic presentation, swirl crème anglaise with contrasting sauces to produce elegant plate designs. Once you get acquainted with this chameleon of a dessert sauce, you'll find endless ways to serve it.

Making Crème Anglaise

The mixture is foamy when you begin cooking.

The foam subsides as the sauce starts to heat.

To test for doneness, run a finger across the back of the spoon. The sauce should stay separated.

Crème anglaise is easy to make. Be vigilant when cooking it, however, to avoid overcooking the eggs.

Ingredients Crème anglaise can be made with whipping cream, half-and-half or milk. These recipes use a combination of whipping cream and milk; the cream adds richness while the milk keeps the sauce light. For a richer sauce, use all whipping cream or heavy cream. If using milk, whole milk works best.

Egg yolks should be at room temperature. To achieve a creamy texture, take your time when beating them. They should be pale yellow and form a ribbon of batter that stays on the surface for a few seconds when the beater is lifted.

Flavoring Always use top-quality ingredients. Vanilla beans should be soft and supple, and the seeds should be moist when scraped out of the bean. When adding other ingredients, such as fresh ginger, chopped espresso coffee beans or toasted nuts, let them soak in the cream mixture for at least 30 minutes to allow the flavors to infuse. Do not use acidic ingredients because they cause the milk to curdle. For citrus flavor, use lemon or orange peel instead of juice.

Cooking Because there is no starch in crème anglaise, it can curdle if overheated. It is not necessary to cook this sauce in a double boiler, however, as long as you are careful; stir constantly, and don't leave the stove while the sauce is cooking. If you are vigilant about the heat and consistency of the sauce, you should not have problems. Use a heavy saucepan, preferably one with a rounded bottom so a spoon easily can get into the corners of the pan. Cook the sauce over medium-low to medium heat, stirring constantly.

The mixture is very foamy to begin with, but once it starts to heat, the foam subsides, steam begins to rise and the sauce thickens slightly. The custard is done when it coats the back of a spoon. To test for doneness, lift the spoon and run a finger down the center. The sauce should stay separated, not flow back together. Do not let the sauce boil or it will curdle. If you begin to see a bubble or two, immediately remove the pan from the heat and strain the sauce into a bowl. (Once you become familiar with the stages the sauce goes through, you may be able to increase the heat, but you'll need to be extra careful or the eggs will scramble and the sauce will curdle.) Refrigerate the sauce immediately, placing plastic wrap directly on its surface to prevent a skin from forming; or cool the sauce to room temperature, stirring occasionally, before refrigerating it (a skin will not develop).

Cranberry Upside-Down Tart with Vanilla Bean Crème Anglaise

TART
- 4 cups fresh or frozen cranberries
- 1 cup diced peeled Golden Delicious apple (about 1 large)
- 1¾ cups plus 1 tablespoon sugar
- ¼ cup all-purpose flour
- 2½ teaspoons cinnamon
- 1 sheet frozen puff pastry (from 17.3-oz. pkg.), thawed

CREME ANGLAISE
- 1 vanilla bean, halved lengthwise
- 4 tablespoons sugar
- ½ cup whipping cream
- ½ cup whole milk
- 3 egg yolks, room temperature

1 Heat oven to 400°F. In large bowl, stir together cranberries, apple, 1¾ cups of the sugar, flour and 2 teaspoons of the cinnamon. Place in 9x1½-inch round baking pan. Place puff pastry over berry mixture; trim puff pastry even with edge of pan.

2 In small bowl, stir together remaining 1 tablespoon sugar and ½ teaspoon cinnamon; sprinkle over pastry. Bake 35 to 45 minutes or until golden brown and fruit is tender. (Check after 25 minutes. If browning too quickly, cover with foil.)

3 Meanwhile, with small knife, scrape each vanilla bean half to remove seeds. With seeds on cutting board, sprinkle seeds with 2 tablespoons of the sugar. With side of knife, work vanilla bean seeds and sugar together to combine. (Sugar helps separate seeds so they will disperse in sauce easier.) Place vanilla seeds and sugar along with vanilla pod in large saucepan. Add cream and milk. Cook over medium heat until small bubbles appear around outside edge of saucepan.

4 Meanwhile, in medium bowl, beat egg yolks and remaining 2 tablespoons sugar at medium speed 5 to 6 minutes or until pale yellow, thick and mixture forms a ribbon on surface when beater is lifted. Slowly pour hot cream mixture into egg yolks, beating at low speed. Return mixture to saucepan; place over medium-low heat. Cook, stirring constantly, until sauce coats back of spoon. Do not let mixture come to a boil.

5 Immediately pour through strainer into medium bowl. Cool to room temperature, stirring occasionally. Cover; store in refrigerator. Serve warm or at room temperature.

6 To serve, cut tart into wedges; place in shallow bowls. Spoon remaining fruit in pan over crust. Pour sauce around tart. Refrigerate leftovers.

8 servings

PER SERVING: 505 calories, 22 g total fat (9 g saturated fat), 4 g protein, 75.5 g carbohydrate, 105 mg cholesterol, 90 mg sodium, 3 g fiber

Ginger-Poached Pears with Ginger-Honey Crème Anglaise

CREME ANGLAISE
- ½ cup whipping cream
- ½ cup whole milk
- 3 (¼-inch) slices fresh ginger
- 3 egg yolks, room temperature
- ¼ cup honey

PEARS
- 6 firm but ripe pears
- 1½ cups sugar
- 1 cup water
- 2 tablespoons lemon juice
- 2 tablespoons grated fresh ginger

GARNISH
- 18 dried apricots
- 2 tablespoons chopped pistachios

1 In medium saucepan, heat cream and milk over medium heat until hot. Do not boil. Add sliced ginger. Partially cover; let stand 30 minutes.

2 In medium bowl, beat egg yolks and honey at medium speed 5 to 6 minutes or until pale yellow, thick and mixture forms a ribbon on surface when beater is lifted.

3 Reheat cream mixture until hot; slowly add to yolk mixture, stirring constantly. Return mixture to saucepan; reduce heat to medium low. Cook until sauce coats back of spoon, stirring constantly. Do not let mixture come to a boil.

4 Immediately pour mixture through strainer into medium bowl. Cool to room temperature, stirring occasionally. Cover; refrigerate until chilled.

5 Meanwhile, peel pears, leaving stem on. Cut small slice off bottom of each pear so they will stand upright. With apple corer or small knife, remove core through bottom of pear.

6 In large saucepan, stir together sugar, water, lemon juice and 2 tablespoons ginger. Bring to a boil over medium-high heat, stirring until sugar dissolves. Place pears in syrup; cover. Reduce heat to medium low; boil gently 10 minutes.

7 Add apricots; cook an additional 10 to 15 minutes or until pears and apricots are tender, turning pears occasionally. Remove fruit with slotted spoon; place on plate to cool. Reserve syrup for another use.

8 To serve, spoon about ⅓ cup crème anglaise onto each of 6 large dessert plates. Place pears in center of plates. Arrange apricots around pears. Sprinkle with pistachios. Refrigerate leftovers.

6 servings

PER SERVING: 345 calories, 11 g total fat (5.5 g saturated fat), 4 g protein, 62 g carbohydrate, 130 mg cholesterol, 30 mg sodium, 5.5 g fiber

Mastering Meringue

Lemon-Lime Meringue Pie

Apple pie may get billing as the all-American dessert, but we're betting lemon meringue is a close second. Sweet yet tart; rich yet light—it's no wonder lemon meringue pie is so popular. But it's also one of those desserts that can pose problems for the cook—usually because of the meringue. It doesn't whip up properly, it shrinks, it beads up or it weeps. Success lies in the technique.

To help ensure the perfect meringue, I've incorporated a food-styling trick into the recipe: adding cornstarch to the egg whites to stabilize the meringue, making it less likely to bead up or shrink from the edges during baking. I learned this technique from fellow food stylists and have used it during photo shoots to produce beautiful pies. Now I use it for the pies I bake at home, too.

Meringue Techniques

MAKING CREAMY FILLINGS

The fillings in these pies are simple egg custards thickened with cornstarch. Whole eggs as well as egg yolks are used to add body and richness to the filling.

Whisk constantly Use a wire whisk to stir the cornstarch, sugar and water mixture while it cooks to keep lumps from forming.

Pour slowly When adding the hot cornstarch mixture to the egg yolks, place the bowl on a damp towel to keep it stable while you whisk. Spoon in the hot mixture slowly. Eggs need time to adjust to heat; they curdle if they're exposed to heat too quickly.

Cook thoroughly Once the eggs are added to the filling, they must be cooked thoroughly. This not only kills bacteria but also ensures the eggs will not break down the cornstarch and cause the filling to be runny.

Timing's important Lemon and lime juice are added after the filling is thoroughly cooked. If they're added sooner, they can affect the cornstarch's ability to thicken.

Make it hot Heat the filling immediately before pouring it into the pie shell and topping with the meringue. Do not allow the filling to cool down before the meringue has been spread or the pie may weep because the cool filling prevents the meringue from baking completely.

MAKING THE MERINGUE

The key to perfect meringue is the cornstarch-water mixture that is added to the egg whites. Cornstarch produces tender meringues that are less likely to shrink, bead or weep. Add the mixture to the egg whites a tablespoon at a time while the mixture is still warm.

Beating egg whites For maximum volume, use room temperature egg whites.

1. Begin beating the egg whites slowly, increasing speed when they are frothy and beating until soft peaks just begin to form.

2. Continue beating, slowly adding the sugar and then the cornstarch mixture.

3. Beat the egg whites until stiff peaks form—this takes a little time. Egg whites are ready when the beaters leave ridges in the whites and they are glossy and hold a stiff peak when the beaters are lifted out.

4. Spread one-half of the meringue over the hot filling, starting at the outside edge. Make sure the meringue touches the crust around the entire edge to avoid shrinkage. Pile the remaining meringue on top and swirl it with a knife or spoon.

Lemon Meringue Pie

FILLING
- 2 eggs
- 4 egg yolks
- ¼ teaspoon salt
- 1¼ cups sugar
- ⅓ cup cornstarch
- 1½ cups water
- ¼ cup unsalted butter, cut up, softened
- 2 teaspoons grated lemon peel
- ½ cup fresh lemon juice

MERINGUE
- ⅓ cup water
- 1 tablespoon cornstarch
- 4 egg whites
- ½ teaspoon fresh lemon juice
  Dash salt
- ½ cup sugar
- 2 teaspoons grated lemon peel

PIE SHELL
- 1 (9-inch) baked pie shell

1 Heat oven to 350°F. To make filling, in large bowl, whisk eggs, egg yolks and ¼ teaspoon salt until well blended. Set aside. In medium saucepan, combine 1¼ cups sugar and ⅓ cup cornstarch; mix well. Stir in 1½ cups water. Bring to a boil over medium heat, stirring occasionally. Boil 1 minute, stirring constantly. (Mixture will be very thick.)

2 Slowly add hot cornstarch mixture to egg mixture, whisking constantly. Return mixture to saucepan. Bring to a boil over medium heat. Boil 30 seconds, stirring constantly. Remove from heat. Add butter; stir until melted. Stir in 2 teaspoons lemon peel and ½ cup lemon juice. Cover; let stand while making meringue.

3 To make meringue, in small saucepan, combine ⅓ cup water and 1 tablespoon cornstarch; mix well. Bring to a boil over medium heat. Boil 30 seconds, stirring constantly. Set aside.

4 In large bowl, combine egg whites, ½ teaspoon lemon juice and dash salt; beat at medium-low speed until egg whites are frothy. Increase speed to medium; beat until egg whites hold a soft peak. With mixer running, slowly add ½ cup sugar and cornstarch mixture. Increase speed to medium high; beat until mixture is glossy and egg whites hold a stiff peak. Lightly fold in 2 teaspoons lemon peel.

5 Heat filling over medium-high heat until very hot, stirring constantly. Pour into pie shell. Spoon half of meringue evenly over hot filling, making sure meringue covers all filling and touches crust on all edges. Spoon remaining meringue onto pie and spread evenly. Add decorative swirls with back of spoon.

6 Bake 15 to 18 minutes or until meringue is dry to the touch and light brown. Place on wire rack; cool 2 hours or until room temperature. Refrigerate 3 to 4 hours or until chilled. Store in refrigerator.

8 servings

PER SERVING: 385 calories, 15 g total fat (6 g saturated fat), 6 g protein, 59 g carbohydrate, 175 mg cholesterol, 260 mg sodium, .5 g fiber

Lemon-Lime Meringue Pie

FILLING
- 2 eggs
- 4 egg yolks
- ¼ teaspoon salt
- 1 cup sugar
- ⅓ cup cornstarch
- 1½ cups water
- ¼ cup unsalted butter, cut up, softened
- 2 teaspoons grated lime peel
- ¼ cup fresh lime juice
- ¼ cup fresh lemon juice

MERINGUE
- ⅓ cup water
- 1 tablespoon cornstarch
- 4 egg whites
- ½ teaspoon fresh lime juice
  Dash salt
- ½ cup sugar
- 2 teaspoons grated lime peel

PIE SHELL
- 1 (9-inch) baked pie shell

1 Heat oven to 350°F. To make filling, in large bowl, whisk eggs, egg yolks and ¼ teaspoon salt until well blended. Set aside. In medium saucepan, combine 1 cup sugar and ⅓ cup cornstarch; mix well. Stir in 1½ cups water. Bring to a boil over medium heat, stirring occasionally. Boil 1 minute, stirring constantly. (Mixture will be very thick.)

2 Slowly add hot cornstarch mixture to egg mixture, whisking constantly. Return mixture to saucepan. Bring to a boil over medium heat. Boil 30 seconds, stirring constantly. Remove from heat. Add butter; stir until melted. Stir in 2 teaspoons lime peel, ¼ cup lime juice and lemon juice. Cover; let stand while making meringue.

3 To make meringue, in small saucepan, combine ⅓ cup water and 1 tablespoon cornstarch; mix well. Bring to a boil over medium heat. Boil 30 seconds, stirring constantly. Turn off heat; cover to keep warm.

4 In large bowl, combine egg whites, ½ teaspoon lime juice and dash salt; beat at medium-low speed until egg whites are frothy. Increase speed to medium; beat until egg whites hold a soft peak. With mixer running, slowly add ½ cup sugar; spoon in warm cornstarch mixture. Increase speed to medium high; beat until mixture is glossy and egg whites hold a stiff peak. Gently fold in 2 teaspoons lime peel.

5 Heat filling over medium-high heat until very hot, stirring constantly. Immediately pour into pie shell. Spoon half of meringue evenly over hot filling, making sure meringue covers all filling and touches crust on all edges. Spoon remaining meringue onto pie and spread evenly. Add decorative swirls with back of spoon.

6 Bake 15 to 18 minutes or until meringue is dry to the touch and light brown. Place on wire rack; cool 2 hours or until room temperature. Refrigerate 3 to 4 hours or until chilled. Store in refrigerator.

8 servings

PER SERVING: 365 calories, 15 g total fat (6 g saturated fat), 6 g protein, 52.5 g carbohydrate, 175 mg cholesterol, 260 mg sodium, .5 g fiber

Cool and Creamy Sorbet

Honey-Watermelon Sorbet

Sorbets, once icy palate cleansers served between courses, have evolved into creamy, intensely flavored-yet-light desserts. To create this luscious texture, chefs often use a little milk, gelatin and various forms of sugar. Milk adds creaminess without masking the fruit and other flavors in the sorbet. Gelatin helps stabilize the sorbet, keeping it from becoming grainy or icy and prolonging freezing time. Corn syrup, honey and other sugars provide creamy texture and a softer consistency. They're a perfectly refreshing ending to any meal.

Sorbet Basics

Sorbet, sorbetto, sherbet. These are all names for the same thing: a frozen mixture of sugar, water, and fruit or flavoring. Sorbet and sorbetto are the French and Italian words, respectively, for sherbet. Traditionally, sherbet was slightly different than sorbet because it contained milk. Today, however, the distinction no longer exists. Many sorbets contain milk along with other ingredients, such as gelatin, to prevent ice crystals. But they all still differ from ice cream because they never contain cream or eggs. As a result, they are lower in fat and have more intense flavors.

INGREDIENTS

Because there are so few ingredients in sorbet, the quality of those ingredients determines the intensity of the flavor. When using fresh fruit, it should be very ripe and flavorful. For the best-tasting sorbets, use fruit that is in season.

Milk makes the texture creamier in these recipes. Whole milk provides the creamiest texture, but low-fat or even nonfat milk also can be used.

Unflavored gelatin also contributes to a creamy texture by helping to prevent the formation of ice crystals. In addition, it aids in keeping the sorbet scoopable for several days.

TECHNIQUE

Pour chilled mixture into ice cream maker.

Sorbet is easy to make. The only time-consuming task is cutting up the fruit. Because the sugar needs to be dissolved before the mixture is frozen, the sugar is added to a warm liquid and stirred until dissolved. To quickly chill the mixture, place it in a large metal pan and let it cool in the freezer 15 to 20 minutes or until chilled. If the mixture is not heated, use superfine sugar, which dissolves quickly in liquid.

Puree the fruit in a blender or food processor before adding it to the sorbet mixture. Be sure the mixture is very smooth before adding it to the ice cream maker because any large pieces of fruit will freeze solid, resulting in little ice chunks in the sorbet.

When the sorbet comes out of the ice cream maker, it can be eaten immediately, although it will be very soft. For a firmer consistency, transfer it to a freezer container and freeze. Two to three hours should be sufficient time to allow the sorbet to harden to a scoopable consistency.

EQUIPMENT

Sorbet is soft when it comes out of the ice cream maker.

An ice cream maker is necessary to make this sorbet recipe. There are many types, from old-fashioned hand-crank models to deluxe machines with built-in refrigeration units. The small electric machines that require no rock salt or elbow grease are very easy to use and relatively inexpensive (about $50).

If you don't have an ice cream maker, you can freeze the mixture in a large metal pan, stirring occasionally as it begins to freeze. However, the texture will be fairly icy and granular.

Honey-Watermelon Sorbet

- 1 teaspoon unflavored gelatin
- 2 tablespoons water
- ½ cup milk
- 3 cups seeded chopped watermelon (1-inch pieces)
- ½ cup superfine granulated sugar
- ¼ cup mild honey, warm
- 1 tablespoon fresh lime juice

1 Combine gelatin and water in small cup; let stand to soften gelatin. Heat milk in small saucepan over medium heat until small bubbles form around outside edge; remove from heat. Add gelatin; stir until melted. Cool to room temperature.

2 Meanwhile, place watermelon in blender or food processor; blend until pureed. Add sugar, honey and lime juice; blend until smooth. Add gelatin mixture; blend to combine. Freeze in ice cream maker according to manufacturer's directions.

6 (½-cup) servings

PER SERVING: 145 calories, .5 g total fat (.5 g saturated fat), 1.5 g protein, 35 g carbohydrate, 0 mg cholesterol, 15 mg sodium, .5 g fiber

Chocolate and Cream

**Amazingly Decadent
Chocolate Sauce**

What if all you need to turn your chocolate desserts into pastry shop-style confections are just two ingredients? The simple combination of chocolate and cream, called *ganache* [pronounced *gahn-AHSH*], produces shiny glazes, frostings, truffles, mousse cakes and decadent tarts, as well as the richest sauce you'll ever taste. These two ingredients can be poured, shaped, rolled or whipped. The outcome varies, depending on the proportion of chocolate and its temperature.

Making ganache takes only a few minutes: Bring whipping cream to a boil and pour it over finely chopped chocolate; then stir until the chocolate is completely melted. Use it as is for a chocolate sauce. Use more chocolate and chill the mixture for truffles. Cool slightly and pour the ganache for a glossy coating. Cool longer and spread it as a frosting. Whip it for a mousse cake. Such versatility and richness are bound to make ganache one of your favorite choices for desserts.

Ganache: 3 Simple Steps

1. Chop the chocolate Because ganache has just two ingredients, use high-quality chocolate for best flavor. For large blocks of chocolate, use a heavy chocolate chopping tool or a large chef's knife to break the chocolate off the bar in chunks. Then use a chef's or serrated knife to chop the chocolate into finer pieces; this helps the chocolate melt evenly when the cream is added.

2. Add hot cream Bring the cream to a boil on the stovetop or in the microwave and immediately pour it over the chocolate. Do not let a skin form on the cream or it will affect the final texture of the ganache.

3. Stir immediately Stir the chocolate with a spoon until it's completely melted. Don't use a whisk; it could produce air bubbles. If tiny specks of unmelted chocolate remain, gently heat the mixture in a microwave set on high for 10 to 20 seconds or just until it's warm enough for the chocolate to completely melt. If you wish, add 1 to 3 teaspoons of flavoring to the ganache, such as liqueur, coffee, extract or syrups.

Amazingly Decadent Chocolate Sauce

- 8 oz. semisweet or bittersweet chocolate, finely chopped
- 1 cup whipping cream

Place chocolate and cream in medium saucepan over medium to medium-low heat; cook until chocolate is melted and smooth, stirring constantly. Serve warm. Cover and store in refrigerator up to 1 month.

1¾ cups

PER 2 TABLESPOONS: 150 calories, 12 g total fat (7 g saturated fat), 1 g protein, 12.5 g carbohydrate, 20 mg cholesterol, 10 mg sodium, 1 g fiber

Warm Chocolate Ganache Tart with Toasted Pecan Crust

CRUST
- 1½ cups chopped pecans
- 2 tablespoons sugar
- 3 tablespoons unsalted butter, melted

FILLING
- 12 oz. semisweet chocolate, coarsely chopped
- 1¼ cups whipping cream
- 1 egg

1 Heat oven to 375°F. Place pecans and sugar in food processor; pulse until finely ground. Add butter; pulse until moistened. (Crust also can be made by hand.) Press into bottom and up sides of 9-inch tart pan with removable bottom. Bake 12 to 14 minutes or until light brown.

2 Meanwhile, place chocolate in food processor; pulse until finely chopped. Microwave cream in medium glass measuring cup on high 1 to 2 minutes or until cream comes to a boil. With processor running, pour cream into chocolate; blend until smooth. Add egg; pulse until well blended. (Filling also can be prepared by hand.) Pour chocolate mixture into tart shell.

3 Bake 15 to 20 minutes or until slightly puffed and cracked on edges and center jiggles slightly when tapped but is not liquid. (Filling will firm up slightly as it cools.) Cool on wire rack 15 minutes; serve warm. (Tart can be made up to 8 hours ahead. Cool completely; cover and refrigerate. Reheat at 350°F. for 5 to 10 minutes or until warm.)

8 servings

PER SERVING: 515 calories, 44 g total fat (19 g saturated fat), 5.5 g protein, 34 g carbohydrate, 80 mg cholesterol, 25 mg sodium, 4.5 g fiber

Rich Dark Chocolate Glaze or Frosting

- 8 oz. semisweet or bitter-sweet chocolate, finely chopped
- ¾ cup whipping cream
- 2 tablespoons unsalted butter, softened

1 Place chocolate in medium bowl. Microwave cream in medium glass measuring cup on high 1 to 2 minutes or until cream comes to a boil. Immediately pour cream over chocolate; stir until smooth. Cool until just slightly warm (95°F. to 100°F.); stir in butter until melted.

2 To glaze cake: Brush off any loose crumbs from cake; place on wire rack set over rimmed baking sheet. With metal spatula, spread about one-third of the ganache over top and sides of cake to set crumbs. Refrigerate 10 minutes or until cold. Return cake to rack; pour remaining ganache over cake, spreading quickly over top and sides. (The less you touch the cake, the shinier the glaze will be.)

To frost cake: Cool ganache 5 minutes or until of spreadable frosting consistency. Spread ganache over cake as desired.

1⅔ cups glaze or frosting

PER 2 TABLESPOONS: 140 calories, 11.5 g total fat (7 g saturated fat), 1 g protein, 11.5 g carbohydrate, 20 mg cholesterol, 5 mg sodium, 1 g fiber

Chocolate-Raspberry Mousse Cake

CRUST
- 1½ cups chocolate cookie crumbs
- 6 tablespoons unsalted butter, melted
- ¼ cup raspberry preserves

FILLING
- 8 oz. semisweet chocolate, chopped
- 2 tablespoons raspberry flavoring syrup, divided
- 2½ cups whipping cream, divided
- 1 tablespoon sugar

TOPPING
- 6 oz. semisweet chocolate, chopped
- ¾ cup whipping cream

1 Heat oven to 375°F. In medium bowl, stir together cookie crumbs and melted butter. Press into bottom of 9-inch springform pan. Bake 10 minutes or until set. Remove from oven; gently spread preserves over crust. Cool completely on wire rack.
2 Meanwhile, place 8 oz. chocolate and 1 tablespoon of the raspberry syrup in large bowl. Heat 1½ cups of the cream in medium saucepan over medium heat or in microwave on high until cream comes to a boil. Immediately pour cream over chocolate; stir until smooth. Let stand until cool but still liquid (about 65°F.). (To speed up process, place bowl with chocolate in bowl of ice water; stir constantly.) Beat at medium speed 2 to 4 minutes or until slightly soft peaks form; spread over crust. Refrigerate.
3 In large bowl, beat remaining 1 cup cream, remaining 1 tablespoon raspberry syrup and sugar at medium speed until firm but not stiff peaks form. Spread over chocolate filling. Refrigerate.
4 Place 6 oz. chocolate in large bowl. Heat 3/4 cup cream in small saucepan over medium heat or in microwave on high until cream comes to a boil. Immediately pour cream over chocolate; stir until smooth. Cool until slightly thickened but still pourable (about 75°F.). Spoon over raspberry filling. Cover and refrigerate until set, at least 8 hours or overnight. (Cake can be made up to 2 days ahead.)
5 To cut cake, leave cake in springform pan; use hot dry knife to cut through top layer. Refrigerate.

When ready to serve, remove springform pan ring; slice completely. Store in refrigerator.

12 servings

PER SERVING: 485 calories, 37.5 g total fat (22.5 g saturated fat), 4 g protein, 40 g carbohydrate, 85 mg cholesterol, 110 mg sodium, 2.5 g fiber

Chocolate Raspberry Mouse Cake

Nine easy ways to use ganache

Follow the directions for making ganache in "Ganache: 3 Simple Steps," and use the proportion of 8 ounces chocolate to 3/4 cup cream for these quick ganache treats.

1 Pour coffee-flavored ganache into purchased individual tart shells and refrigerate until chilled. Garnish with a chocolate-covered coffee bean.
2 Frost a pan of brownies with chocolate ganache.
3 Cool ganache until it holds a firm peak; then pipe it, using a pastry bag and star tip, into purchased miniature phyllo shells.
4 Serve warm ganache with fresh fruit for a quick chocolate fondue.
5 Dip the tops of cupcakes into slightly cooled ganache.
6 Spread ganache between cookies for sandwich cookies.
7 Spoon warm orange-flavored ganache over poached pears.
8 Fold cooled, liquid ganache with sweetened whipped cream for an instant chocolate mousse.
9 Stir ganache into warm milk for the ultimate hot chocolate.

Lacy Wraps

Molten Chocolate Crepes with Mango Coulis and Raspberries

I t's fun to swirl and flip crepes. If you've never made them, flex your wrist and give it a try; you'll be pleased at how easy it is. If it's been a while since you've made crepes, head to the stove and rediscover the pleasures of this great classic.

Making Crepes

Creamy batter Crepe batter should be smooth and creamy, like heavy whipping cream before it has been whipped. Keep the batter light by mixing the ingredients just until smooth. To ensure tender crepes, let the batter rest for 30 minutes. This resting time allows the starch in the flour to absorb the liquid and the gluten to relax.

Swirling and cooking Cooking crepes is not difficult, but you do need to work quickly. First, heat the crepe pan until it's hot. Brush it lightly with oil and heat it briefly until the oil is hot. Lift the pan slightly away from the heat, pour in the batter and swirl the batter over the bottom. Pour out any excess batter (there should be just a thin coating on the bottom of the pan), and place the pan directly over the heat. Cook the crepe until the top is dry and the bottom is lightly browned; turn it and cook the second side.

Swirl the batter.

Pour out any excess.

Cook until lightly browned.

Plan on throwing away the first crepe—it's a test to help you adjust the heat and amount of batter. Adjust the heat during cooking if the crepes seem to be browning too much or cooking too slowly. Brush the pan with oil only when crepes begin to stick; it shouldn't be necessary to oil it between each crepe. Stack the completed crepes on top of each other to keep them moist and flexible (they will not stick together).

Filling and shaping Crepes have two distinct sides: The side that is cooked first has a lacy golden-brown finish and should always be on the outside, while the second side has a pale speckled brown finish. The crepes can be rolled, folded in half, folded into squares or triangles, or ruffled and tied into pouches.

Make ahead Unfilled crepes can be covered and refrigerated for up to 3 days. They also can be frozen for up to 2 months. Once filled, crepes usually can be refrigerated for up to 1 day.

Crepe pans You can use a variety of pans ranging from imported crepe pans to simple nonstick skillets. Traditional crepe pans are made of black carbon steel and have wide, flat bottoms and narrow 1-inch sides. As with cast-iron pans, traditional crepe pans need to be kept seasoned, but they deliver delicate golden-brown crepes every time. Nonstick and regular skillets can be used as long as they have wide bottoms and sloping sides.

Molten Chocolate Crepes with Mango Coulis and Raspberries

FILLING
- ½ cup heavy whipping cream
- 1½ tablespoons unsalted butter
- 6 oz. bittersweet or semisweet chocolate, chopped

CREPES
- 1 egg
- 1 egg yolk
- ½ cup milk
- ¼ cup water
- 2 tablespoons unsalted butter, melted
- 1 tablespoon sugar
- ¾ cup all-purpose flour
- ¼ cup ground almonds
  Vegetable oil for cooking crepes

GARNISH
- 1 mango, peeled, diced (about 1 cup)
- ¼ cup water
- 2 tablespoons lime juice
  Powdered sugar
- 1¼ cups fresh raspberries

1 Place cream and 1½ tablespoons butter in medium heavy saucepan; cook over medium heat until bubbles begin to form around edges. Remove from heat. Add chocolate; stir until chocolate is melted and mixture is smooth and glossy. Pour into small bowl. Cover; refrigerate until cool but still slightly soft.

2 Meanwhile, in large bowl, whisk together egg and egg yolk until combined. Add milk, ¼ cup water, 2 tablespoons melted butter and sugar. Slowly whisk in flour and almonds. Cover; refrigerate 30 minutes.

3 Meanwhile, combine mango, ¼ cup water and lime juice in blender; blend until smooth.

4 To make crepes, heat 6-inch crepe pan or nonstick skillet over medium-high heat until hot. Brush lightly with vegetable oil; heat briefly. Pour 3 tablespoons crepe batter into pan; immediately swirl to coat bottom of pan. Cook 30 seconds or until lightly browned; turn and cook 20 seconds or until light brown and dry. Place crepe on plate. Continue with remaining batter, stacking crepes on plate.

5 Spray shallow baking pan with nonstick cooking spray. Place crepes on work surface. Place about 1 tablespoon filling in center of each crepe. Fold two edges into center of filling, overlapping slightly. Fold crosswise in half; place in pan. Cover with foil. Refrigerate until ready to bake. (Crepes can be made up to 1 day ahead.)

6 Heat oven to 350°F. Bake, covered, 5 to 8 minutes or until chocolate is melted. Place 2 crepes in center of each plate; sprinkle with powdered sugar. Drizzle mango sauce around crepes. Garnish with raspberries.

12 crepes; 6 servings

PER SERVING: 440 calories, 28.5 g total fat (14.5 g saturated fat), 7 g protein, 45.5 g carbohydrate, 115 mg cholesterol, 35 mg sodium, 5 g fiber

Chervil-Tarragon Crepes with Shrimp and Sugar Snap Peas

CREPES
- 3 eggs
- 1 cup milk
- 1 tablespoon olive oil
- ¼ cup chopped fresh tarragon, chervil and/or Italian parsley
- ¼ teaspoon salt
- 1 cup all-purpose flour
  Vegetable oil for cooking crepes

FILLING
- 3 tablespoons unsalted butter
- ¼ cup finely chopped shallots
- 1 lb. shelled, deveined uncooked medium shrimp
- 1 cup diagonally sliced (¼ inch) sugar snap peas
- 3 plum tomatoes, finely chopped
- ½ cup reduced-sodium chicken broth
- 1 tablespoon lemon juice
- 1 tablespoon water
- 1 tablespoon cornstarch
- ⅛ teaspoon salt

SAUCE
- ½ cup chopped fresh Italian parsley
- 3 tablespoons chopped fresh tarragon
- ¼ cup reduced-sodium chicken broth
- 2 tablespoons extra-virgin olive oil

1 Place eggs, milk, 1 tablespoon olive oil, tarragon and ¼ teaspoon salt in blender; blend until smooth. Add flour; blend just until smooth, scraping sides if necessary. Pour into small bowl; cover and refrigerate 30 minutes.

2 To make crepes, heat 6-inch crepe pan or nonstick skillet over medium to medium-high heat until hot. Brush lightly with vegetable oil; heat briefly. Pour 3 tablespoons batter into pan; immediately swirl to coat bottom of pan. Cook 30 seconds or until lightly browned; turn and cook 20 seconds or until light brown and dry. Place crepe on plate. Continue with remaining batter, stacking crepes on plate.

3 Melt 2 tablespoons of the butter in large skillet over medium heat. Add shallots; cook and stir 1 to 2 minutes or until shallots just begin to soften. Add shrimp, peas and tomatoes; cook 2 to 3 minutes or until shrimp turn pink and peas are crisp-tender. Place in medium bowl.

4 Return skillet to medium-high heat. Add ½ cup broth and lemon juice; bring to a boil. In small bowl, stir together water, cornstarch and ⅛ teaspoon salt. Add to broth mixture; cook until mixture thickens, stirring occasionally. Add to shrimp mixture; stir to mix.

5 Spray 13x9-inch glass baking dish with nonstick cooking spray. Place crepes on work surface; divide filling evenly among crepes. Roll up; place in baking dish. Melt remaining 1 tablespoon butter; brush over crepes. Cover with foil; refrigerate until ready to bake. (Crepes can be made up to 1 day ahead.)

6 Heat oven to 350°F. Bake, covered, 20 to 30 minutes or until hot.

7 Meanwhile, combine all sauce ingredients except 2 tablespoons olive oil in blender; blend until smooth. Slowly add oil until blended. Drizzle sauce around crepes.

12 crepes; 6 servings

PER SERVING: 335 calories, 18 g total fat (6 g saturated fat), 20 g protein, 23.5 g carbohydrate, 230 mg cholesterol, 390 mg sodium, 2 g fiber

Sweet and Citrusy

Lemon Curd

One of the most heavenly creations to grace desserts and breakfast breads is made with fresh-squeezed citrus juice sweetened with sugar, enriched with butter and thickened with egg yolks. Unfortunately, this sensuous, rich cream is called a curd, a name that doesn't do it justice. Apparently, when first created, it brought to mind the creamy, soft curd that forms during cheese making.

Name aside, citrus curds are the darlings of the pastry world. Their sweet-tart flavors are vibrant and fresh, adding spark to many pastry creations. Lemon curd, with its puckery-tart flavor and creamy texture, is the classic standard and was traditionally spread on fresh-baked scones. Today, it's also used as a filling for tarts, layered in cakes, spread on toast and, for the true devotees, spooned right from the jar. Curds are simple to make, and a variety of citrus juices can be used. Along with lemon, the best curds are made from fresh limes, both Persian and Key, and oranges.

Steps to Making Citrus Curd

Making citrus curd is easy, and often the ingredients are right on hand. Follow these few steps for smooth, creamy results.

1 For best flavor, always use fresh-squeezed juice. Make sure your citrus is warm before squeezing so you get the most juice from it.

2 Slowly whisk the hot, melted butter into the egg yolk mixture; don't add it too quickly or the egg yolks will overheat.

3 Although traditional recipes call for a double boiler, using one isn't necessary as long as you watch the mixture carefully and don't walk away while it's cooking.

4 Whisk constantly during cooking, making sure the whisk gets into the corners of the pan. A long, skinny whisk with a narrow end works best.

5 The curd is cooked when the foam begins to subside and the mixture becomes shiny, gelatinous in texture and slightly thickened. Do not let the mixture come to a boil or the egg yolks will curdle.

6 To prevent a skin from forming during cooling, place plastic wrap directly on the surface of the curd and cut slits in the wrap with a knife to allow the steam to escape.

mesh strainer into small bowl; stir in lemon peel. Place plastic wrap directly on surface of curd. Using knife, cut several slits in plastic wrap to allow steam to escape. Refrigerate 2 hours or until well-chilled. Curd can be stored in refrigerator up to 1 week or frozen up to 1 month.

1¼ cups

PER 2 TABLESPOONS: 110 calories, 7 g total fat (3.5 g saturated fat), 1.5 g protein, 11 g carbohydrate, 120 mg cholesterol, 5 mg sodium, 0 g fiber

Blood Orange Curd

⅓ cup unsalted butter
4 egg yolks
½ cup fresh blood orange juice (3 to 4 oranges)
⅓ cup sugar

1 Melt butter in heavy medium saucepan over medium-low heat. Remove from heat.
2 In small bowl, whisk egg yolks, blood orange juice and sugar until blended; slowly whisk in melted butter. Return to saucepan.
3 Cook over medium heat, stirring constantly, 2 to 3 minutes or until mixture thickens and coats back of spoon (175°F.). Do not let mixture boil.
4 Immediately pour through fine mesh strainer into small bowl; place plastic wrap directly on surface of curd. Using knife, cut several slits in plastic wrap to allow steam to escape. Refrigerate 2 hours or until well-chilled. Curd can be stored in refrigerator up to 1 week or frozen up to 1 month.

1 cup

PER 2 TABLESPOONS: 135 calories, 10 g total fat (5.5 g saturated fat), 1.5 g protein, 10 g carbohydrate, 125 mg cholesterol, 5 mg sodium, 0 g fiber

Lemon Curd

¼ cup unsalted butter
5 egg yolks
½ cup fresh lemon juice (2 to 3 lemons)
½ cup sugar
1 teaspoon grated lemon peel

1 Melt butter in heavy medium saucepan over medium-low heat. Remove from heat.
2 In small bowl, whisk egg yolks, lemon juice and sugar until blended; slowly whisk in melted butter. Return to saucepan.
3 Cook over medium heat, stirring constantly, 2 to 3 minutes or until mixture thickens and coats back of spoon (175°F.). Do not let mixture boil.
4 Immediately pour through fine

Key Lime Curd

⅓ cup unsalted butter
4 egg yolks
½ cup Key lime juice (about 20 small Key limes)
¼ cup sugar

1 Melt butter in heavy medium saucepan over medium-low heat. Remove from heat.
2 In small bowl, whisk egg yolks, Key lime juice and sugar until blended; slowly whisk in melted butter. Return to saucepan.
3 Cook over medium heat, stirring constantly, 2 to 3 minutes or until mixture thickens and coats back of spoon (175°F.). Do not let mixture boil.
4 Immediately pour through fine mesh strainer into small bowl; place plastic wrap directly on surface of curd. Using knife, cut several slits in plastic wrap to allow steam to escape. Refrigerate 2 hours or until well chilled. Curd can be stored in refrigerator up to 1 week or frozen up to 1 month.

1 cup

PER 2 TABLESPOONS: 125 calories, 10 g total fat (5.5 g saturated fat), 1.5 g protein, 7.5 g carbohydrate, 125 mg cholesterol, 10 mg sodium, 0 g fiber

Lime Curd

¼ cup unsalted butter
5 egg yolks
½ cup fresh lime juice (about 3 limes)
½ cup sugar
1 teaspoon grated lime peel

1 Melt butter in heavy medium saucepan over medium-low heat. Remove from heat.
2 In small bowl, whisk egg yolks, lime juice and sugar until blended; slowly whisk in melted butter. Return to saucepan.
3 Cook over medium heat, stirring constantly, 2 to 3 minutes or until mixture thickens and coats back of spoon (175°F.). Do not let mixture boil.
4 Immediately pour through fine mesh strainer into small bowl; stir in lime peel. Place plastic wrap directly on surface of curd. Using knife, cut several slits in plastic wrap to allow steam to escape. Refrigerate 2 hours or until well chilled. Curd can be stored in refrigerator up to 1 week or frozen up to 1 month.

1¼ cups

PER 2 TABLESPOONS: 110 calories, 7 g total fat (3.5 g saturated fat), 1.5 g protein, 11 g carbohydrate, 120 mg cholesterol, 5 mg sodium, 0 g fiber

Sweet Orange Curd

⅓ cup unsalted butter
4 egg yolks
½ cup orange juice
⅓ cup sugar
1 tablespoon grated orange peel

1 Melt butter in heavy medium saucepan over medium-low heat. Remove from heat.
2 In small bowl, whisk egg yolks, orange juice and sugar until blended; slowly whisk in melted butter. Return to saucepan.
3 Cook over medium heat, stirring constantly, 2 to 3 minutes or until mixture thickens and coats back of spoon (175°F.). Do not let mixture boil.
4 Immediately pour through fine mesh strainer into small bowl; stir in orange peel. Place plastic wrap directly on surface of curd. Using knife, cut several slits in plastic wrap to allow steam to escape. Refrigerate 2 hours or until well chilled. Curd can be stored in refrigerator up to 1 week or frozen up to 1 month.

1 cup

PER 2 TABLESPOONS: 135 calories, 10 g total fat (5.5 g saturated fat), 1.5 g protein, 10.5 g carbohydrate, 125 mg cholesterol, 5 mg sodium, 0 g fiber

Uses for Citrus Curd

If your citrus curd can outlast eager tasters, use it to top pound cake, cheesecake or fresh fruit, to fill cream puffs or to make parfaits. Or try one of the following ideas.

Key Lime Tartlets Spoon Key Lime Curd into individual baked tarts or meringue shells.

Lemon Mousse Pie Fold sweetened whipped cream into Lemon Curd and pile it into a baked pie shell.

Fresh Orange Napoleons Alternately layer Sweet Orange Curd and sweetened whipped cream between sheets of baked puff pastry.

Sensational Sabayon

Frozen Chocolate Cream Sabayon

The stunning dessert known as *sabayon* (*sah-bah-YAWN*) is actually a simple custard elevated to delicate, creamy new heights. It's the French equivalent of the great Italian dessert, *zabaglione* (*zah-bahl-YOH-nay*). Egg yolks, sugar and fruit juice or wine are combined and then whisked while the mixture cooks. The result is an exquisite foamy sauce that can be used in an array of elegant desserts.

Orange Sabayon over Strawberries (pg. 158) showcases the sauce in its traditional form, as an elegant topping for fresh fruit or slices of pound cake. In Warm Lemon Gratin of Fresh Fruits (pg. 158), sabayon is spooned over crumbled shortbread and fruit and then glazed under the broiler to a golden hue. Frozen Chocolate Cream Sabayon (pg. 158) transforms the sauce into my favorite version, an ice-cold, silky-smooth custard. You can start with these recipes, but once you master the technique for sabayon, you'll soon discover countless other ways to use this versatile sauce.

Perfect Sabayon

Watch the temperature The key to success with sabayon is controlling the temperature of the mixture. Because it relies entirely on egg yolks for thickening, it must be handled carefully. Heat it slowly over low heat and it will perform perfectly. Let it get too hot or heat it too quickly, however, and you'll be left with a curdled, oatmeal-like mixture.

Heat slowly.

Make the sabayon Mix the ingredients in a mixing bowl. Then fill a saucepan with 1 to 2 inches of water and bring it to a simmer. Set the bowl over the saucepan, making sure the bottom of the bowl does not touch the water. Cooking over water shields the eggs from direct heat. Keep the water barely simmering; do not let it boil rapidly. This slowly heats the eggs and results in the greatest volume when you whisk them.

Cook over water.

The first few minutes of cooking The eggs will slowly begin warming; you will not notice a change in consistency during this time. As it begins to cook, the sabayon will slowly thicken. Continue cooking and whisking until the consistency is that of lightly whipped cream and the temperature reaches 160° F. to 165° F. on an instant-read thermometer; this takes from 7 to 10 minutes. To test if the sauce is done, lift the whisk and let the sauce drip back into the bowl. If it forms a slowly dissolving ribbon on the surface, it's ready.

Whisk.

Warm or cold? Warm sabayon is like a soufflé—it must be served immediately after making it. The delicate, creamy result is worth the last-minute preparation. For convenience, you can also make the sauce ahead and serve it chilled. After cooking, put it in the refrigerator or place it over a pan of ice water, stirring occasionally to avoid separation. The mixture will deflate slightly but the sauce is still outstanding.

Check your equipment The proper equipment helps ensure success:

- Use a stainless or copper mixing bowl. An aluminum bowl will react with the acid in the fruit juice and cause the egg yolks to turn gray.

- Use a balloon whisk; it has a large, bulbous tip that adds air and volume to the sabayon. Whisk constantly while the mixture cooks to keep it evenly heated.

- The saucepan should be the proper size. If it's too large, it may become too hot and the mixture will cook too quickly.

Frozen Chocolate Cream Sabayon

SABAYON
- 3 egg yolks
- ¼ cup sugar
- 1 cup whipping cream
- 2 tablespoons dry Marsala wine
- 2 oz. bittersweet chocolate, finely chopped

SAUCE
- ¼ cup whipping cream
- 2 oz. bittersweet chocolate, chopped

1 In medium stainless steel bowl, combine egg yolks and sugar; beat with wire whisk until light and creamy. Add ¼ cup of the whipping cream and Marsala; mix well.
2 Place bowl over a saucepan of *barely* simmering water. (Bowl should not touch water.) Cook 7 to 10 minutes, whisking constantly, until mixture is thick and foamy and temperature reaches 160°F. to 165°F. Turn off heat; remove bowl. Add finely chopped chocolate; stir gently until melted. Refrigerate until cool.
3 Meanwhile, line bottom of 4 (½-cup) ramekins with parchment paper. In medium bowl, beat remaining ¾ cup whipping cream until soft peaks form. Gently fold whipped cream into cooled chocolate mixture. Spoon into ramekins. Cover; freeze at least 4 hours or up to 24 hours.
4 To make chocolate sauce, in small saucepan, combine ¼ cup cream and chopped chocolate; cook over low heat, stirring until melted.
5 To serve, unmold frozen sabayon onto individual dessert plates. Let stand 5 to 10 minutes to slightly thaw. Drizzle with chocolate sauce and serve.

4 servings

PER SERVING: 450 calories, 35.5 g total fat (20.5 g saturated fat), 240 mg cholesterol, 35 mg sodium, 1.5 g fiber

Warm Lemon Gratin of Fresh Fruits

SABAYON
- 4 egg yolks
- ⅔ cup sugar
- ¼ cup fresh lemon juice
- 2 tablespoons cream sherry, if desired
- 1 teaspoon lemon peel

GRATIN
- 1½ cups crushed shortbread cookies
- 3 to 4 cups fresh fruit (sliced peaches, halved strawberries, raspberries and/or blueberries)
- 2 teaspoons sugar

1 In medium stainless steel bowl, combine egg yolks and ⅔ cup sugar; beat with wire whisk until light and creamy. Add lemon juice and cream sherry; mix well.
2 Place bowl over a saucepan of *barely* simmering water. (Bowl should not touch water.) Cook 7 to 10 minutes, whisking constantly, until mixture is thick and foamy and temperature reaches 160°F. to 165°F. Turn off heat; remove bowl. Stir in lemon peel. (Sabayon can be made ahead up to this point; cover and refrigerate 1 to 2 hours.)
3 Place oven rack 6 inches from heat; heat broiler. Spread shortbread cookies over bottom of 6-cup oval gratin or shallow baking dish. Top with fruit. Spoon sabayon over fruit; sprinkle with 2 teaspoons sugar. Broil 3 to 5 minutes or until golden brown. Serve immediately.

6 servings

PER SERVING: 426 calories, 19 g total fat (4.5 g saturated fat), 140 mg cholesterol, 190 mg sodium, 3.5 g fiber

Orange Sabayon over Strawberries

- 3 egg yolks
- ¼ cup sugar
- ⅓ cup fresh orange juice
- 1 tablespoon Grand Marnier or other orange-flavored liqueur
- 1 teaspoon grated orange peel
- 4 cups halved strawberries

1 In medium stainless steel bowl, combine egg yolks and sugar; beat with wire whisk until light and creamy. Add orange juice and Grand Marnier; mix well.
2 Place bowl over a saucepan of *barely* simmering water. (Bowl should not touch water.) Cook 7 to 10 minutes, whisking constantly, until mixture is thick and foamy and temperature reaches 160°F. to 165°F. Turn off heat; remove bowl. Stir in orange peel. Serve warm or refrigerate until cool.
3 To serve, place strawberries in individual stemmed glasses or dessert bowls. Spoon sabayon over strawberries.

4 servings

PER SERVING: 160 calories, 4.5 g total fat (1 g saturated fat), 160 mg cholesterol, 5 mg sodium, 3.5 g fiber

Index